"These are turbulent times for o
hearts of many to seek His King
been more important for the Chu
the work of the Holy Spirit and this book is a clarion call to men and
women to do just that."

**Rev. Anne Dunn**

*Minister at Stonehouse Community Church*

"There is no substitute for the work of the Holy Spirit in today's church, an amazing gift of the Father. It is available to all who believe – receive it, embrace it with all your heart. This book will inspire you to passionately seek the fullness of the Spirit, enabling you to be a living witness of our Lord and Saviour, Jesus Christ."

**Rev. Peter J. Boyd**

*Senior Minister at St. Paul's Church Worcester*

"Tony Chamberlain is an anointed Bible teacher, a very experienced church minister and one of the best preachers I have heard. His book brings to life the reality of the Holy Spirit that is available to all Christians. Unfortunately, so many only have a theoretical knowledge of the subject and of the nature of Holy Spirit baptism, and have yet failed to experience the reality of those special and sometimes powerful moments when we are *filled* with the Spirit. This may come upon us like "heaven's electricity", or a flooding of the warmth and closeness of God's love, or a myriad of other impressions. And sometimes we experience and use those supernatural Gifts of the Spirit described in the Bible, in 1 Corinthians chapter 12.

Tony's book clearly lays down the wealth of scriptural evidence, and explains the reality of Holy Spirit ministry in the lives of those who are open and wiling to receive him. This is a very detailed study of the subject, and I recommend it to all Christians, whether you are an *ordinary* Christian, or student at Bible College, or a church minister."

**Philip Tory, BSc(Hons)**
*Evangelist and Lay Preacher*

# THE PROMISE OF
# THE FATHER

# *The* PROMISE *of the* FATHER

*ANTHONY K. CHAMBERLAIN*

Published by Zaccmedia
www.zaccmedia.com
info@zaccmedia.com

Published May 2017

ISBN: 978-1-911211-55-6

*British Library Cataloguing-in-Publication Data*
A catalogue record for this book is available from the British Library.

# CONTENTS

# FOREWORD

The Bible teaches that we can have fellowship with God the Father, God the Son and God the Holy Spirit. We believe in one God in three distinct personalities. Jesus says to enter the kingdom of God we must be born again of the Holy Spirit – we need a spiritual birth. Some Christians and churches believe in God the Father, God the Son and the holy Bible! That is not the Trinity. God the Holy Spirit must not be absent or neglected from our experience. Followers of Jesus are encouraged to be continually filled with the Holy Spirit. We are told to keep in step with the Spirit, live by the Spirit, and not to grieve the Holy Spirit of God, who we should remember is sensitive.

Anthony Chamberlain's book is a timely message to the church – a message which too often is forgotten or ignored. Anthony is bringing an important truth to our attention, so we can be released and renewed. We must be baptised in the Holy Spirit and empowered. About a year after I was born again I was baptised in the Holy Spirit and began to share Christ boldly.

I have sought to be filled with the Holy Spirit continually every day, and increasingly I seek to walk in fellowship with the Holy Spirit along with Jesus and my heavenly Father.

When we are baptised in the Spirit and walk in the Spirit we are able to receive the gifts of the Holy Spirit, which we are told to "eagerly desire". We need both the gifts and the fruit of the Holy Spirit which provide power and purity in our lives. You will be blessed as you read Anthony's excellent book which is challenging, inspiring and Biblical. Seek the Lord and His Spirit with all your heart. Jesus invites us, saying *"How much more will your Father in heaven give the Holy Spirit to those who ask him"* (Luke 11:13 NIV). Just ask.

**Rev. Andy Economides**
*Founding Director of Soteria Trust*

# PREFACE

THE BIBLE CONTAINS MORE THAN 3,500 PROMISES. NONE of them are trivial. In fact, most are crucial! Under the Old Covenant with Israel, God said, *"No, I will not break my covenant; I will not take back one word of what I said"* (Psalm 89:34 The Living Bible Translation). Joshua's testimony was that *"not one word has failed of all the good things that the LORD your God promised concerning you. All have come to pass for you; not one of them has failed"* (Joshua 23:14 NKJV). Within the New Covenant, Peter tells us, *"By His own glory and goodness He has given us exceedingly great and precious promises"* (2 Peter 1:3–4) by which we share in the divine nature. 2 Corinthians 1:20 says that all the promises of God in Christ are *"Yes and Amen"* to the glory of God *"through us"*. Here God's positivity and our involvement are emphasised.

Congregations have been asked, "Are you standing on the promises, or merely sitting in the premises?" This challenge reinforces the idea that many of God's promises require a solid and positive response from us. Some promises God will fulfil despite us, but the majority demands our solid acceptance by faith. For several minutes I have been trawling through internet websites concerning the promises of God. What shocked me is that not one single site mentioned the words of Jesus when He spoke about the *promise of the Father*. These words and our Lord's explanations of them are omitted! Is it accidentally overlooked or purposefully ignored by so many preachers, churches and denominations? Think for a moment, when did you last hear a message, or receive a Bible study on this subject? You might be asking already, "What is the Promise of the Father?"

This book sets out to answer that very question, but with a radical difference. Too many offer humanistic opinions, or simply cling to what others have said, which has been so often wrong, unscriptural, or even anti-scriptural! We evangelicals proudly maintain that our doctrines are totally Bible-based, yet some of what we teach appears to have no Biblical basis at all. For example, the idea that the gifts of the Holy Spirit were for the early Church only remains unsupported by Biblical evidence. It's a human theory reliant on strained Bible interpretations at best, and generally proffered to excuse the lack of Spirit manifestations in a believer's life today.

A return to a Biblical approach is essential if we are serious with God. Jesus said it is the truth which sets us free, not spurious speculation. Therefore this book rests its case on what the Scriptures actually state, and what Jesus actually said. In many cases we are required to return to the New Testament Greek text, and diligently avoid loose, inaccurate English translations. For this reason I rarely use the seemingly popular New International Version (which has been altered and amended over the years) because in many places it paraphrases verses to the detriment of an accurate translation. In general I have used the Authorised Version which includes only a few inaccuracies, but in most cases I have resorted to my own translation, for two reasons: firstly to modernise the King James language and secondly to present the most accurate translation from the majority of Greek texts. All Scripture quotations are italicised.

Doctrine must be established only from the clear statements of Scripture, and never deduced from our personal experience of being a Christian. Our own experiences might fall far short of what it should be, for example, are we *"tasting the powers of the Age to come"*? Experiences can endorse doctrine, but also they might run counter to what the Bible says, often as a result of a shallow walk with the Lord.

In many places I have used the word *Pentecostal* and I owe you an explanation. I am not referring to particular denominations which use this word in their descriptive titles. Neither am I referring to the annual Old Covenant Jewish feast of Pentecost, except that it was then that the first Christians experienced Spirit baptism. My use of the word *Pentecostal* indicates that a believer has experienced his own personal baptism in the Holy Spirit in the Biblical way; he is thus 'Pentecostal' by experience; he has received what the first believers received from the Lord Jesus on the Day of Pentecost, ten days after Jesus ascended into heaven. Irrespective of our denomination, all born-again believers should be Pentecostal by experience, because this is the *"Promise of the Father"*.

Anthony K. Chamberlain
Gloucester 2016

# CHAPTER ONE

# MY STORY

ORNITHOLOGY CONSUMED MY WEEKENDS, BUT MY SCHOOL friend Gordon would never accompany me on Sundays because on that day he attended church three times, with his parents. I hated church. I didn't understand it and literally had no time for it. I made up my mind that Gordon would never get me to church, but after a whole year of persuasion I struck a compromise. I agreed to accompany my friend to watch a film being shown in his church hall.

The film portrayed different people struggling with their religious convictions. I was not struggling since I did not have any religious convictions. Then, in the film, a man began to sing "He's Got the Whole World in His Hand". I liked that song, and by the third verse a powerfully clear voice spoke to me! "Tony, I've got you in my hands. I know where you are and what you're thinking and I know what you're planning for the future." That last bit about 'planning for the future' shocked me. Even my parents did not know that! It was clear who had spoken to me so meaningfully with penetrating truth – it was the voice of God Himself! Of course, I could deny it; indeed, I mused that all this could be the result of my progress through puberty and that the voice was no more than a mere hormonal reaction. However, every attempt to repudiate what had really happened was pathetically feeble and wretched compared with the reality of His voice.

I wanted to know more about God. Gordon's minister at Brunswick Baptist Church, Gloucester was Rev. Walter Quicke, who was affectionately known as Wally. On this occasion it was me who felt like a wally when he asked, "What did you want to talk to me about?" I didn't want to talk to him, so I said nothing. Wally went on to tell me something or other, which I did not take in, because an idea came to me which I reckoned would be like a broadside against the good ship Church! I butted in, "But you don't have to go to church to be a Christian." I think I had heard that somewhere before and it made good sense to me. However, my broadside missed the mark completely, and triggered a powerful rebuff from Rev. Quicke. "I have never met with a more selfish attitude," he said, and went on, "To want God all on your own in your little corner and not to share His love with others who know Him too."

I felt ashamed and wished I had said nothing. There was silence before Wally asked me something that nobody had ever asked me before: "Would you like me to pray for you, Tony?" I thought it was the most wonderful question in the world, and without hesitation I replied, "Yes, please." I closed my eyes as Wally voiced his prayer. What he actually said or asked, I didn't take in at the time, nor do I remember his words to this present day, but this I knew, in some way or another it was "OK between little me and the big God high in the sky"! I came away sensing that this God loved me. He was not against me. He was on my side and He was my heavenly Father. Even though I had constantly rejected Him, He still wanted me! Such a thing was wonderful to know, and I felt strong all over. Nobody had taught me, but instinctively I knew what a great heavenly Father God truly is.

So it happened that I was saved in the Raikes Hall of Brunswick Road Baptist Church in Gloucester one Saturday evening in November 1956. My school friend Gordon Totterdell had steered me to the place where God could speak to me, save me and give me an amazing assurance: that the Creator God was now my heavenly Father – He loved me and I belonged to Him! I became a member of Brunswick Road Baptist Church and grew in knowledge and faith.

Not long after I had become a Christian, another school friend, Derrick Isles, came with me to a Sunday school anniversary at church, and he got saved too. I thought the Baptist church was tops, although some people at Trinity Baptist Church called Brunswick Road Baptist Church "the morgue"! Trinity had been started by believers from Brunswick Road founding a 'daughter' church, but it had become an Independent Baptist Church, meaning it was not affiliated to the Baptist Union. With their leaning towards Reformed doctrine and their influence by the Brethren, they had become proud of their status, part of which involved seeing other Christians as lesser beings. "Brunswick Road Baptist Church is not a morgue," I said to some members of Trinity Baptist. "God saved me and my friend Derrick at Brun, so how can it be dead if God is there?"

As time passed, I learned much about different Christian denominations, and still thought that the Baptists were best, until I was seventeen years of age and training as a laboratory technician at Southmead Hospital in Bristol. There I travelled past an intriguing building called the 'City Temple'. I thought it must be some Eastern religion, since it used the word *temple*.

3

The building was modern and attractive with a colourful noticeboard at the front. On the board I read, 'Bible Study Wednesdays at 7.30 p.m.'

I longed to know and understand the Bible better, and so the words *Bible Study* gripped me. Currently I was attending Broadmead Baptist Church in Bristol which, like the Baptists in Gloucester, had a prayer meeting and Bible study combined in one evening. I always came away thinking the prayer time was too short, and the Bible study was reduced to a small homily. I left unsatisfied and still very hungry to know God's Book. This 'City Temple' organised Bible study separate from its prayer meeting, and I felt drawn to attend the Bible studies, and prayed that if this place was a cult, or if they were twisting Bible truths, that God would clearly show me and keep me safe from error.

I entered the City Temple with trepidation, but I was warmly welcomed by an attendant on the door who handed me a hymn book. About fifty people were already seated in the brightly lit building – a good number I thought, since our Baptist churches saw only about half this number at the midweek prayer-cum-Bible-study meeting.

The City Temple was also called the Elim Church, about which I knew nothing. It was a large building holding several hundred people, and the platform had a massive notice above it, stating in huge white block letters on a bright red background, "HE IS RISEN". That is true, I said to myself! Then I looked at the hymn book they had given me. It was called the *Redemption Hymnal* and some of the hymns were in ancient poetic style, but many others used more modern language and were easy to understand. I knew you could learn a lot about what a church believes from the content of its hymn book, and with the *Redemption Hymnal* I discovered Bible-honouring doctrine on page after page, and its design with major section headings seemed to honour and glorify the Father, Son and Holy Spirit.

By now about 100 people had gathered and there was an atmosphere of expectation as two men came and sat on the platform. I learned later that the younger one was a student minister, and the other one (I estimated in his late thirties) was the senior minister, but what I noticed about them was that they were both smiling! Smiling in church? Didn't they know that due reverence and propriety was necessary as people gather before a holy God?

The first hymn was announced, number 629, and this was it:

There's a sweet and blessed story
Of the Christ who came from glory,
Just to rescue me, from sin and misery.
He in loving kindness sought me,
And from sin and shame has brought me,
Hallelujah! Jesus ransomed me.

What a hymn, written by Julia H. Johnston (1849–1919), which explained in simple terms what Jesus had come to do, and what He had done for me personally. However, the best was yet to come. Not the atmosphere, not the music, not the singing nor the songs, but the Bible teaching. The minister, Rev. Ron Jones, was taking a series of studies from the Book of Exodus, and this week he was teaching about the golden candlestick made by Moses for the Tabernacle (the tent where God would dwell among His people, Israel). My soul thrilled with excitement from the explanations and the dynamic truths imparted by Pastor Ron directly from the Scriptures. He preached for over an hour, and I did not want him to stop! I could have sat all night and all the next day at his feet, listening to God's word, just like Paul preached well into the night, and caused a young man to fall asleep and tumble from the window where he was sitting. The only difference was that I as a young man would never fall asleep during the preaching of the Rev. Ron Jones. I left about nine o'clock feeling exhilarated and blessed beyond measure.

What made the Elim Church different from the Baptists? Oh! I know the style of the services and what they entailed was different, but why were they different? What was behind it all? Just like Elim people, I was saved, born again, and in love with the Lord Jesus, but somehow I lacked their joy, faith, Scripture knowledge and the reality which they exhibited in their lives.

After a number of Wednesday night visits, before going home I asked an elderly lady why Elim is so different. Gently she responded, "Ah! It's the baptism in the Holy Spirit, dear." I had never heard about such a baptism, and not long after that, while at home in Gloucester I sat in the garden on a beautiful summer's afternoon and wrote out my first Bible study. It was entitled 'The Baptism with the Holy Spirit'. My outline comprised questions and answers. For example, 'Where is the baptism with the Holy Spirit mentioned in the Bible?' Each answer came directly from the Scriptures.

However, I was not yet baptised in the Holy Spirit. I knew the Holy Spirit was with me, just as the disciples experienced before the events recorded in Acts chapter two. Jesus told them something else. Although they knew the Holy Spirit, they were not to begin the work of spreading the gospel message, but rather to wait in Jerusalem until they received the *"Promise of the Father"* (Luke 24:49) which He further explained was the *"Baptism in the Holy Spirit"*, which would give them *"power"* to be (His) witnesses (Acts 1:4–8).

Now, my position was very similar to the disciples. I knew I was saved and born again; I knew that my sins were forgiven;

and I knew that I was a child of God. I also had the Holy Spirit, but I lacked power for service. I needed to be baptised into the Holy Spirit by the Lord Jesus, as John the Baptist had emphasised.

In addition, God had commissioned me. It happened one evening after an hour or more in prayer in my little dark and cold room where I lodged in Bristol. At the end of my long prayer session, when I had brought each member of the Brunswick Baptist Church's young people before the Lord, Jesus came very near to me, so near I wanted to reach out my hand – and I knew I would touch Him. My inner trepidation caused me to refrain from physically reaching out to Him. Then gently but firmly He said, *"I want you to preach the gospel."* I replied that I was not a good speaker, and that my personality was somewhat reserved and retiring; I was a 'behind-the-scenes' rather than an 'up-front' person! The Lord told me He had not made a mistake, that I was the one He wanted to preach, and that I need not make several excuses, as Moses had done!

Shortly afterwards I left my training and work at Southmead Hospital in Bristol and returned home to Gloucester in order to save up money for Bible college. Then I began to seek the Lord for the baptism in the Holy Spirit. Soon I left Brunswick Baptist Church and began to attend the Gloucester Elim Church. The minister there was the Rev. George Canty whose faith and Bible knowledge was astounding. I saw miracles performed on people who were sick, and almost every week in the Sunday services people were saved by committing their lives to Christ. It was a thrilling time, I made many new friends, but I especially sought to be baptised in the Holy Spirit.

Fred and Margaret Cooper became my best friends and they encouraged me greatly in the things of God. They too were anxious for me to be baptised in the Holy Spirit. However, it seemed the more I asked and pleaded with God, the more disappointed I became because nothing happened. I became disconsolate, and after many months depression set in, and the joy I had previously experienced in the dynamic services at church was gone. I felt a failure. I was sure that I was the problem, and that it was not the Lord's fault!

After one Sunday evening service, Fred and Margaret invited me back to their house where they would pray for me to receive the baptism in the Holy Spirit. I cycled from the church to their home in Hucclecote. Fred opened the Scriptures, and carefully explained that Jesus said, *"If we ask we shall receive."* I had been asking for months, with no result! Then Fred said all I had to do was receive the Spirit by faith and then I would find I could speak in tongues as the Spirit enabled me, just like the disciples on the Day of Pentecost. Simple! So we prayed and I tried to believe, but nothing really happened and I could not speak in tongues.

We ate some supper, and I said to Fred, "If I am baptised in the Spirit while riding home, will I fall off my bike?" Fred pointed out that God is *"not the God of confusion"*, so it would be all right.

On my way home cycling down the Barnwood Road, I confessed my lack of faith to the Lord and said sorry for my shortcomings. The last thing I wanted to do was to offend the precious Holy Spirit, so I tried to speak in tongues! I actually said some funny words and the smallest sense of excitement went through me. Could this be it? Am I now baptised in the Holy Spirit? Has the Lord at last been gracious and given me the desires of my heart? I told Fred and Margaret about this mini experience and they were sure I had been baptised in the Holy Spirit, and it was not long before news of this spread through the congregation.

For a little while I felt a release of tension – at least I didn't need to seek for this baptism any more – but strangely I continued to feel cold and empty inside; in fact, I seemed little different from before.

After a number of months I said to Pastor George Canty, "I'm disappointed with my baptism in the Holy Spirit." George looked at me and said, "No one is ever disappointed with their baptism in the Holy Spirit." I noticed that he had not said that I was not baptised in the Spirit, but the implication was there, and I began to sense that what had happened on my bike was nowhere near the real thing! As months went by I became sullen and depressed; my spiritual life seemed static and unfulfilled. I continued to attend church but I had very little joy in my soul.

After an evening service at Elim, George Canty announced that there would be a further meeting for seeking God and the fullness of His Holy Spirit. I did not want to stay and prepared to cycle home, but Fred and Margaret said that if I stayed I could go to their house afterwards and have some supper. Therefore, for their sake, or perhaps for the sake of the supper, I stayed. About twenty people were there and I sat on the back row behind them all. George began to lay hands on their heads and many people were blessed, as indicated by their tears of joy, their speaking out in tongues, and by their holy laughter. However, I felt dead inside, and made only faint-hearted attempts to pray to the Lord.

After a while, George walked along the empty row behind me, and as he passed me he very gently laid his hand upon my right shoulder. It was then that something remarkable happened. I had a vision. I saw the Lord Jesus Himself standing in the water along the shoreline, and facing me. His arms were open wide. He beckoned me to come to Him. I began to walk slowly towards Him as I told Him I loved Him. An amazingly strong elation welled up within me and joyous feelings intensified, beginning deep inside my stomach and flowing down to my feet, but I kept my eyes on the Lord and I told Him, "I don't want joy or gifts, I want You, Lord Jesus!"

Then the bubbling joy began to rise upwards to my head, and I could do not refrain from crying out, "Jesus, I love You." Spontaneously a stream of bubbling language poured out from my soul and through my mouth – I was "speaking in tongues"! Then the Lord Jesus took my hand and we began to rise. Yes! I was rising up out of my seat, towards the high church roof, then through the roof and out into the night air, but still travelling on towards the stars and space. I had always suffered from a fear of heights, but during this experience I had no fear, I was at perfect peace. Eventually I stopped travelling and found myself surrounded by a beautiful light. I knew Jesus was that light, and although I could not see Him, I worshipped Him. What I actually said I do not know as unknown languages streamed from my soul in adoration of my Saviour. After what seemed to be no more than ten minutes the light receded, and I felt myself returning through space and earth's atmosphere towards Gloucester, then through the church roof and back into my seat, where for some moments I continued to speak in tongues.

I had been caught up to Paradise, and like Paul I can say, *"Whether in the body or out of the body I do not know."* However, what I know for certain is that when at last I came to full consciousness of my surroundings, I looked up with the biggest smile imaginable on my face, and saw Pastor George with Fred and Margaret Cooper standing waiting for me. Everyone else had gone and what I thought had been about ten minutes in glory had been well over half an hour!

"You've had a great time," Margaret said, and I simply replied, "Yes!" Now I felt a great love for people. It was a deep, living feeling, far more powerful and beautiful than anything I had encountered previously. I wanted to dance – I felt I loved everybody! Something else I surely knew: that was my baptism in the Holy Spirit! What I had sought over many months Jesus had done, and I was not, nor ever would be, disappointed with that! Rightly or wrongly, I never told Fred and Margaret that Jesus had baptised me in the Holy Spirit that night at Elim. I did not want them to be hurt or belittled. They thought I had been baptised cycling home many months before. This book will inform them otherwise.

Now, those who suggest that we are automatically baptised by Jesus into the Holy Spirit at the moment of our conversion will be required to explain what happened to me. They may suggest a number of things. They might say that Paul described how he was taken up into Paradise, but there is no indication in Scripture that he was baptised into the Holy Spirit during that experience. That is true, and I do not say one has to be caught up into Paradise to be baptised in the Holy Spirit. Indeed, my own experience is that Jesus baptised me into the Holy Spirit as I saw the vision of Him on the seashore. After that, I was caught up, but that was an additional blessing given through His grace and mercy. Neither do I say that one has to have a vision of Jesus to be baptised into the Spirit – that was simply how it happened for me. God deals with individuals in different ways, but one thing is certain: we will all know when we are baptised into the Spirit, whatever else accompanies our experience, or whatever does not accompany it. So what will those who teach that we are baptised into the Holy Spirit automatically at our conversion say about my experience?

They might suggest I was merely "filled with the Spirit", in which case is it the filling that enables us to speak with tongues? If I had been filled, why is the filling more powerful and exhilarating than the baptism? How is it that the *baptism in the Holy Spirit* at conversion is less dynamic than the subsequent fillings of the Spirit? Surely a strange doctrine is emerging here, which the Bible fails to support!

# CHAPTER TWO

# CLARIFYING TEACHING ABOUT THE HOLY SPIRIT

THERE REMAINS VAGUENESS IN PEOPLE'S MINDS ABOUT THE Holy Spirit. He is often seen as the One who works unseen and unfelt. His activities are viewed as operating in the spiritual realm only, so that expectations of sensing His presence in the Church today remain minimal. Often He is side-lined and any reality of interacting with Him is stifled. Preaching and teaching more than often circumvent the major work of the baptism in the Holy Spirit. Great doctrine inspires great songs, but because there is little mention of Spirit baptism, no songs on this subject are produced today. Many songs mention the Holy Spirit, but omit the crucial key to His activities in an individual's life.

The era between the first coming of Christ as Saviour and His second coming as King has traditionally been called the Gospel Age, and latterly the Kingdom Age. According to Jesus it is the Holy Spirit Age, because it rested on Jesus leaving earth in bodily form. *"If I do not go the Spirit will not come,"* He said. In other words, the ascension of Jesus must occur before the Spirit comes at Pentecost. These two are crucially linked together – you can't have the latter without the former. The absence of Jesus in bodily form is replaced with *"another Comforter"*, which is the Holy Spirit. Jesus stated that it was to our advantage that He left us in bodily form and that the Spirit continued with us in a new and special way.

However, Pentecost was not a simple arrival of the Holy Spirit, either into the world or upon the Church as a gathered group. In the sense of arriving, the Spirit had already come. He was present from creation onwards. Jesus told the disciples that the Spirit was already with them, and later Jesus breathed on them to receive the Holy Spirit, prior to His ascension.

To understand what truly took place on the Day of Pentecost we must carefully read Acts chapter 1, where the words of Jesus provide a precise answer. The Lord referred to the *"Promise of the Father"* and further explained that this Promise was the baptism in the Holy Spirit, which would be activated for the first time very soon. Notice the Lord did not say the Spirit would arrive, or that the Spirit would establish the Church, or any such thing. He said to His disciples, *"You will be baptised with the Holy Spirit not many days from now."* According to Acts chapter 2, the only thing which *came* was the Day of Pentecost itself! Any explanation of what occurred on that Day must not negate, nor override what Jesus said would take place. Crucially Pentecost was not the coming of the Person of the Holy Spirit, but the coming of the baptism in the Holy Spirit.

The question is often asked, "When does a believer receive the Holy Spirit?" Is it at the point of conversion, or is it later? Unfortunately the word *receive* in this question can be misleading. The Holy Spirit *interacts* with a person from the moment of their conviction, and if He is obeyed He leads them into conversion. Once converted (saved, regenerated, redeemed), the believer can be baptised in the Holy Spirit, which the Anglicans call confirmation. So conviction can lead to conversion which can lead to confirmation!

The question is better put by asking, "When does a believer receive the baptism in the Holy Spirit?" In Bible days water baptism and Spirit baptism were an integral part of a complete salvation, which took place very soon after a person repented. Today, due to ignorance of the Bible and spiritual matters generally, both water baptism and Spirit baptism are postponed until the convert is immersed in teaching and instruction about these subjects. In some circles both subjects are ignored, especially in those sections of the Church which sprinkle infants.

Just as the crucifixion came before Pentecost, so conversion comes before Spirit baptism. Indeed, the Lord said that the world cannot see or know the Holy Spirit, who is given only to those who believe and obey (John 14:17; Acts 5:32). Where the word *promise* is linked to the Holy Spirit, the referral is to the baptism in the Spirit known as the *"Promise of the Father"* (Luke 24:49; Acts 1:4, 2:33,39; Galatians 3:14; Ephesians 1:13). Ephesians 1:13 says we believe in Christ before we are sealed with the Holy Spirit of promise, confirming that a believer is sealed through Spirit baptism after being saved (2 Corinthians 1:21–22; Ephesians 1:13, 4:30).

Holy Spirit understanding has been homogenised! His various activities and operations are intermixed. Isolated verses have been blended to produce a melded cluster of teaching which fails to distinguish the Spirit's primary work from His general work, and the Person of the Spirit from the baptism in the Spirit. Passing light through a prism displays seven distinctive colours: red, orange, yellow, green, blue, indigo and violet. The seven colours always appear in the same order, and each has its own distinct properties, but mixed together they make white light. Coloured paint is different, because if red, blue and green

15

are mixed together the result is black, not white. This is called subtractive mixing, since each colour degenerates towards the neutral colour black, but used separately the colours add a distinctive vibrancy to life. Suppose we give conviction by the Spirit the colour blue; regeneration by the Spirit the colour red, and baptism in the Spirit the colour green. Mixing them together like paint will produce a muddy mess! Failure to separate the Spirit's activities results in a confusing picture of His work. We must rightly divide God's Word.

When we consider Christ, we break down into separate parts the varied aspects of His life and work. By this means, our understanding of Him is significantly increased as we examine in detail each aspect of His ministry. We can consider separately His pre-incarnate glory, His human birth, His earthly ministry, His miracles, His teaching, His mission, His arrest, His trial, His scourging and death, His resurrection, His ascension and His return as King. Many other factors can be investigated too, such as His Person and Name.

The wisdom of God has granted us four Gospels. One large harmonised account would not have enabled us to clearly distinguish the separate aspects of Christ's being. Matthew depicts Christ as the Messiah King. Mark illustrates the Lord as the sacrificial Servant. Luke reveals Christ's humanity as the Son of Man. John discloses Christ's divine nature as the Son of God. In Eden there was one river, but beyond the garden it divided into four separate streams. Similarly we who now live beyond Eden need separate streams of revelation to enable us to grasp the individual facets of God.

Concerning the Holy Spirit, where shall we begin? We see Him at work throughout the pages of Scripture, yet often the separate references seem little more than clues as to His operating procedures. How shall we unravel the varied aspects of His ministry? Most believers understand far more about Father God and Jesus, the Son of God, than about the Holy Spirit, despite the fact that we live in the dispensation of the Holy Spirit. The Lord emphasised that His absence and the Spirit's presence was to our advantage, indicating that the New Covenant experience of God would be radically different from all that had occurred beforehand.

Two principal activities of the Holy Spirit reserved for God's New Covenant people can be distinguished from all the other aspects of His general work in the believer. They are firstly being born of the Spirit, and secondly being baptised in the Spirit. The former has been thoroughly understood and taught down the years by most orthodox denominations, but being baptised with the Spirit has been woefully neglected. Indeed, many evangelicals have merged these two activities together, claiming that coverts are baptised in the Spirit at the moment they are born again. Such a notion generally strips Spirit baptism of its identity and urgency. New birth by the Holy Spirit is the starting point for every Christian disciple, and Spirit baptism is the starting point for a Spirit-empowered ministry and a life immersed in the service of God. Jesus told His followers not to begin the work of publishing the gospel until they had been baptised in the Holy Spirit. He instructed them to wait for the endowment of power from on high, but before we proceed with this theme, it is necessary to appreciate who the Holy Spirit is. We also need to understand the differences between the Holy Spirit's working in Old Testament times from His working in New Testament times.

# CHAPTER THREE

# THE PERSON OF
# THE HOLY SPIRIT

A PERSON HAS THE ABILITY TO KNOW, FEEL AND CHOOSE. The Bible shows that God's Spirit is not merely an influence or power, but a real person. Since we are created in God's image, we too have the qualities of personality – mind, emotion and will.

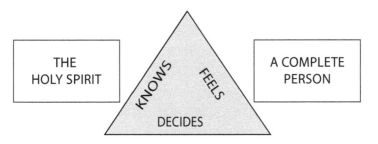

## 1. THE SPIRIT'S MIND

The Holy Spirit acts with intelligence and wisdom. In Romans 8:27 Paul states that the Holy Spirit knows God's will and the needs of the people, and this makes Him an effective intercessor. The Holy Spirit is also an excellent counsellor, confirming what action should be taken, as Acts 15:28, *"It seemed good to the Holy Spirit and to us . . ."* 1 Timothy 4:1 tells us that the Spirit speaks, so His thoughts can be verbalised and expressed in human language.

## 2. THE SPIRIT'S FEELINGS

The Holy Spirit has an emotional quality. His feelings include the ability to love. In Romans 15:30 Paul says he begs the brethren *"through the Lord Jesus Christ, and through the love of the Spirit . . ."* Romans 5:5 says, *"The love of God has been poured out in our hearts by the Holy Spirit."* The Spirit also has the ability to suffer grief and pain, and believers are instructed not to grieve nor quench Him. We should not lie to Him, nor resist Him, nor insult Him, and speaking against or blaspheming the Holy Spirit cannot be forgiven!

## 3. THE SPIRIT'S WILL

The Spirit is shown in Scripture as One who is able to choose, to make decisions and to give directions. He exercises His sovereignty, His supreme will, as illustrated in Acts 13:1–4, where The Holy Spirit told the disciples to separate Barnabas and Saul for the work to which He was calling them. 1 Corinthians 12:7–11 tells us that the Spirit distributes His gifts to individual people *"as He wills"*. This deliberate selection is the personal act of the Holy Spirit, and He reveals His presence through the various gifts as listed.

## 4. THE SPIRIT'S PERSONAL PRONOUN

The Bible assigns personal names to the Holy Spirit, and in fact His personal name *"Holy Spirit"* is mentioned over ninety times in Scripture. This emphasises His own essential character, and distinguishes Him from any other spirit, whether angelic, human or satanic.

Jesus used the masculine personal pronoun *"He"* and *"His"* ten times in John 16:13–15. *"When He, the Spirit of truth, has come, He will guide you into all truth, for He will not speak of Himself, but whatever He hears He will speak, and He will declare to you things to come. He will glorify Me, for He will receive what is Mine and declare it to you. All things that the Father has are Mine. Therefore I said that He will take of Mine and declare it to you."* New Testament Greek does not generally use separate words for pronouns, rather the pronoun gender is indicated by various verb endings.

## 5. THE SPIRIT'S DIVINITY

Peter shows that a sin against the Holy Spirit is a sin against God Himself, asking, *"Why has Satan filled your heart to lie to the Holy Spirit? You have not lied to men but to God."* (See Acts 5:3–4). Clearly the Holy Spirit must be God! Although the Spirit is a distinct Person within the Godhead, His associations with the other members of the triune God is so close that He is called:

1. The Spirit of God – Romans 8:9,14

2. The Spirit of your Father – Matthew 10:20

3. The Spirit of the Lord – Acts 5:9, 16:3

4. The Spirit of Christ – Romans 8:9; 1 Peter 1:11

5. The Spirit of Jesus Christ – Philippians 1:19

6. The Lord is the Spirit – 1 Corinthians 3:17

The New Testament uses the Greek word Θεοτης or Θεοιν and the word is translated *"Godhead"* in the AV; *"Divine Nature"*, NKJV; *"divine being"*, NIV.

21

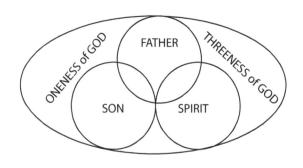

| ETERNAL ATTRIBUTES | GOD THE FATHER | GOD THE SON | GOD THE HOLY SPIRIT |
|---|---|---|---|
| **GOD** | 1Timothy 1:2 | Isaiah 7:14 | Matthew 1:20, 3:16 |
| **ETERNAL** | Psalm 90:2 | John 8:56–58 | Hebrews 9:14 |
| **CREATOR** | Genesis 1:1 | John 1:3 | Psalm 104:30 |
| **ONLY SAVIOUR** | Isaiah 43:3,11 | Acts 4:12 | Titus 3:5 |
| **OMNIPOTENT** | Matthew 19:26 | Matthew 28:18 | Zechariah 4:6 |
| **OMNISCIENT** | Psalm 139:2–3 | John 16:30 | 1Corinthians 2:10–11 |
| **OMNIPRESENT** | Psalm 139:7–12 | Matthew 18:20 | Psalm 139:7–10 |
| **CHANGELESS** | Malachi 3:6 | Hebrews 13:8 | Ephesians 2:18–22 |
| **HOLY** | Isaiah 6:3 | Luke 1:35 | Luke 11:13 |
| **WORSHIPPED** | Revelation 22:9 | Matthew 14:33 | John 4:24; Phil. 3:3 |
| **DIVINE LOVE** | John 3:16 | 2Corinthians 5:14 | Romans 15:30 |
| **DIVINE GRACE** | Titus 2:11 | Philemon 1:25 | Hebrews 10:29 |
| **FORGIVES SIN** | Psalm 103:3 | Mark 2:5 | 1Corinthians 6:11 |
| **TITLE LORD** | Matthew 22:37 | Ephesians 6:23–24 | 2Corinthians 3:17 |

Acts 17:29, Romans 1:20, Colossians 2:9 indicate that the Being of God is complex, and other references show the *Oneness* and the *Threeness* of God.

We can appreciate that God comprises a Three-in-One Being since the Father, Son and Holy Spirit all possess the same Godly attributes and qualities, as shown by the table above.

The above table has at least two weaknesses, namely not all the attributes of God are listed, and for each attribute generally only one verse of Scripture is given, whereas the Bible gives multiple verses in almost all cases.

We often use the word *Trinity* to describe this Bible truth. The Bible shows that the Holy Spirit is God, just as the Father is God and the Son is God, and many times these three Persons are seen acting together. Here are some examples: at Christ's water baptism, Matthew 3:16. Jesus' water baptismal formula, Matthew 28:19. The Father sends the Spirit in Christ's name, John 14:26. Jesus sends the Spirit, who proceeds from the Father, John 15:26. Paul writes about the Spirit, the Lord (Jesus) and the (Father) God in 1 Corinthians 12:4–6 and gives the tripartite blessing in 2 Corinthians 13:14. The Father, Spirit and Son are mentioned together in Ephesians 3:14–16 and 4:4–6. The three Persons are grouped together in Hebrews 9:14, also in 1 John 3:23–24 and 5:7. The Spirit, the Father God and the Lord Jesus are linked together in Jude 20–21. The three Persons of the Godhead are cited in Revelation 1:4-6. Jehovah's Witnesses are quick to point out that the word *Trinity* is not mentioned in the Bible. They should realise that the word *theology* is not mentioned either, but there is a wonderful amount of it in the Bible! Although the actual word *Trinity* is not used, the precept and reality of one God comprised of three Persons is firmly established in Scripture.

Jesus emphasised that the only sin which cannot be forgiven is blasphemy against the Holy Spirit, see Matthew 12:31–32;

Mark 3:28–29; Luke 12:10. For the Jews, blasphemy was an act of cursing or reviling God. Blasphemy is a sin against God Himself, so the Holy Spirit must be God, and His deity is confirmed by the fact that He can be blasphemed. Note, it is only in later times that Muslims applied blasphemy to objects and persons other than God, but in Jesus' day it was understood that it was a sin against God only.

Many examples of the close involvement of the Holy Spirit in the major acts of God could be given, including the following:

Creation – Genesis 1:2,26

Jesus' Birth – Matthew 1:18–23

Christ's Ministry – Isaiah 61:1–2; Luke 4:14–21

Christian Baptism – Matthew 28:19–20

Apostolic Blessing – 2 Corinthians 13:14

The Threeness of God's nature is reflected in the created universe. Consider a few examples:

Family – Dad, Mum, son = three persons but one family

Man – Spirit, soul, body = three parts but one person

Universe – Space, matter, time = three dimensions but one universe

Space – Length, breadth, height = three dimensions but one entity

Fire – Heat, light, energy = three factors but one source

Musical Note – Heard, seen, felt = three senses but one sound

Mathematically – $1 \times 1 \times 1 = 1$

# CHAPTER FOUR

# THE DIFFERENCES BETWEEN THE SPIRIT'S OT AND NT MINISTRY

THE HOLY SPIRIT IS GOD, AND WE KNOW THAT GOD DOESN'T change, He is immutable. However, the activities of God are variable dispensationally. The fact that He originated what we now call an Old Covenant, and later designed a New Covenant illustrates this. Paul speaks about many diverse activities and gifts which are all worked by the same God.

Here are some of the activities of the Holy Spirit in Old Testament times:

1.  In CREATION – Genesis 1:1–2,26; Psalm 104:30; Job 26:13, 33:4

2.  In JUDGMENT – Genesis 6:3

3.  In SERVICE – Exodus 31:3; Luke 1:15

4.  In POWER – Numbers 11:29, 24:2

5.  In LEADERSHIP – Judges 3:10, 6:34

6.  In VICTORY – Judges 14:6,19, 15:14

7. In PROPHESYING – 1 Samuel 10:10

8. In RULING – 1 Samuel 16:13, 19:20–24

9. In MIRACLES – 2 Kings 2:9,14,15

10. In SPEAKING – 2 Chronicles 20:14; Luke 1:41–42,67

11. In REVELATION – 1 Peter 1:10–12; Luke 2:26–27

12. In FILLING – Exodus 31:3; Luke 1:15,41,67

13. In SPECIAL CONCEPTION – Luke 1:35

14. In PRODUCING SCRIPTURE – 2 Peter 1:20–21

It is evident that the Holy Spirit was active in many ways in the lives of people during the Old Testament dispensation. It is also evident that the Spirit's New Testament ministry would be remarkably different. This difference is pinpointed by John, who writes a commentary about Christ's words, stating, *"But this He spoke concerning the Spirit, which those who believe in Him would receive; for the Spirit was not yet, because Jesus was not yet glorified"* (John 7:39). The text is as follows:

> ουτω  γαρ ην  πνευμα
> not yet for  was   Spirit

This can be rendered into better English with a slight change in word order: *"for not yet was Spirit"* or *"for (the) Spirit was not yet"*. The definite article is added to make better English, and although the Greek text does not use a capital letter (Π) for πνευμα, the context confirms that it is indeed the Holy Spirit of God which John is referring to, therefore in English a capital first letter is required for the word *Spirit*.

What does John mean by *"for not yet was Spirit"*? His phrase seems grammatically incomplete in English, and attempting to make better sense some translators add the word *given* causing the text to read, *"the Spirit was not yet given"* (NKJV includes *given* in italics to indicate the word is absent from the Greek text. The NIV uses the word *given* without any indication of textual absence). Adding a word avoids the impression that the Spirit did not exist prior to that point. However, this is hollow and unnecessary, because the Bible shows clearly that the Holy Spirit was abundantly active in the world from creation onwards.

The Darby translation honours the Greek text by simply saying, *"[the] Spirit was not yet"*. Most other English translations provide a dynamic translation which offers the sense of what John was saying, rather than a formal word-for-word rendering. Here are some alternative translations:

> Common English Bible: *"but they hadn't experienced the Spirit yet ..."*
>
> God's Word Translation: *"The Spirit was not yet evident, as it would be ..."*
>
> Holman Translation: *"the Spirit had not been received ..."*
>
> Mounce Reverse Interlinear: *"the Spirit was not yet present ..."*
>
> The Voice: *"the Spirit had not yet arrived ..."*

Each of these indicate a translator's varied interpretation about the Holy Spirit, and they seem to permit a Bible student adding his own choice of words such as the Spirit was not yet 'operating', 'available', 'provided', 'active' , 'commissioned' , 'dispensed' and so on. I am not opposed to adding a word but its inclusion must not alter the apostle's meaning. John is saying that not yet, but later, after Jesus is ascended and glorified, the Holy Spirit will accomplish something new, different, vital and extraordinary, something which would first occur on the Day of Pentecost.

What John DOES NOT mean by *"for not yet was Spirit"*:

1. That God the Holy Spirit did not exist before the Day of Pentecost

2. That the Spirit was absent on earth before His outpouring at Pentecost

3. That no one knew the Spirit's presence in their lives before Pentecost

4. That there was a different Spirit operating in Old Testament times

5. That John is mistaken and writing words which are untrue

6. That the OT references to the Holy Spirit are erroneous mistakes

What John DOES mean by *"for not yet was Spirit"*:

John means that the Holy Spirit phenomenon which would be experienced on the Day of Pentecost according to Acts chapter 2 was not yet activated. Permitting the addition of a word enables us to gain a fuller understanding.

1. Not yet was Spirit (given) in the way He would be dispensed from Pentecost onwards

2. Not yet was Spirit (operating) in that particular manner as at Pentecost onwards

3. Not yet was Spirit (experienced) with that special effect as at Pentecost onwards

4. Not yet was Spirit (arriving) with that extraordinary power as at Pentecost onwards

5. Not yet was Spirit (available) for that particular purpose as at Pentecost onwards

6. Not yet was Spirit (evident) as He would be experienced at Pentecost onwards

7.  Not yet was Spirit (received) with the evident dynamic as at Pentecost onwards

8.  Not yet was Spirit (fulfilling) what God had promised believers at Pentecost onwards

9.  Not yet was Spirit (present) with that physical vitality as at Pentecost onwards

10. Not yet was Spirit (providing) the power He would grant at Pentecost onwards

11. Not yet was Spirit (released) to impart the effects as at Pentecost onwards

12. Not yet was Spirit (the baptismal medium) that Jesus would immerse us into.

## *The import of what John is saying:*

John 7:39 confirms that the future operation of God the Holy Spirit in the lives of men and women would be entirely new and distinct from all that He did beforehand. John's *"not yet"* shows that something more and something new is on the way! He indicates a major difference between the Old Testament ministry of the Spirit and His New Testament ministry. Something new would be activated later, on the Day of Pentecost, ten days after Jesus visibly ascended and was glorified.

This leads us to ask the question: "What happened on the Day of Pentecost?" At first glance this question appears easy to answer. We only need to read Acts chapter 2 for a full explanation. However, when this question is put to a group of believers, their forthcoming divergent answers expose inherent difficulties. Some will say, "It was the arrival of the Holy Spirit." Others, "It was the coming of the Holy Spirit upon the Church." Others say, "It was the birthday of the Church" and Billy Graham states,

"Pentecost instituted the Church."[1] Rather than giving a straightforward Biblical answer, we are plunged into the realm of interpretation, opinion and speculation. Some will even suggest that there isn't a straightforward Biblical answer to this question. With this I firmly disagree, because what actually happened on the Day of Pentecost is clearly spelt out by Jesus in Acts 1:4–8. These words are the key to understanding what actually happened at Pentecost, and they are also the key to understanding all the subsequent events recorded in the Book of Acts.

Let's rephrase the question: "What did Jesus say would happen to the disciples on the Day of Pentecost?" His answer is typically concise and clear: *"In a few days you will be baptised in the Holy Spirit"* (Acts 1:5). Therefore the Day of Pentecost saw the first Christians baptised in the Holy Spirit. To leave us in no shadow of doubt, Jesus referred to John the Baptist, who baptised in water. John was the greatest of all the Old Testament prophets and he prophesied that Jesus would baptise people in the Holy Spirit. In Acts 1:4 Jesus allayed any doubts about the baptism with the Spirit by describing it as *"The Promise of the Father"*. The NIV offers a mellow and inaccurate paraphrase here, translating Acts 1:4 *"wait for the gift my Father promised"*. The word *gift* is absent from the Greek text, which reads: αλλα περιμενειν την επαψψελιαν του πατρος and which should be translated simply into English as *"but await the promise of the Father"*.

So the Day of Pentecost saw the disciples receiving exactly *the promise of the Father*, which is the baptism in the Holy Spirit. Any other answer or explanation perilously sidesteps Christ's words. We might argue amongst ourselves, but we must never argue with our Lord and Master. John's words of explanation in John 7:39 now make sense. Although the Holy Spirit was already present in the world, and with the disciples, the Spirit was not yet the baptising medium into which Jesus would plunge and immerse His disciples. That would occur after Jesus was glorified, after He had physically ascended into the heavens. Obviously believers need much more than to interact with the Person of the Spirit in a general way; they need to have received the baptism in the Spirit before commencing ministry for God.

Now we can highlight the principal differences between the Spirit's operations in New Testament times, from His workings in Old Testament times:

## 1. DIFFERENCE OF DISPENSATION

The Old Testament is the dispensation of law (Galatians 3:24) which Jesus came to fulfil (Matthew 5:17). Jesus is our second or last Adam (1 Corinthians 15:45) who completely adhered to every Old Testament precept, and fulfilled every Old Testament prophecy about His first coming into the world. The perfect Son of God is qualified to be our Saviour through death and resurrection and having procured salvation, Christ Jesus introduces to us new life in the Holy Spirit (Romans 7:6, 8:2; Galatians 3:13–14). The abundant life in Christ moves us from the former dispensation of law into the new dispensation of the Spirit (John 3:5, 14:16–18,26, 15:26, 16:7–15). This new era is known by different names:

1. The New Covenant Age
2. The New Testament Age
3. The Church Age
4. The Gospel Age
5. The Age of Grace
6. The Kingdom Age
7. The Holy Spirit Age

In many respects all of these designations are valid, and we can use whichever one we wish, but since Jesus has ascended into the heavens, and replaced His physical presence with the Holy Spirit, this new dispensation should best be called the age of the Holy Spirit. The other designations are automatically included and embraced by this phrase, because:

1. The Holy Spirit is referred to many times in a New Covenant context (Romans 8:1–27)

2. The Holy Spirit is the sacred author of the New Testament (Ephesians 6:17; 2 Peter 1:20–21)

3. The Holy Spirit dwells in the Church as His temple (1 Corinthians 3:16)

4. The Holy Spirit confirms the gospel with a seal and signs (Ephesians 1:13; Mark 16:15–18)

5. The Holy Spirit is received by grace through faith (John 1:15–17; Galatians 3:2–5)

6. The Holy Spirit characterises the Kingdom of God (Romans 14:17)

## 2. DIFFERENCE OF DISTRIBUTION

In the Old Testament era the Spirit empowered only a few individuals at particular times, but the promise of God for the New Testament era is that everyone may know the intimate touch of God's Spirit upon their lives, as Joel and Peter confirmed. When the Lord says, *"I will pour out My Spirit upon all flesh"*, He does not mean on all without exception (every living soul), but on all flesh without distinction. In Joel 2:27 God refers to *"My people"*, those who belong to Him (as opposed to the devil's children for example, John 8:44). His people are those related by Spirit rebirth (John 3:3–8) and on these God pours out His Spirit, irrespective of their gender, social status, age or ability, as the context of Joel shows.

However, some believers are reluctant to accept that God will pour out His Spirit on their flesh! They will only accept the Spirit's presence in their soul, in an unseen, unfelt, inner way. This is a grave error. Truly it is better for us to be totally compliant with the Spirit's will, than to try bending His operations to our personal preferences. In the Bible, salvation is applied to the whole person, not just the soul! Some might say that Joel's use of the word *flesh* simply means human beings, but remember that *"your body is the temple of the Holy Spirit"* (1 Corinthians 6:19).

## 3. DIFFERENCE OF DEGREE

In the Old Testament people were convicted, quickened, filled, guided, clothed with, transported and energised by the Holy Spirit. They also experienced many gifts of the Spirit, including prophecy, healing and miracle power. However, the New Testament era began with a new and distinct experience, different from anything that had happened before – they were baptised in the Holy Spirit! Under the Old Covenant the deepest degree of intimacy that a person could experience was to be filled with the Holy Spirit. Something on a higher level is planned for New Testament saints, namely to be baptised in the Holy Spirit (Matthew 3:11; Acts 1:4–5). While the filling with the Spirit was restricted to a few people in Old Testament times, the New Testament baptism with the Spirit is a profound experience promised to all and providing a continuous outflow and an unrestricted and constant filling. What is the difference between being "filled with" and being "baptised in" the Holy Spirit? When you are filled with the Spirit, you have the Holy Spirit. When you are baptised in the Spirit, the Holy Spirit has you! The illustrations below show the difference:

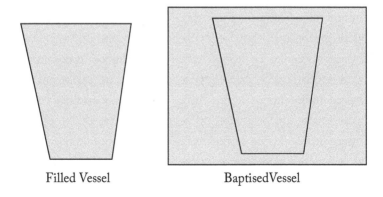

Filled Vessel                                   BaptisedVessel

It is important to realise that a believer is baptised in the Spirit only once, just as they are baptised in water only once. There is one baptism, not multiple baptisms, and the one baptism is sufficient to accompany the person right into eternity. Spirit baptism is the initial thrust leading to a constant filling.

## 4. DIFFERENCE OF DURABILITY

Samson knew both the presence and the absence of the Holy Spirit upon his life (Judges 14:6; 16:20), and the cry of David was, *"Take not Your Holy Spirit from me"* (Psalm 51:11). But Jesus gave His followers a new promise that the Counsellor (Comforter, Helper or Holy Spirit) would *"abide with you for ever"*. The Spirit comes to live within us and to stay. The Holy Spirit was never given in this way previously, and it is the baptism in the Spirit which causes the anointing to remain with us. 1 John 2:27 says, *"The anointing which you have received from Him abides with you."* 1 John 3:24 explains that it is the abiding Spirit which lets us know the abiding presence of the Lord Jesus: *"By this we know that He abides in us, by the Spirit whom He has given us."* Clearly, if the Spirit didn't live in us continually, we would have only intellectual assent that the Lord was still with us!

It is the baptism in the Holy Spirit which enables us to be constantly filled with the Spirit, and a literal translation of Ephesians 5:18 is *"Be being filled with the Spirit"*. Those already baptised in the Holy Spirit might attend meetings seeking to be recharged with the Holy Spirit. But they do not receive Spirit baptism again. When a person yields more of their life to the Lord, or surrenders more areas of their soul to Him, they can experience a new filling of the Spirit. Also, they will have a richer emotional feeling and the reassurance that the Spirit in fact had never left them. The original anointing of the Spirit remains, as John says. The other factors are that seeking the Lord very often provides them with a clean conscience, through confession of their sins and their unworthiness. All this enables them to leave the meeting feeling closer to God and refreshed.

One of the devil's tricks is to cause a believer to think that the Spirit has left him, and that he needs to seek the Lord for the Spirit to come back. This is the Old Testament way, and quite distinct from the New Testament promise of an abiding Spirit's presence. Of course, the Holy Spirit within the believer can be grieved by sin and repetitive disobedience, and His activities can be quenched if we are critical of Him, or if we deliberately prevent Him from operating. In these cases He patiently waits for that person to repent and submit to the Lord – this enables the Spirit to fill the believer afresh and to re-establish His Lordship in their life.

## 5. DIFFERENCE OF DESIGNATION

A new descriptive name is introduced to describe the action of the Spirit in a believer's life in the New Testament age: BAPTISM – immersed, plunged, submerged and engulfed. Jesus said that John the Baptist was the greatest of the Old Testament prophets, and it was this same John who prophesied

| BAPTISM | PURPOSE | BAPTISER | BAPTISED | MEDIUM | SCRIPTURES |
|---------|---------|----------|----------|--------|------------|
| CEREMONIAL WASHINGS | Set apart | Jewish Priests | People and artefacts | Water | Matthew 23:25 –26 <br> Mark 7:1–5 |
| JEWISH PROSELYTES | Conversion to Judaism | Pharisees | Converts to Judaism | Water | Matthew 23:15 Acts 13:43 |
| JOHN'S BAPTISM | Repentance | John the Baptist | Repentant people | Water | Matthew 3:6 <br> John 1:25–26 |
| SUFFERINGS OF CHRIST | Provision of salvation | Powers of Darkness | Jesus Christ | Scourging, cross, death | Matthew 20:22 –23 <br> Mark 10:38 |
| BELIEVER'S BAPTISM | Confirming salvation | Christian minister | Born-again believers | Water | Matthew 28:19 Mark 16:16 |
| BAPTISM IN HOLY SPIRIT | Power for service | Jesus Christ | Born-again believers | Holy Spirit | Matthew 3:11 <br> Luke 3:16 <br> Acts 1:4-8 |
| BAPTISM OF FIRE | Judgment | Jesus Christ | Unsaved | Fire | Matthew 3:11 <br> Luke 3:16–17 |

about the baptism in the Holy Spirit. His words are recorded in all four Gospels – this does not make them more accurate, but establishes their importance. Jesus Himself used the term *"baptism in the Holy Spirit"* in Acts 1:5, indicating what would occur after His ascension.

There are at least seven different baptisms referred to in the Bible, and we need to distinguish them. The table above illustrates the differences.

John Baptist clearly taught that Jesus would baptise people in the Holy Spirit, but Matthew and Luke add two small words, *"and fire"*. It has been assumed that these words exemplify and elucidate Spirit baptism, that it is accompanied by divine fire! The fact that *"tongues of fire"* rested on each believer on the Day of Pentecost seems to endorse this view. However, other Scripture references to *"fire"* concern judgment, and the contextual verses of both Matthew 3:10–12 and Luke 3:9,17 lead to the conclusion that John the Baptist is speaking about two distinct baptisms – baptism in the Holy Spirit for believers, and a separate, contrasting baptism of fire for unbelievers.

# CHAPTER FIVE

# THE BAPTISM IN
# THE HOLY SPIRIT

A T THE OUTSET IT SHOULD BE UNDERSTOOD THAT BAPTISM *with* the Spirit is the same as baptism *in* the Spirit, just as baptism with water is the same as baptism in water. The English language allows baptism to be described either way. We prefer the conjunction *in* because *baptism* signifies immersion whether in water or in the Spirit. Every verse in the New Testament referring to Spirit baptism uses the NT Greek preposition εν (meaning *in*) followed by a dative noun. The phrase 'baptism *of* the Spirit' is not scriptural and implies that it is the Spirit Himself who is baptised!

Before the eventful Day of Pentecost recorded in Acts 2, people were convicted, quickened, filled, guided, clothed with and energised by the Holy Spirit. But on that day Christ's disciples experienced the Holy Spirit in a new and distinct manner from anything that had happened before – they were *baptised* in the Holy Spirit! The phenomenon of the baptism in the Holy Spirit on the Day of Pentecost will be examined under eight headings:

# 1. THE PEOPLE OF PENTECOST

Acts 1:12–15 says the people included the eleven apostles (Judas had committed suicide), with Jesus' mother and brothers, some of the women, plus other disciples – about 120 persons.

*Their position – born again*

These people were already saved, regenerated, forgiven, justified and spiritual members of the Church of Jesus Christ. They loved the Lord Jesus and obediently they waited in Jerusalem for what He had promised them. Consider the following facts:

Luke 10:20 – their names were written in heaven (Jesus said this to the seventy).

Matthew 16:15–20 – God's revelation showed them that Jesus was God's Son.

Luke 9:1–6, 10:1–24 – they had been sent out to preach, heal and deliver.

John 13:10 – they were clean.

John 14:17 – they had the Spirit dwelling with them already.

John 17:6–14 – Jesus' prayer words regard them as regenerate persons.

John 17:20–22 – Jesus said others would get saved through their ministry.

John 20:19–23 – they received the Person of the Holy Spirit as Jesus breathed on them.

Matthew 28:18–20 – Jesus commissioned them to preach.

Luke 24:49; Acts 1:4–8 – Jesus commanded them to wait for the baptism in Holy Spirit.

It is plain to see these people belonged to the Lord before the Day of Pentecost. They were reconciled to God, born again and saved. It is an unworthy and unscriptural argument to suggest that they were born again on the Day of Pentecost! Support for this erroneous view is made by suggesting that the Day of Pentecost was the 'birthday of the Church' (implying it was a once-for-all happening). However, such theories are totally without scriptural warrant.

Also, it is unethical to use John's words *"because the Spirit was not yet (given)"* to suggest that they had a born-again experience at the same time as their baptism with the Spirit! We have already seen that the words *"because the Spirit was not yet (given)"* does not mean the Spirit was absent or ineffective, or that He had not yet arrived on earth. Jesus told His disciples that the Holy Spirit was already with them. However, the Spirit had not yet been given as the medium into whom Christ Himself would baptise believers. The disciples on the Day of Pentecost were the first Christians to be baptised in the Holy Spirit, therefore they set the pattern for us all: firstly born again, then secondly baptised with the Spirit.

*Their condition – not equipped*

Remarkably these disciples were ill-equipped and unfitted for the task ahead of them. They had been three years in the Master's Bible School; they had listened to His teaching; they had asked Him many questions; they had watched Him perform miracles; they had been sent out by the Lord to do the same things that He did; they had seen Him suffer and die; they had witnessed His bodily resurrection and seen His physical ascension into heaven; and they had been commissioned to take the gospel to all the world, and many had received the Holy Spirit when Jesus breathed on them. Despite all these things, they were told not to begin the work of publishing the gospel, but to wait for the *"power from on high"*, which Jesus referred to as the *"Promise of the Father"* and the *"baptism in the Holy Spirit"* (Luke 24:49; Acts 1:4– 8).

*Their submission – obediently compliant*

Acts 5:32 says that *"the Holy Spirit is given to those who obey Him"*. Mary the mother of Jesus was present on the Day of Pentecost and she had said long before, *"Whatever He says to you, do it"* (John 2:5 NKJV). So compliantly they waited in Jerusalem for Spirit baptism. There seems to have been no disapproval from the disciples about waiting, although they could have protested and raised many seemingly valid arguments against needing something more:

> We've learned from You, Lord, for three years, we know how to operate.

> We've already become children God and our names are written in heaven.

> We've learned how to pray, and what to pray for, just as You taught us.

> We've witnessed your sufferings, and Your resurrection glory.

> We've already received the Holy Spirit, when You breathed on us.

> We've already been commissioned by You, and we know what to do.

> We've seen Your amazing bodily ascension into heaven.

> We've got Your promise: You're always with us, even to the end of the age.

These and many more protestations could have been made by the disciples.

# 2. THE PHENOMENON OF PENTECOST

Here is a list of the main points taken from Acts 2:1–4.

1. *They were all with one accord in one place.* Together in unity.

2. *Suddenly.* There was no slow build-up or warning signs.

3. *There came a sound from heaven.* A heavenly source, not from earth.

4. *Like a rushing mighty wind.* It could be heard, felt and its effects seen.

5. *It filled the whole house where they were sitting.* Everywhere, not just a corner!

6. *There appeared to them separated tongues of fire.* Visible phenomenon.

7. *One sat on each of them.* An individual experience for each person.

8. *They were all filled with the Holy Spirit.* Spirit baptism includes filling of the Spirit.

9. *Began to speak with tongues.* A beginning generally leading to a continual act.

10. *As the Spirit enabled them.* Holy Spirit ability, not the result of human emotion.

## Its designation

Consider the words, names, titles and terms used in the New Testament for this event:

1. The promise of the Father. Luke 24:49; Acts 1:4, 2:33,39; Galatians 3:14

2. The baptism in the Holy Spirit. Matthew 3:11; John 1:33; Acts 1:5, 11:16

3. The Holy Spirit comes upon and falls on you. Acts 1:8, 10:44

4. Filled with the Holy Spirit. Acts 2:4

5. Pour out My Spirit upon. Acts 2:17

6. Gift, and Gave the Holy Spirit, just as He did to us. Acts 2:38, 11:16–17, 15:8

7. Sealed, deposit, foretaste. 2 Corinthians 1:21–22, 5:5; Ephesians 1:13, 4:30

8. Endued (clothed) with power from above. Luke 24:49; Acts 1:8

9. Received the Holy Spirit just as we have. Acts 10:47

10. Anointed. 2 Corinthians 1:21; 1 John 2:20,27

Each term is significant. The *promise* means it is backed up by God's immutable word and emphasises the faithfulness of God. *Father* confirms that Spirit baptism is for God's children. *Baptism* indicates immersed, deluged, drenched, submerged and overwhelmed. *Baptises* refers to Jesus who does the baptising, and the Holy Spirit who is the medium into whom He immerses you. *Comes upon* and *falls* confirms that Spirit baptism is from outside a person's life. *Filled* affirms that Spirit baptism results in being abundantly satisfied. *Poured out* means Spirit baptism is a copious supply. *Gift* and *gave* shows that Spirit baptism isn't a reward and cannot be earned. *Sealed* means that Spirit baptism stamps the mark of Christ upon us. *Deposit* specifies that Spirit baptism grants a foretaste of heaven. *Endued* attests that Spirit baptism clothes, enables and enhances life and service. *Power from above* denotes that Spirit baptism concerns divine power, not human or earthly power. *Received* indicates that Spirit baptism is to be willingly accepted. *Anoints* points out that Spirit baptism bestows a blessing for ministry and service.

## 3. THE PROMISE OF PENTECOST

Most Christians accept without question what happened to the disciples on the Day of Pentecost. The experience of millions of believers in recent years has shown that what the disciples received then, we can receive today! Indeed, the Bible shows that the baptism in the Holy Spirit is promised to all believers. Who spoke of this promise?

*The prophet Joel – Joel 2:28–32*

These verses clinch the matter. The Lord will *"pour out His Spirit on all flesh . . . in those days"*. Those days last until the sun is darkened at the return of Christ to earth. So the promise is for all generations. As long as people can call upon the Name of the Lord for salvation, so they can know the outpouring of the Spirit on their lives. The context of Joel confirms that the Holy Spirit is poured out up to the time of the Lord's return to earth.

*John the Baptist – Matthew 3:5,11; Mark 1:5,8; Luke 3:7,16; John 1:33; Acts 1:4–5, 11:16*

John the Baptist spoke to all who came to him about Jesus being the One who *"baptises in the Holy Spirit"*.

*The Lord Jesus – Matthew 28:19–20*

All that Christ had taught His disciples they in turn were to teach others to observe *"to the end of the age"*. I'm included in that! Christ taught His disciples that they needed the baptism in the Spirit, the dynamic power from above, to be His effective witnesses. They taught this not only by words, but by example and practice.

*The apostle Peter – in Acts 2:33,38–39*

Peter said the promise of the baptism in the Spirit is for *"as many as the Lord our God shall call"*. The Father's promise of Spirit baptism is for every believer, in every generation since the Day of Pentecost, and thus for you and me today!

## 4. THE PERPETUATION OF PENTECOST

Scripture declares that what happened on the Day of Pentecost was not a one-off occurrence. The New Testament shows that others were baptised in the Holy Spirit subsequent to the Day of Pentecost.

*Samaritan Believers – Acts 8:14–17*

The believers in Samaria were born again and baptised in water by Philip. Subsequent to this, Peter and John arrived and *"prayed for them that they might receive the Holy Spirit. For as yet He had fallen upon none of them: they had only been baptised* (in water) *in the name of the Lord Jesus"*. It was after they believed the gospel and were saved that Philip baptised them in water. It was after all this that Peter and John *"laid their hands on them, and they received the Holy Spirit"*. How long did it take for news of the Samaritan revival to reach Jerusalem? And how long did it take for Peter and John to reach Samaria and find Philip? This would have taken at least a number of days. We see that just as the 120 disciples were baptised in the Holy Spirit some time after they were saved, so the pattern remained true for the Samaritan believers.

*Saul of Tarsus – Acts 9:1–7,17*

Almost without controversy Christians accept that Saul was saved on the road while travelling to Damascus. During this encounter it is significant that twice Saul called Jesus *"Lord"*. Later Saul (now Paul) writes in 1 Corinthians 12:3 that *"no one can say that Jesus is Lord except by the Holy Spirit"*. So it is evident that Saul had experienced the Holy Spirit in his life as he was bathed in light from heaven and as Jesus spoke to him. For three days Saul remained without sight. He receives a prophetic vision about Ananias who arrives and says he has come to restore Saul's sight and cause him to be filled with the Holy Spirit. Here is another Biblical instance where a person is saved some days before he is filled with the Spirit. Recall that the 120 disciples were filled with the Spirit when they were baptised in the Spirit, and doubtless the same procedure happened to Saul – he was filled with the Spirit as a result of being baptised in the Spirit.

*Cornelius and his household – Acts 10:34–48*

Peter's visit to Cornelius took place between ten and twelve years after the events on the Day of Pentecost. Peter visited Cornelius after God showed him that Gentiles were not unclean but acceptable to God through believing the message of salvation. We generally believe that Cornelius and his household were not saved believers when Peter began preaching the gospel to them. Then, while Peter continued his message, something wonderful occurred. The Holy Spirit fell upon all who heard the word, resulting in the Jewish Christians amazement that the gift of the Holy Spirit was poured out on Gentiles.

How did Peter and his Jewish companions know that the Holy Spirit had been poured out upon Cornelius and his household? *"They heard them speak with tongues and magnify God."* Peter went on to say that they *"have received the Holy Spirit just as we have"*, and later Peter explains the whole episode to the Jewish believers in Jerusalem, stating that *"the Holy Spirit fell upon them, as upon us at the beginning"*. This can only mean one thing: what Cornelius and his household received was the same as that received by the 120 many years earlier on the Day of Pentecost. Then Peter recalled the words of Jesus, *"John indeed baptised with water, but you shall be baptised with the Holy Spirit"*, and this is exactly what had happened to Cornelius and his household. It is after these Gentiles are saved and baptised in the Holy Spirit that Peter baptises them in water.

In this instance we have a difference of order. Firstly Cornelius was born of the Spirit and perhaps within moments, baptised in the Holy Spirit. This means that Spirit birth and Spirit baptism can occur at almost the same time, although it appears to be an exception in God's dealings. Notice the evidence that people had been baptised in the Spirit was outward, audible, visible, physical and dynamic. It was not based on an assumption that Spirit birth and Spirit baptism always occur together with little or no outward evidence, as some teach.

### The Ephesian converts – Acts 19:1-6

Protagonists against being baptised in the Holy Spirit today have gone to great lengths to explain that these *believers* were not saved, they were unregenerate disciples of John the Baptist.

Paul, however, recognises them as *"disciples"* who *"believed"*. Interestingly he does not ask them if or how they were saved, but: *"Did you receive the Holy Spirit when you believed?"* (NKJV). His question indicates that it is possible to *believe* but not *receive* the baptism in the Holy Spirit. Their literal answer, *"We have not heard whether holy Spirit there is."* So Paul questions their water baptism. If they had experienced believer's water baptism they would have heard about the Holy Spirit since Jesus instructed the tripartite title of God to be used (Matthew 28:19).

Now the crunch comes. If these *believers* were just John the Baptist's converts, and not truly saved Christian believers, why did Paul baptise them in water? He did so because at that point they were born-again believers. There is no instance or doctrine in the Scriptures to suggest we should be baptised in water before we are born again! Infant baptism remains an unscriptural formality based on misunderstanding.

After the Ephesians are saved and baptised in water, Paul lays his hands upon them and they are baptised in the Holy Spirit. Once again we know they were baptised in the Spirit because *"they spoke with tongues and prophesied"*. It was not merely assumed that they were baptised in the Spirit independently of outward evidence.

### Church history

Let me say straight away that it is not acceptable to believe and cite particular activities in Church history, while ignoring others. There is ample evidence of the manifestations (gifts) of the Spirit in use within the Church down the centuries. For example, Augustine in the fourth century wrote, "We still do what the apostles did when they laid hands on the converts to receive the Holy Spirit. It is expected that the converts will speak in tongues."

Various theories have been invented by unscrupulous believers to account for the Bible's repeated instances of the baptism in the Spirit subsequent to the Day of Pentecost. The Plymouth Brethren said that what happened on the Day of Pentecost was never repeated! They taught this despite the repeated instances cited in the Acts of the Apostles and despite the testimony of Church history. In order to twist the Bible to fit their own theory, they suggest that the four repeated instances of Spirit baptism in Acts arose because each case was special rather than typical, although the Bible is silent about such a theory.

They postulate that the Samaritans were a mixed race and their Pentecostal experience was necessary to show they were included in God's call to salvation. Then they say, Saul received a Pentecostal experience because he was to be the apostle to the Gentiles. Similarly, Cornelius and his household received a Pentecostal experience because they were the first Gentiles to be saved. The Ephesian converts were really disciples of John the Baptist, not of Jesus Christ. So they received a Pentecostal experience to confirm that they were saved. None of these suppositions are endorsed by Scripture, they are manmade contrivances to wriggle out of accepting the validity of the baptism in the Holy Spirit today. Leaning on one's own understanding rather than trusting the Word of God gives rise to many inventions totally unsupported by Scripture. How tragic that false teaching is taught to unsuspecting believers to deprive them of a blessing which God has promised to *"as many as the Lord our God shall call"*.

## 5. THE PURPOSE OF PENTECOST

*Power for service*

Remember that what occurred on the Day of Pentecost was not the simple arrival of the Holy Spirit, either into the world or into the first disciples. It was the arrival of a new experience termed the *baptism in the Holy Spirit*. The baptism in the Spirit enables believers to be effective witnesses of Christ and to have faith in God to perform miracles. Power for service is its principle purpose. Jesus said, *"I send the Promise of My Father upon you; but wait in the city of Jerusalem until you are endued with power from on high"* (Luke 24:49 NKJV). He continued, *"you shall be baptized with the Holy Spirit not many days from now . . . you shall receive power when the Holy Spirit has come upon you; and you shall be witnesses to Me"* (Acts 1:5,8 NKJV).

Consider the first disciples who had been in Christ's 'School of Ministry' for three years, but who Jesus indicated remained ill-equipped to implement the Great Commission until they had been baptised in the Holy Spirit. It is evident that having the Holy Spirit is different from having the baptism in the Holy Spirit. Doubtless we interact with the Holy Spirit when we are born again, but we remain ill-equipped without the power and dynamic of God until we have been baptised by Jesus in the Holy Spirit.

After Jesus had been crucified, the Scriptures acknowledge that the first disciples were very afraid of reprisals. As they gathered together they locked the doors, fearing the Jewish authorities would endeavour to find them and kill them. The Scriptures also show how bold these same disciples were after Pentecost. For example, Peter blatantly accused his hearers of being responsible for Christ's death. *"Whom you crucified,"* he said (Acts 2:23,36; 4:10), and when commanded by members of the Sanhedrin not to preach in Jesus' Name, unflinchingly they replied that they ought to obey God rather than men (Acts 5:29).

## Provision of spiritual gifts

It is possible to exercise some of the manifestations (gifts) of the Holy Spirit before being baptised in the Spirit, as did the Old Testament saints, with prophecy, healings and miraculous happenings. But the New Testament indicates that the initial baptism in the Holy Spirit opens the way for the exercise of His special gifts in a believer's life. Whilst the Holy Spirit operates freely according to His own will, His general *modus operandi* is that the *baptism* leads to the *filling*, and then to the *gifts* and the *fruit* of the Spirit.

Out of the nine manifestations of the Spirit, two were absent in Old Testament times, being reserved for the New Covenant age of the Holy Spirit. These unique New Covenant gifts are speaking in tongues and the interpretation of tongues, of which the former is especially operational when a believer is baptised in the Holy Spirit.

1 Corinthians 12:4 says, *"There are diversities of gifts [charismata] but the same Spirit."* 1 Corinthians 12:8–11 lists nine specific manifestations of the Spirit: word of wisdom, word of knowledge, faith, gifts of healings, working of miracles, prophecy, discerning of spirits, different languages and the interpretation of languages. Then we read that one and the same Spirit works all these things, distributing to each individually as He wills. Each manifestation of the Spirit is supernatural in its origin. They can be imitated or replaced with human substitutes, of course, but the genuine gifts of the Spirit do not come through study, practice or mimicry. They are manifestations of the Spirit; that is, they are the Holy Spirit revealing Himself in these extraordinary ways. This is one reason why we are told not to despise them.

John 14:12 says, *"he who believes in Me, the works that I do he will do also; and greater works than these because I go to the Father."* The last phrase *"because I go to the Father"*, refers to the fact that when Jesus ascends to Father God, the Holy Spirit would come as the baptismal medium, enabling miracle works to be performed. John 16:7 records the words of Jesus, *"Nevertheless I tell you the truth. It is to your advantage that I go away; for if I do not go away, the Helper will not come to you; but if I depart, I will send Him to you."* The word *Helper* refers to the Holy Spirit who is also an intercessor, comforter, advocate, counsellor and encourager. The Holy Spirit would more than compensate for the loss of the bodily presence of Jesus, and the historical account of the early Church in the Book of Acts records numerous miracles through the ministry of believers, made possible by the baptism in the Holy Spirit.

*Production of Fruit – purity*

Galatians 5:22–23: *"The fruit of the Spirit is love, joy, peace, longsuffering, kindness, goodness, faithfulness, meekness, self-control. Against such there is no law."*

Romans 14:17: *The kingdom of God is not eating and drinking, but righteousness and peace and joy in the Holy Spirit."*

The truth is that despite believers being *"born again"* and being *"new creations in Christ"*, they themselves lack the capacity to produce the excellent fruit of character. Such fruit can be produced only by the Holy Spirit. It is not a coincidence that John 15 about believers bearing fruit is sandwiched between chapters 14 and 16 which talk about the Holy Spirit. John 15 contains a key to fruitfulness. Nowhere in this chapter does it mention that the believer must *produce* fruit! In verses 2–8 the Greek word *phero* is used six times and it means to carry, or in older English, to bear. Jesus carefully shows that it is the vine (Jesus Himself) which produces the fruit, but each branch must bear that fruit.

Some people are morally better than others. Some have a quieter and more refined disposition. Some have a good character with acceptable qualities such as honesty, truthfulness and reliability. There is nothing wrong with such human traits, but they are no substitute for the fruit of the Spirit which is produced in believers by the Spirit Himself.

# 6. THE PRODUCT OF PENTECOST

Jesus made it clear that the baptism in the Spirit provides power for service, and leads to the gifts of the Spirit and the fruit of the Spirit. These are the three principal purposes of the baptism in the Spirit. However, special products are mentioned in Scripture.

They are not the reason for the baptism in the Spirit, but something which emanates and derives from it. Acts 2:4: *"And they were all filled with the Holy Spirit and began to speak with other tongues as the Spirit gave them utterance."* The two products mentioned in the above verse are the *filling* with the Holy Spirit and s*peaking with other languages.*

## Filled with the Spirit

It is impossible to be *baptised* in the Spirit without being *filled* with the Spirit. The baptism includes the filling, and the filling accompanies and ensues from the baptism. Many Old Testament people were *"filled with the Spirit"* (Exodus 31:3, for example), but none were baptised in the Spirit, that is a new dynamic reserved for the New Testament age.

Spirit baptism produces something unique in the believer's life. We could describe it like the construction of a causeway down which the Spirit can travel; or we could say it produces a channel through which the river of God's Spirit can flow, just as Jesus said, *"Out of his belly will flow rivers of living water, but this He spoke concerning the Spirit."* It is interesting to find that some Christians happily accept the filling of the Spirit as a legitimate New Testament experience, but shy away from Bible teaching about the baptism in the Spirit! However, it's almost a case of "you can't have one without the other", because Spirit baptism includes the filling, and a continual filling emanates from the baptism. Reasons why some prefer to speak of filling rather than baptism are many, including the fact that the filling is perceived as a spiritual happening – unseen, unfelt, unaccompanied by physical evidence. While the baptism includes physical overtones such as tongues and other manifestations, which are feared or considered unacceptable! This brings us to the second product of the baptism in the Spirit.

## Speaking with other languages

*"And they were all filled with the Holy Spirit and began to speak with other tongues as the Spirit gave them utterance"* (Acts 2:4). Spirit baptism produces characteristics quite distinct from any other operation of the Spirit. One of these is the ability to *"speak with tongues"*, meaning languages which have not been previously learned by the speaker.

Let's examine the Scriptures to see where speaking with tongues applies to the baptism in the Spirit.

## The disciples on the Day of Pentecost – Acts 2:1–13

How did the people in Jerusalem know God had met with the believers in that special way which Jesus had described as *"The Promise of the Father"* and *"The Baptism in the Holy Spirit"*, Acts 1:4–5? We might also ask, "How did the believers themselves know that what happened to them was exactly what Jesus had promised as they waited in Jerusalem?" It is not recorded that Jesus described in detail what would happen when His followers were baptised in the Spirit. When it happened, it seems that they knew instinctively and spiritually what was taking place. It was the same for me; nobody told me I had been baptised in the Spirit, but I knew without doubt exactly what had happened and when it occurred! This is how real spiritual things are. Perceptions, knowledge and understanding are all increased and elevated to the highest level possible for mortals to experience! The phrase "we know that we know that we know" is used to describe with certainty the indisputable nature of an experience with God. The evidence of what actually happened when believers were baptised in the Spirit in the Bible is often given. On the Day of Pentecost certain outward, tangible and physical phenomena are described:

1. A sound from heaven like a mighty, rushing wind.

2. The sound filled the house.

3. Tongues of fire separated and sat on each of them.

4. They were all filled with the Spirit.

5. They began to speak with other tongues as enabled by the Spirit.

### The Samaritan believers – Acts 8:14–24

Verse 17 says, *"Then they laid hands on them, and they received the Holy Spirit."* So hands were laid upon the believers, but no outward evidence is described – neither wind, nor fire, nor tongues are mentioned. Something outstanding did occur, however, because it impressed Simon so much he offered money to possess the power to baptise people in the Holy Spirit! These Scriptures confirm that the baptism in the Spirit is not merely an unseen and unfelt inward, spiritual experience, but a spiritual experience revealing itself with outward, physical effects. However, in this particular case, the outward effects are not described.

### Saul of Tarsus – Acts 9:1–22

> *"Brother Saul, the Lord Jesus, who appeared to you in the way as you came, has sent me that you may receive your sight and be filled with the Holy Spirit."*

Doubtless Ananias laid hands on Saul, but did other manifestations occur such as wind, fire and tongues? The Bible gives no descriptive details. We know, however, that Saul did speak in tongues, as he confessed later, *"I thank my God I speak with tongues more than you all."*

If it is asked, "When did Saul first speak in tongues?", we have no clear Bible statement. But the mention of his powerful and persuasive preaching points to the fact that he was baptised in the Spirit when Ananias prayed for him, and doubtless tongues began then. It is the baptism in the Spirit which gives power and gifts (including tongues) and initiates the Spirit filling a believer's life. So the outward evidence in Saul's case is:

1. Hands laid on Saul by Ananias.

2. Saul receives his sight.

3. Saul is filled with the Holy Spirit.

4. Saul preaches Christ with convincing power.

5. Saul (later named Paul) claims to speak copiously in tongues (1 Corinthians 14:18).

*Cornelius and his household - Acts 10:34-48*

Here godly but unsaved Gentiles hear the gospel as Peter preaches. They are saved and baptised in the Holy Spirit before Peter has finished speaking. Peter testifies that it was in exactly the same way that the Spirit fell on the disciples on the Day of Pentecost, Acts 10:47, 11:15–17. But how did Peter and the other Jews with him know that Gentiles had been baptised in the Holy Spirit? Were hands laid upon them? Was there a mighty wind? Were there tongues of fire? Did they immediately begin preaching powerfully? No, there were none of these things. The answer is, *"They heard them speak with tongues and magnify God."*

The evidences in this case are:

1. The gospel is preached to Gentiles.

2. The Gentiles are baptised in the Holy Spirit.

3. The Gentiles speak with tongues and magnify God.

4. The Gentiles are obviously saved, and they are baptised in water later.

## *The Ephesian converts – Acts 19:1-6*

In this chapter we have ardent disciples of John the Baptist, who strangely have not heard of the Holy Spirit, although John the Baptist spoke about the Spirit. Paul explains that John the Baptist pointed forward to Jesus Christ, whom they should now believe. It is evident that they did believe in Christ because Paul baptises them in water. After that Paul lays his hands upon the believers and the Holy Spirit comes upon them. Again we ask how Paul knew that the Holy Spirit had come upon them. Did Paul accept they were baptised in the Spirit by what we might describe as purely by faith? Was it a spiritual and physically undetectable event, or was there some outward, tangible evidence? The Scriptures clearly say that they spoke with tongues and prophesied. Here are the facts in this case:

1. John's followers become Christ's followers.
2. The believers are baptised in water.
3. Paul lays hands on the believers.
4. The believers are baptised in the Holy Spirit.
5. The believers speak with tongues and prophesy.

Above are the only instances in Scripture where baptism in the Spirit is cited, and we see that it is a definite event taking place after conversion. Putting these instances into the chart below reveals some interesting facts:

The chart indicates which effects are similar in each event. The order of events in three cases out of five is that conversion and baptism in water occur in a believer's life before they are baptised in the Spirit. Concerning Saul of Tarsus, the Scriptures do not cite the moment he was baptised in water or in the Spirit, although both occurred some days after his conversion. The

| EVENT | TEXT | SAVED | WATER BAPTISM | WAITING | LAYING ON HANDS | SPIRIT BAPTISM | FILLED | SPEAKING IN TONGUES |
|---|---|---|---|---|---|---|---|---|
| PENTECOST | Acts 2:1–39 | ✓ | ✓ | Years | Wind and fire | ✓ | ✓ | ✓ |
| SAMARITANS | Acts 8:14–24 | ✓ | ✓ | Weeks | ✓ | ✓ | ✓ | Not described |
| SAUL (PAUL) | Acts 9:1–22 | ✓ | ✓ | Days | ✓ | ✓ | ✓ | ✓ |
| CORNELIUS | Acts 10:34–48 | ✓ | ✓ later | Minutes | – | ✓ | ✓ | ✓ |
| EPHESIANS | Acts 19:1–6 | ✓ | ✓ | Hours | ✓ | ✓ | ✓ | ✓ |

occasion with Cornelius and his household shows they were all saved and baptised in the Holy Spirit and spoke in tongues before being baptised in water. Despite the exceptions we rightly conclude that the usual pattern of events is:

1. Conversion
2. Water baptism
3. Baptism in the Holy Spirit
4. Speaking in tongues

However, God is sovereign and this order of events is not a straight-jacket timeline! An un-churched young man in Leyton, London got saved, and the same week attended the prayer meeting where the Lord baptised him in the Holy Spirit, although he had not yet been baptised in water. Very wisely Scripture does not allow us to put God into a rigid mode or bind Him to a set order of functioning. Remember, the Holy Spirit acts as He wills to act, and not according to our preferences, ideas or regulations. Laying on hands is applied in three out of the five cases. Where no laying on hands occurs is firstly with the disciples on the Day of Pentecost when they obediently waited on God for the baptism in the Spirit, not knowing when or what would happen. Secondly in Cornelius' house where they were saved and baptised in the Spirit while Peter preached the gospel. Speaking in tongues is described clearly in three out of five instances. The remaining two instances are firstly the Samaritans, where no description of what happened is given. Yet here Simon saw something remarkable take place and wanted the power to do it! The second instance is with Saul, where once again no description of what happened is given, but later Saul (who became Paul) says that he spoke with tongues more than all the Corinthians. It is reasonable and plausible to conclude that speaking with tongues was manifested in both these instances, at the time of the baptism in the Holy Spirit.

Do all believers speak in tongues when they are baptised in the Spirit? Are tongues a sign or evidence that someone has been baptised in the Spirit? Some teach that speaking with tongues is the *initial evidence* of being baptised in the Spirit, and generally this is so. The Bible does not spell this out so dogmatically, however, and I prefer to say that speaking with tongues is *an evidence* of being baptised in the Spirit. Tongues are often the first evidence, but not always. This sits comfortably with Scripture, and also fits in with my own experience, which shows that most do speak with tongues at the time they are baptised in the Holy Spirit.

With God there are often exceptions. Let me tell about, the young student who called at my house saying urgently, "Pastor, can we pray?" Immediately we sat in a side room and knelt to pray, but instead of praying, James began prophesying! A lengthy stream of inspiring and God-magnifying prophecy flowed from his being like a mighty river, and after some time with beaming eyes we looked at each other and he asked, "What has happened to me?" I said, "You have been baptised in the Holy Spirit." "But I haven't spoken in tongues!" was his immediate reply, and in turn I answered, "Don't you worry about that; you may well speak with tongues later, just as the Lord decides."

A few days later James told me he had been looking up into the night sky, seeing a multitude of stars, and praising the Lord, when suddenly, like the prophecy, speaking with tongues began pouring out of him. Wonderful! Interestingly it says about the Ephesian converts that they *"spoke with tongues and prophesied"*. In this instance they did both, whereas my student friend prophesied firstly, then spoke with tongues later.

# 7. THE PICTURES OF PENTECOST

*A well*

Isaiah 12:3 speaks about the wells of salvation. In John 3:3–8 Jesus describes the need to be born again, or born of the Spirit, which He illustrates in chapter 4 as a well or fountain, bubbling up into eternal life. Near Jacob's well, Jesus asks a Samaritan woman for a drink of water. She is puzzled that a Jew should ask anything from a Samaritan woman, but Jesus said whoever drinks His water will never thirst because His water will be in them a well of water springing up into everlasting life. So a well depicts salvation – eternal life.

*A river*

In contrasts with his earlier words the prophet later speaks of *"rivers in the wilderness"* (Isaiah 43:19). Jesus draws a similar contrast, by referring to *rivers* in John 7:37–39, *"If anyone thirsts, let him come to Me and drink. He who believes in me, as the Scripture has said, out of his belly will flow rivers of living water. But this He spoke of the Spirit whom those who believed in Him should receive; for the Holy Spirit was not yet (given), because Jesus was not yet glorified."* In this context, rivers refer to the baptism in the Holy Spirit and the ongoing fullness and life in the Spirit which God has promised to every believer.

*"The last day of the feast"* refers to the tenth and final day of the Jewish Feast of Tabernacles (Booths or Ingathering held on the fifteenth day of the seventh month – see Leviticus 23:33–43, Numbers 29:12–39). On that last day the priests brought water in a golden pitcher from the pool of Siloam to the Temple where it was poured out. It was symbolic of the water which God supplied from the rock in Exodus 17:1–7. As the water was poured out, Jesus cried out with a loud voice, because He is the

Rock and the Living Water of Life (1 Corinthians 10:4). His words *"As the Scripture has said"* certainly refer to Isaiah 43:19–20 where the Lord says, *"I give waters in the wilderness and rivers in the desert, to give drink to My people, My chosen."* So the picture of a well of water illustrates the refreshment of salvation in the wilderness of this world's existence. But the picture of flowing rivers epitomises the fullness of the Holy Spirit in our lives. After their initial salvation experience, most believers instinctively know there is more to come. Indeed, how sad it would be if they assumed that being born again (or drinking from the well of salvation) was all there was! Wonderfully, God has more for us all.

## The Red Sea

Back in Exodus 14:21–31 God's people were given a way out of slavery, and it involved crossing a river – the Red Sea. There was also a cloud which brought darkness on the Egyptians but which provided light for the Israelites. In 1 Corinthians 10:1–2, Paul explains that being under the cloud and passing through the sea was a baptism into Moses at that time. The guiding and shielding cloud and the Red Sea crossing symbolised salvation – coming out of Egypt (typically, the godless world). After crossing the Red Sea, the whole company of Israelites found themselves in the Sinai wilderness! There they followed the cloud which would lead them to the Promised Land of Canaan. Such a journey would take less than a year.

They encountered difficulties as well as delights, just as we do after we are first saved. They came to the bitter waters of Marah, then travelled on and rested at an oasis called Elim. God provided food in the form of manna, and on at least two occasions, water from the rock. The Lord cared for them, guided them and provided for all their needs – even their shoes didn't wear out, we are told! He fought their battles for them, and won. But it was a hot, dry period in their lives, and regretfully many of them grumbled about God and about their circumstances. They also failed to honour God's Law, and many lost their lives in the wilderness, as 1 Corinthians 10:1–13 and Hebrews 3:16–19 explains. It is sobering that the journey from Egypt to Canaan took forty times longer than it should have done, because of the people's disobedience and unbelief!

## The river Jordan

But through God's grace after forty years of wandering around in the desert, they reached another river which they had to cross – the river Jordan. Now, it is often interpreted that the Jordan River represents physical death. We see it referred to in the great hymn by William Williams (1717–91), 'Guide me, O Thou great Jehovah.' His third stanza reads:

> *When I tread the verge of Jordan,*
> *Bid my anxious fears subside:*
> *Death of death, and hell's destruction,*
> *Land me safe on Canaan's side;*
> *Songs of praises, songs of praises*
> *I will ever give to thee.*

The "When" in the opening line has more recently been amended to "If" because some Christians will be alive when Jesus returns and will not experience physical death as we know it, rather they will be *"changed, in a moment, in a twinkling of an eye, at the last trumpet"* (1 Corinthians 15:50–52), and *"caught up in the clouds to meet the Lord in the air"* (1 Thessalonians 4:16–18).

Crossing Jordan being understood as physical death is commonly accepted. Graphically landing on "Canaan's side" is seen as arriving in heaven! I like this hymn, and I do not consider that William Williams is totally in error with his idea that crossing Jordan foreshadows the believer's passage through physical death into heaven. But this is not the Old Testament's primary type and meaning of the river Jordan. The Book of Joshua shows that crossing Jordan was indeed a passage from the wilderness into the Promised Land. Many things in the Promised Land were certainly inconsistent with events in heaven. Straight away there were battles to fight – a victory to win at Jericho. Then there was sin in the camp by Achan, resulting in a defeat at Ai, and Achan being stoned to death. There was an unwise treaty made with the deceiving Gibeonites. The Amorite kings were executed. Both the southern and northern territories were conquered. Later, cities of refuge were appointed, to which transgressors could resort to prevent their premature death by avengers! None of this is consistent with the Promised Land representing heaven!

What does the river Jordan typify? The Promised Land of Canaan was designated the place where God's covenant people, Israel, would live in victory. Just as crossing the Red Sea illustrates conversion and salvation, so crossing Jordan illustrates the baptism in the Holy Spirit. It was not the Lord's intention that Israel should remain in the wilderness after crossing the Red Sea. Although God provided for and guided His people there, it was intended to be a short time before entering the Promise Land. This fits the New Testament evidence that after a born-again conversion it should be a short while only before God's servants are baptised in the Holy Spirit.

After being baptised by Jesus in the Holy Spirit, the believer finds that there are battles to fight and victories to be won, just as in Canaan. This is well-illustrated in the lives of the first Christians, where Peter and John bring healing, and then are brought to court to face charges (Acts chapters 3 and 4). Today, when Spirit-filled believers do mighty exploits in the Name of

Jesus, often opposition and accusations come from other religious people, just as Peter and John had to face the Jewish Sanhedrin. Through the Book of Acts we read about many people getting saved and many mighty miracles being performed, and these are interlaced with violent accusations against the apostles and the Christians. It is the New Testament counterpart of the days of Joshua! Why is it like that? Jesus said in John 15:18–20: *"If the world hates you, you know that it hated Me before you . . . Remember the word that I said to you, 'A servant is not greater than his master.' If they have persecuted Me, they will also persecute you. If they kept My word, they will keep yours also."*

## 8. THE POSSESSION OF PENTECOST

At this point it is likely that a person will ask, "How do I get baptised in the Spirit?" It is important to remember that this is the work of Jesus – He is the baptiser in the Holy Spirit, just as He is the Saviour who redeems from sin and death through new birth. It is precisely here that people wrongly play the sovereignty of God card. Unbelievers will say, if He wants to save me it will happen, otherwise there is nothing I can do! A believer will often use a similar argument; if the Lord wants me baptised in the Spirit He will do it, otherwise there is nothing I can do! This is the devil's trap to keep people out of God's Kingdom, or to keep them ineffective if they are believers. Of course we cannot save ourselves nor baptise ourselves in the Holy Spirit, but we know from Scripture that the sovereign God desires all people to be saved and baptised in His Holy Spirit. His sovereignty does not negate human responsibility, however. He says, *"Draw near to Me and I will draw near to you."* The onus rests on us to seek Him, and those who fail to comply with His instruction will remain disappointed. So there are a number of things we should do to place us where the Lord Jesus can baptise us in the Holy Spirit.

*Ask Father*

Jesus said if we know how to give good gifts to our children, how much more will our heavenly Father give the Holy Spirit to those who ask Him? He also said, *"Ask, and it will be given to you; seek, and you will find; knock, and it will be opened to you."* According to the continuous verb tenses used here, the meaning of this verse is, 'Ask and keep on asking; seek and keep on seeking; knock and keep on knocking.' So a very definite note of persistence is sounded here. I asked the Lord for many, many months to be baptised in the Holy Spirit, before it happened. When seeking God for anything, we must demonstrate *"the desire of our hearts"* (Psalm 37:4). Now let us consider a number of words associated with asking in prayer.

**Desire:** Someone has said that "We will receive from God only as much as we really want". One of John Wesley's students commented that he would like to receive a particular gift of the Holy Spirit. Wesley took him to the washroom and asked him to pour a good amount of water into the basin. This done Wesley pushed the student's face into the water and held him there until he thrashed wildly. Releasing him, Wesley said, "When you want a gift of the Spirit as much as you wanted air, you will get it!"

**Motive:** Why do we want to be baptised in the Holy Spirit? Poor motives include not wanting to miss out on what others have, or to banish a feeling of inferiority about not being baptised in the Spirit. Wanting Spirit baptism to prove to others that there is such a thing, will not work, just as wanting to proudly exhibit your personal spirituality to others will not be sanctioned by a holy God. But there are good motives, which include desiring to be fully equipped for God's work, and desiring to be the best that you can be for God. A good motive is longing to see God glorified and people saved. It may be helpful to ask yourself a number of questions, such as, "Do I really want this? How much do I want this? Do I believe that the Lord has promised this? Do I have faith to receive the Holy Spirit in this way?"

**Faith:** James 1:6: *"Let him ask in faith, not doubting, for he who doubts is like a wave of the sea driven and tossed by the wind."* Some come to the Lord in a most half-hearted manner. Some ask casually and are quite happy to leave the matter with God, whether there is an answer or not. Others have little faith, and their expectations are near zero, and after asking the Lord, they are content that the answer is up to Him! Conversely, if nothing actually happens, some are prepared to accept that having asked, God must have given, and accept that they are now baptised in the Holy Spirit, even though it was unaccompanied by any outward evidence or inward conviction! This "by faith" method would not be a true Biblical Spirit baptism, of course.

**Persistence:** Stories are manifold of those who almost reached their goal, but gave up too soon. Jesus said, *"He who endures to the end will be saved."* To endure here means to stand firm, persevere, wait calmly and courageously. Such a stance is not passive resistance to fate, but active resistance to defeat. This applies not only to asking to be baptised into the Holy Spirit, but asking for anything. We fail to see the answers to many prayers because we give up too soon, often sinking into resigned unbelief! Persistence in prayer is taught throughout the Scriptures. Recall Jacob wrestling: *"I won't let you go until you bless me!"* Remember Jesus' parable about the widow and unjust judge in Luke 18:1–8. In this parable the godless judge is contrasted with the benevolence of our Father God. The widow never gave up until she got what was due to her. She believed justice would come. This is why, at the end of the parable, Jesus asked, *"when the Son of Man comes, will He find faith on the earth?"*

**Conviction:** Some disbelieve that there is a baptism in the Holy Spirit for people today, and others teach that believers are baptised in the Holy Spirit at the moment of their conversion, rather like Cornelius, but minus speaking with tongues and magnifying the Lord, of course. Such double-minded instability means they are most unlikely to receive anything from the Lord, as James 1:6–8 records. Rather, we need to come to God in humble faith that He will fulfil His Promise in our lives. The following principles apply to prayer generally, and specifically to receiving the baptism in the Holy Spirit:

Ask with sincere desire.

Ask with a pure motive.

Ask with faith and expectation.

Ask with persistence and stability.

Ask with conviction that what God has promised He will give.

## Examine yourself

2 Corinthians 13:5 says, *"Examine yourselves as to whether you are in the faith. Test yourselves."* Examining ourselves is not meant to increase doubts about our personal salvation and forgiveness. It is meant to reveal spiritual defects which can be put right. Are you living a holy life, separated to God from the world? Are you living in obedience to the known will of God? For example, Jonah set off westward for Spain instead of obeying God and going eastward to Nineveh. Being out of the will of God can prevent Jesus baptising you in the Holy Spirit. The Bible says, *"This is the will of God, your sanctification."* Paul writes in 1 Corinthians 11:28 *"Let a man examine himself, and so let him eat of the bread and drink of the*

*cup.*" If your conscience will not allow you to drink the 'Communion cup', hardly will you be able to drink of the baptism in the Holy Spirit! If our consciences are pricked by our short-comings, rest assured they can all be put right, if we want them to be. Seek and trust God to help you towards repentance and forgiveness. Get right, and then get filled.

### *Have faith and trust the Lord Jesus to baptise you*

Galatians 3:14 says "*. . . that we might receive the promise of the Spirit through faith.*" Faith that the Lord will keep His promise is an essential facet of our Christian life. The baptism in the Holy Spirit is sanctioned by the triune God. It is the Promise of the Father which Jesus performs as He immerses believers into the Holy Spirit. This experience is for all, even *"as many as the Lord our God shall call"* (Acts 2:39).

We must be clear about the fact that no one but Jesus Christ can baptise a person into the Holy Spirit. Neither the minister, pastor, priest, Pope, nor anyone else has the right or the ability to confer this blessing upon others! Of course, God uses people to encourage others, and 'laying on hands' does impart the activity of the Lord into a person's life, be it for healing, blessing or Spirit baptism. But the fact remains that it is Jesus Christ Himself who saves, heals, blesses and baptises in the Holy Spirit! Therefore, keep your eyes upon Jesus (Hebrews 12:2) for whatever you desire from Him. And aim to desire Him more than His gifts! Desire intimacy with Him as a living person, more than anything He can provide. When we love Him deeply, the Father will delight to *"freely give us all things"* (Romans 8:32).

### *Laying on hands*

This is mentioned three times out of the five instances where the baptism in the Holy Spirit is described. This simple act is a God-ordained method for people to be blessed (Acts 8:17; 9:17; 19:6), to be healed (Mark 1:31, 41, 16:18; Acts 9:17) and also for ordaining to ministry (1 Timothy 4:14). Laying on hands is not merely a symbolic act, it is also a point of contact for the Spirit's *"rivers of living water"* to flow from one person to another. Recall that Jesus sensed power going out of Him when a woman who touched Him was healed (Luke 8:46).

Since God uses human channels through whom He imparts blessing, can any believer irrespective of their official status lay hands on converts to receive Holy Spirit baptism? I believe so, because in Acts 9:17 Ananias is sent by the Lord to lay hands on Saul and pray for him, but Ananias was not an apostle! Whoever prays, they must operate in faith. If they do not believe the Lord will fulfil His promise, then generally little or nothing will occur. You see, it is required not only that we see and understand what the Bible says, but that we believe God will do the work He has promised to do. Jesus tells us in Acts 1:4–5 that Spirit baptism is *"the Promise of the Father"*. Let's believe it!

### Be thirsty and drink

Jesus said that those who *"hunger and thirst shall be filled"* (Matthew 6:6). Similarly this applies to being baptised in the Holy Spirit. 1 Corinthians 12:13 says, *"We have all been made to drink one Spirit."* In order to drink we must be thirsty!

When ministering to people to receive the baptism in the Spirit, I have never followed the more recent practice of encouraging the candidates to *try* to speak in tongues. I do not wish upon them my own unfortunate situation when I spoke a few funny words and thought it indicated I was baptised in the Holy Spirit. Rather, if they are baptised by Jesus into the Holy Spirit they will know it and doubtless speak in tongues, or prophesy or experience some other manifestation of the Spirit.

Jeannie Morgan in her excellent book, *Encounter The Holy Spirit*[2] says that the biggest barrier that prevents people receiving the gift of tongues is that after they have asked for the gift, they fail to make a sound. Now, Jeannie may be referring to someone who is already baptised in the Spirit but has only prophesied and never spoken in tongues! But I suspect she is referring to someone who has never been baptised in the Holy Spirit, and I maintain that when we are genuinely baptised in the Spirit, no one will need to prompt us to speak – whether in tongues or in our native language!

Jeannie goes on to tell how sometimes folk say that they have asked God for a prayer language but He didn't give it to them. She replies, yes He did, but you just haven't used it yet!

This sounds very psychological. In a similar situation, I would ask, "Have you been baptised in the Holy Spirit?" If they say, "Yes, I think so," or "Yes, when I was saved," or "I'm not sure," etc. I would simply ask them to describe what they think was their Spirit baptism. In many cases it will be discovered that they have not been baptised in the Spirit at all. If this is so, to encourage them to speak in tongues prior to the baptism is putting the cart before the horse! They will simply go away disappointed and disillusioned. I would rather ask if I could pray for them to be baptised in the Spirit, and when Jesus does that for them, they will speak out spontaneously in tongues or in their native language with prophecy or praise to God. *"Out of the abundance of the heart the mouth speaks"*, said Jesus, and when the heart is full of the Holy Spirit, the same Spirit grants utterance!

# CHAPTER SIX

# VARIETY OF TITLES AND DESCRIPTIONS OF SPIRIT BAPTISM

THE BIBLE USES A WIDE VARIETY OF TERMS TO DESCRIBE Spirit baptism. This need not surprise us. The work of God extends beyond our imagination, and describing it calls for an extensive vocabulary. Only the pedantic will baulk at this. A cut-and-dried attitude towards the working of God will provide more problems than answers. The Lord cannot be contained in watertight compartments – He is bigger than that, and it is folly to attempt restrictive measures upon His Being or His work. Many different words, names, titles and terms are used to describe the phenomena occurring on the Day of Pentecost in Acts chapter two. Such broadly embracing terms demonstrate the magnitude of this experience, which Jesus described as the baptism in the Holy Spirit. Amalgamating each term gives a more complete picture:

*The Baptism in the Holy Spirit is the Father's promised gift that descends from heaven and is poured out upon, falls*

> *upon, comes upon, fills, seals, guarantees a foretaste, anoints
> and endues believers who receive Him with power from on
> high.* [3]

The multiplicity of words used indicates that the baptism in the Holy Spirit is a mighty experience. It has to be. No human being can be immersed in God and sense nothing! It is incredulous that many in the weakness of their own minds have reduced Spirit baptism to what is unseen, unfelt, unnoticed and undetectable. Some appear to hope that what the first believers experienced is unrepeatable today. They cry out, "We don't want tongues, fire, wind, noise, shaking or what we see as ecstatic utterances, disorder, emotionalism, immaturity, and the like! Doesn't the Scripture talk about decency and order?" Yes, 1 Corinthians 14:40 says, *"Let all things be done decently and in order."* However, this is not calling for a stoic British attitude, or a stiff upper lip syndrome. This is referring to God's sense of decency and order which includes miracles and manifestations of the Holy Spirit, such as prophecies, tongues and interpretation.

*What does* "when the Spirit comes" *mean?*

Referring to the Holy Spirit, Jesus twice used the phrase, *"When He comes"* (John 16:8,13). Based on these verses many see the phenomena on the Day of Pentecost as only the *arrival* of the Holy Spirit. However, we know the Spirit was already present in the world from creation onwards. Jesus told His disciples that the Spirit was already with them. In that sense the Spirit had come already. In John chapter 16 the context of Jesus' words is linked with conviction (16:8) and guidance (16:13). Most likely Christ was referring to the Spirit coming as the baptismal medium on the Day of Pentecost and onwards, because Spirit baptism activates conviction and guidance.

*Receive the Spirit*

In John 7:38 Jesus says, *"The one believing in Me ... out of his belly will flow rivers."* Verse 39 continues, *"By this he meant the Spirit, whom those who believed in him were later to receive"* (NIV). The reference to *"rivers"* and *"later to receive"* refers to Spirit baptism as at Pentecost. This indicates that a person must believe before he can receive the Spirit. Indeed, Jesus confirmed that the world cannot receive the Spirit (John 14:17). In his book, *Word and Spirit Together*,[4] David Pawson clarifies the subject by showing that the Biblical order is that we *believe* in Jesus Christ, and then *receive* the Spirit. Yes, indeed!

On the Day of Pentecost Peter told the new converts, *"you will receive the gift of the Holy Spirit, for the promise is to you"* (Acts 2:38–39). Provided we understand that Peter's phrase *"receive the gift of the Holy Spirit"* refers to the baptism in the Holy Spirit, there will no confusion. When Cornelius and his household were baptised in the Holy Spirit, Peter says they *"have received the Holy Spirit, as well as we"* (Acts 10:47). Again, what must not be overlooked is that they received the baptism in the Holy Spirit just like Peter at Pentecost, and as Acts 11:15–16 states. In another instance, Paul asked the Ephesians converts, *"Did you receive the Holy Spirit when you believed?"* (Acts 19:2). Paul proceeded to baptise each convert in water, after which he laid hands on them for Spirit baptism, which occurred and was accompanied by speaking in tongues and prophecy. What each of these received was not the *Person* of the Holy Spirit, but the *baptism* in the Holy Spirit. If this difference is missed, the whole question of *receiving* the Spirit becomes confused. All instances of receiving the Spirit in the New Testament refer to Spirit baptism. Here are some examples:

> Acts 2:33 *"Having received from the Father the promise of the Holy Spirit."* (Spirit baptism)

Acts 2:38 *"You shall receive the gift of the Holy Spirit."* (Spirit baptism)

Acts 8:15,19 *"That they might receive the Holy Spirit."* (Spirit baptism)

Acts 19:2 *"Did you receive the Holy Spirit when you believed?"* (Spirit baptism)

Galatians 3:2 *"Did you receive the Spirit by the works of the law?"* (Spirit baptism)

Unless the word *received* is used carefully in connection with the Holy Spirit there will arise incorrect assumptions which the Bible does not support. For example, it could be assumed that no one *experienced* the Holy Spirit prior to the Day of Pentecost. We know this is untrue because people were *filled* with Holy Spirit in both Testaments before Pentecost! This is at the very heart of what concerns evangelicals. They ask, "When does a believer receive the Holy Spirit?" It is a good question but it is loaded by the word *receive.* Scripturally it would be better to ask, "When does a believer receive the baptism in the Holy Spirit?" In his book, *The Normal Christian Birth,*[5] David Pawson includes four stages of a complete salvation: 1) Repentance 2) Believing in Jesus 3) Water Baptism 4) Receiving the Spirit. This is an excellent clarification, and David makes it clear that 'Receiving the Spirit' means 'Receiving Spirit Baptism'.

There is another question which can clarify this subject, 'When does the Holy Spirit *interact* with a person?' The Scriptures show that the Holy Spirit is involved in all the steps necessary to bring a person to full salvation. He interacts with a person to bring conviction of sin leading to repentance. He reveals Christ, in whom a person must believe in order to be saved. He grants regeneration by which a person is born again. He encourages a person's obedience concerning believer's baptism in water and He makes Himself available as the medium for Spirit baptism in a believer's life. So the question, "When does a believer receive the Holy Spirit?" can be misleading, because a believer receives the Spirit in the sense of interacting with Him from the moment of his conviction onwards.

Before Christ physically ascended we are specifically told in John 20:22 that Jesus breathed on His disciples, saying *"Receive the Holy Spirit."* It would be fair to ask if the disciples received the Spirit then, why they needed to wait for a further infusion at Pentecost. John does not include an explanation of Jesus' words or a clarification of this incident. (John does elucidate in other matters, such as John 7:39; 13:11; 21:23.) Some accept that this was a rehearsal or promise of what was to come at Pentecost. Others think that the breath of Jesus assured the disciples that the Spirit would remain with them during those ten uncertain days between Christ's visible ascension and the Day of Pentecost.

The workings of the Holy Spirit from conviction to water baptism is His general salvation work. During these stages a person corresponds with the Holy Spirit, who brings conviction, reveals Christ, grants new birth, lives with them, encourages and guides them. Viewed this way, the Biblical record is satisfied; and every born-again Christian is assured that God the Holy Spirit is active in their lives. However, there is the specific equipping work of the Holy Spirit to be experienced by believers. Before engaging in the Great Commission, they need Jesus to baptise them in the Holy Spirit. A Biblical Spirit baptism is accompanied by outward, physical, demonstrable signs such as inspired speech and most often speaking in tongues. Spirit baptism is the fountainhead of every dynamic operation in us and through us to others. It is sufficient to equip us for a life of

| HOLY SPIRIT ACTIVITIES IN SAVING AND EQUIPPING | | | | |
|---|---|---|---|---|
| CONVICTION | REGENERATION | ADMINISTRATION | WATER BAPTISM | SPIRIT BAPTISM |
| Reveals sin

Reveals the Saviour

Drawn by Father

Urges confession

Grants faith in Christ | Born again

Saved,

converted, forgiven, justified, redeemed

Child of God

New creation | Assurance of salvation
Guidance, leading, teaching, prompting

protecting | Step of obedience

Declaration of faith in Christ

Public testimony

Imparts blessing

and grace | Immersed, filled, sealed, anointed empowered

Provision of manifestations, and production of fruit |

service and powerful enough to grant a constant filling and to accompany us into eternity.

## The Prepositions 'with' and 'in'

In John 14:17 Jesus addresses His disciples and says about the Spirit, *"He dwells with you and will be in you."* The New Living Translation boldly paraphrases this: *"he lives with you now and later will be in you."* This raises the question, "Was the Holy Spirit merely with, and not in, the disciples, before the cross, the resurrection, the ascension and Pentecost?" Can we say all Christians have the Holy Spirit with them, but only Spirit-baptised Christians have the Spirit in them? This could be our conclusion, but it must not be our creed, because nowhere does the Bible state this! Consequently I am reluctant to firmly press this view, and the following points show adequate grounds for caution:

1. An NIV footnote says that some early manuscripts say he dwells with you *"and is"* in you. This would mean that before

the cross and Pentecost the Holy Spirit had taken up residence within the disciples, in which case they had already knew Him, although at that stage they had not been baptised in Him.

2. This is the only verse in the New Testament which includes *with* and *in* regarding the Holy Spirit. We have no other passage of Scripture to shed light on this. So these words of Christ stand in isolation without further commentary, and therefore must be used cautiously.

3. In both the Old Testament and New Testament, people were *"filled"* with the Holy Spirit, in which case it is hard to argue that the Holy Spirit was not actually in them (Exodus 31:3)! John Baptist was *"filled with the Holy Spirit from birth"* (Luke 1:15). Elizabeth and Zacharias were both filled with the Holy Spirit (Luke 1:41,67). The NT Greek word for *fill* is πλμθω (plêthō), which describes the disciples on the Day of Pentecost (Acts 2:4). The import of the word *fill* is that the Holy Spirit was actually in them. You cannot fill a jug with water while keeping the water outside the jug!

When we read that Zacharias was filled with the Spirit, surely the Spirit was *in* him. Whereas when Jesus was anointed it describes the Spirit as descending, and remaining *on* Him. Later Jesus quoted Isaiah 49:8–9, saying that the Spirit of the Lord was *upon* Him. I consider that the variety of prepositions used is not intrinsically significant. Whether the Holy Spirit is with, in, on or upon you, the effects will be similar, since the Spirit is God! Jesus said He would be with us to the end of the age, but we know that the Lord Jesus Christ also lives in us, according to many New Testament verses. Jesus said that the Father, Son and Holy Spirit (the Trinity of God) will live with us (John 14:16,23) so I conclude that the prepositional differences are far less significant than we might otherwise conclude.

*Restricted use of the term 'baptism in the Spirit'*

It has been pointed out that the phrase *baptise(d) with the Spirit* occurs in only six verses of the Bible. From this fact it is deduced that the subject of the baptism in the Holy Spirit cannot be vitally important. However, limited inclusion does not indicate minor importance! Although this specific phrase is used only six times, the subject itself is scattered widely throughout the Scriptures, as we have already observed. Jesus referred to the baptism in the Spirit as *"rivers of living water"* and as *"the Promise of the Father"* and as the Holy Spirit *"coming upon"* us. Other New Testament writers amply use different phrases when speaking of Spirit baptism.

Consider the fact that the phrase *"born again"* is found only three times in the Bible, while *"born of the Spirit"* and *"born of God"* is used nine times. By this it could be argued that being born again is far less important than being baptised with the Spirit – but such an argument is Biblically unsound.

Consider other matters: only once do we read that Jesus did not Himself baptise people in water. Jesus weeping is recorded only three times. It is evident that the significance of a subject does not depend on the number of times it is included in the Bible. Indeed, there are only four Gospels!

| SUBJECT | SPECIFIC PHRASE USED | SUBJECT REFERRED TO |
|---|---|---|
| Born again | X 3 | X 9 |
| Baptism with Spirit | X 6 | X 53 |

# CHAPTER SEVEN

# COMPLETE AND INCOMPLETE SALVATION

A COMPLETE SALVATION INCLUDES MANY STAGES, FROM initial conviction by the Holy Spirit, through to new birth regeneration, to the outward response of believer's water baptism and to being baptised in the Holy Spirit by Jesus, who at that point will be the convert's Lord and Saviour.

The chart below illustrates the Biblical pattern of a complete salvation experience.

Although repentance, regeneration, water baptism and Spirit baptism are distinctive steps towards a complete salvation, the thin dotted lines between each column indicates that there is a real connection between each step. Each separate stage leads to the next. The first column is repentance, where a person is under conviction and conscious of their own sinfulness. They confess their sin and see Christ as their Saviour. Regeneration in column two continues with a redeemed experience of the new birth. Here people are conscious of being a child of God, and their response leads them to the next stage concerning water baptism,

| THE BIBLICAL PACKAGE OF SALVATION | | | |
|---|---|---|---|
| 1. REPENTANCE | 2. REGENERATION | 3. WATER BAPTISM | 4. SPIRIT BAPTISM |
| Under conviction<br><br>Repentance from sin<br><br>Sincere confession<br><br>Faith in Jesus Christ as personal Lord and Saviour. The Father's drawing power | Converted<br><br>Born again from above. Regenerated<br><br>Saved, a redeemed child of God. Ransomed, forgiven, restored | Believer's baptism in water. A step of obedience. A declaration of faith in Christ. An impartation of grace. An outward testimony | Jesus baptises in the Holy Spirit.<br><br>Immersed, filled, sealed, empowered,<br><br>endued with power from above. Gifts and fruit of the Spirit |
| HOLY SPIRIT ACTION | | | |
| Conviction<br><br>Urging repentance<br><br>Revealing Christ<br><br>Drawing to Christ<br><br>Urging conversion | Regeneration<br><br>New birth<br><br>Child of God. Assurance of forgiveness | Urges obedience<br><br>Imparts blessing<br><br>and grace. Prepares believer for Spirit baptism | Spirit baptism, filling,<br><br>sealing, a deposit, anointing, provision of manifestations and production of fruit of the Spirit |

which is an outward confession of an inward experience of salvation. Water baptism should lead to an experience of Spirit baptism where they are immersed in the Holy Spirit and experience the dynamic of God.

Each stage connects with the other stages, and together they constitute an integrated whole, an amalgamation of the multi-facets of a full salvation. This is the usual way in which God works, but He is not bound by such a pattern, and His dealings with Cornelius in Acts chapter 10 illustrate a difference of order and experience. The important fact is that all four stages of the Salvation Package should be experienced and completed in a person's life.

Current gospel interpretations have tended to do two things with this whole process. Firstly to homogenise the stages, with Spirit baptism occurring (unnoticed) at the moment of being born again. If the person was christened when a baby, then the whole package of salvation is considered complete when he is later converted or confirmed! Another method of interpretation is to time-separate the stages by extraordinary lengths, so that water baptism of a baby occurs many years before conviction, conversion or confirmation! In evangelical circles, often believer's water baptism is administered months, if not years, after conviction and conversion, while Spirit baptism is ignored altogether! The New Testament pattern is that each stage occurred within a short space of time – waiting between them was limited.

## AN INCOMPLETE INITIAL SALVATION

Recently I listened to a message about the disciples that Paul discovered on his initial visit to Ephesus. The speaker began by quoting Acts 2:39 about the gift of the Holy Spirit, and saying quite rightly that this isn't just for the people whom Peter was speaking to, it is for us as well. He continued to say:

> If God has called us; if we repent of our sins and turn to God and are baptised in the Name of Jesus Christ, our sins will be forgiven and we receive the Holy Spirit. It is like a package deal. The Holy Spirit is everything we need to live the Christian life. We don't receive more of the Holy Spirit later on. It's like a package deal; it's done; you have received the Holy Spirit!

Alarmingly he continued to quote Romans 8:9, stating:

> Paul is very clear that you have either got the package deal
> – you've repented, been baptised and you've received the
> Holy Spirit – or you haven't got the package deal. You're
> either in or out – that's Paul's thinking.'

Romans chapter 8 deals with our son-ship in Jesus Christ, applied by the Holy Spirit. The preacher's view on Romans 8:9 fails
to distinguish between having the *Person* of the Holy Spirit, who
initiates our conversion, and being *baptised* in the Holy Spirit
subsequent to conversion – a crucial difference. Listening to the
above message made it seem as though being Spirit-baptised is
automatic, that it is so much part of the package that it is all
done, and that there is nothing more to come. The speaker said,
"We don't receive more of the Holy Spirit later on," but we
might well do, because such a statement contradicts the Biblical
trend, as we shall see.

The preacher's illustration of salvation being like a package-
deal holiday is helpful, but as with all human illustrations we
must be careful not to oversimplify it, nor to increase the com-
plexity of its meaning beyond that which Scripture permits.
Paul accepts there is such a thing as an *incomplete salvation*, just
as he discovered on his arrival in Ephesus. According to the
record of events in the Bible, it is possible for certain elements
of salvation to be applied to our lives, while other factors have
yet to be experienced. To suggest you have everything at the
moment you are regenerated disagrees Biblically and experien-
tially.

When we liken salvation to a package deal, it is vital to
acknowledge the importance of time-gaps between each stage:

1. Booking the package at the travel agent and receiving the
   tickets

2. Journeying to the airport and flying to your destination

3. Passing through immigration and customs and travelling to the hotel

4. Booking additional tours during the holiday

5. Returning home – with its multiple stages: journeying back to the airport; flying; travelling from the airport to home.

There is an inevitable time-gap between each stage, some longer and some shorter, so that booking the package at the travel agent, or even arriving at the hotel, does not mean you have received the whole package! It is the same with conversion; you may have repented and believe, and been baptised in water, but it does not mean you have immediately experienced the whole package! Certainly the potential for the whole package is there, as each stage with its time-gap is passed through, but the package illustration shows we do not get everything at once. Let's examine a number of Bible cases where a complete salvation package was not granted in one moment, but spread over a period of time, and in one case curtailed.

### The apostles of Christ

Before He went to the cross, Jesus said the apostles already had the Holy Spirit dwelling with them, then after His resurrection, Jesus breathed the Holy Spirit into them, but instructed them not to begin spreading the gospel until the Promise of the Father clothed them with power from on high, which Jesus further explained was the baptism in the Holy Spirit. That occurred ten days after Jesus' visible ascension, so the preacher's statement, "We don't receive more of the Holy Spirit later on" is at best misleading and at worst untrue.

### The thief on the cross

Here one of the criminals confesses that his punishment is deserved, and that Jesus is innocent. Then he prays to the Lord

Jesus, saying, *"Lord, remember me when you come into Your Kingdom."* That is all. At best it seems a poor example of a sinner's prayer; but it was enough. The prayer was from the heart to the saving Son of God, and the reply establishes the fact that this criminal was saved. *"Truly, I say to you, today you will be with Me in Paradise."* His name was in the Book of Life; the great redeeming work of God was done in his broken life which would soon end. During his remaining hours he experienced an incomplete salvation in so far as he could not be baptised in water or baptised in the Holy Spirit. This did not negate his forgiveness or his entrance into heaven. Those who have the opportunity to live on as witnesses of Jesus Christ should not use this case to suggest that water baptism and Spirit baptism remain unimportant or unnecessary for them.

## The Samaritan believers

In Acts 8:1–25 Philip is powerful in word and deed, resulting in many being converted. The Samaritans heard the gospel, repented, and many were healed and delivered from demonic spirits, and they all were baptised in water. In this instance the Samaritan believers hadn't received the baptism in the Holy Spirit. That didn't happen until much later after Peter and John arrived from Jerusalem, and laid their hands on them. So before then, were they "in" or "out", as the preacher above suggests? Was the whole package deal received by them or not? Obviously they had only part of the package since there more of the Spirit to come later!

## The apostle Paul

Saul (who later named himself Paul) was confronted by the living Christ on the road to Damascus. He fell to the ground shocked, challenged and physically blinded. There on the road

Saul twice called Jesus "Lord" and responded in humble obedience to the Lord's instructions. I believe he was saved through this experience. After this he is found to be praying and he has a vision from God. The Lord told Ananias that Saul was a chosen vessel of His (not "he will be" but "he is") confirming Saul is already saved. Later Ananias finds him and at least four things occur: his blindness is removed, he is baptised in water and he is filled with (baptised in) the Spirit and he eats. The visit of Ananias was not to get Saul saved, but to get him healed, filled/baptised with the Spirit and baptised in water. It was to complete the package of his salvation. He was justified and redeemed a number of days before he reached Damascus and met Ananias.

### Cornelius and his household Acts 10:44–48

As Peter preaches the gospel, his audience suddenly bursts out with speaking in tongues and magnifying the Lord. Although unusual (the only case recorded in the Bible) it was perfectly consistent with the ways of God – regenerated and baptised in the Spirit within the same few moments. But at that stage there was more to come, because they hadn't been baptised in water. That had to be done to complete the salvation package.

### The Ephesian converts

About twelve disciples had received John the Baptist's water baptism for repentance, but they had not heard about the Holy Spirit, nor had they received believer's water baptism. Doubtless they were saved, forgiven, justified, redeemed (just as the thief on the cross had been) but their experience was incomplete – it fell short of the fullness intended by the Lord. To remedy this situation they were firstly given believer's baptism in water (which proves they were saved). Secondly they were baptised in the Holy Spirit as Paul laid his hands upon them. And they spoke in tongues and prophesied, and their initial salvation experience was then complete. Paul asked the Ephesians, *"Did you receive the Holy Spirit when you believed?"* because people often are not baptised in the Spirit at the moment they believe in Christ. All Biblical examples of people being baptised in the Holy Spirit occurred sometime after they were saved, with the exception of Cornelius and his household who were all saved and baptised in the Spirit almost at the same time. In their case, even water baptism came later.

## Apollos

Apollos was an eloquent Jew from Alexandria who arrived in Ephesus about AD54. He was instructed in the way of the Lord, and he taught passionately and accurately the truths he had received, although he knew only the baptism of John (Acts 18:24–28). He knew the Old Testament well, but it was evident that something was missing from his experience. When Paul arrives in Ephesus he discovers disciples who know only an incomplete salvation. Did they become believers through the ministry of Apollos? Apollos by this time had moved on to Greece, having been taught *"the way of God more accurately"* by Aquila and Priscilla. We are not told exactly what they taught, but it seems that after their ministry this eloquent man emerged as a water-baptised and Spirit-baptised firebrand for the Lord. Very often people stand in the shoes of Apollos with an incomplete salvation. They have gone out to minister and spread the gospel. Like Apollos, they may be mighty in the Scriptures, ably teaching God's word, but how much more could they have achieved for eternity had they been baptised in the Spirit. The Lord has only the material available to Him, and if we are ignorant of Spirit baptism His resources in our lives are curtailed. Plainly we see that there can be an incomplete salvation experience due to missing elements from a person's initial conversion experience, but this does not mean such believers are unregenerate – "out", as the preacher put it! Neither are they to be considered "second class Christians" (as you might attribute to the criminal on the cross who turned to the Lord). Wonderfully, there is more to come, and they all should rejoice in that!

# CHAPTER EIGHT

# THE EARLY CHURCH: PENTECOSTAL BY EXPERIENCE

S OME WILL FAIL TO BE ENAMOURED WITH THE WORD *Pentecostal*, but I am using it in a definitive sense to describe the experience of believers in the early Church – they all were Pentecostal by experience because they had been baptised in the Holy Spirit. This includes the 120 disciples in Jerusalem, and the 3,000 who responded to Peter's preaching, and later converts. Peter told them to repent and be baptised in water, also that they would receive the Promise of the Father, namely the baptism in the Spirit. It would be inconsistent to think that only the first two factors mentioned by Peter were actioned (repentance and water baptism) and that the third factor (Spirit baptism) was omitted. All three were a vital part of their salvation experience.

The Scriptures allow no doubts about the fact that all believers in the early Church were Spirit-baptised. In the province of Galatia, Churches had been established in Antioch, Iconium,

Lystra and Derbe and Paul writes reminding them how they received the promise of the Spirit through faith (Galatians 3:14). The Corinthian believers were Pentecostal, as was Paul himself, who spoke in tongues more than all the Corinthians! The import of this fact is that all the New Testament letters were written to people who were Pentecostal by experience. They all had heard the gospel, repented, been baptised in water and received Spirit baptism, and when the apostle spoke about the Holy Spirit and His manifestations in their lives, they knew by experience what he was talking about. They had all become partakers of the Holy Spirit, and tasted the powers of the age to come. Since the New Testament books were written by Pentecostals and for Pentecostals, those not Spirit-baptised will encounter two great difficulties. They will have little personal experience of what the New Testament writers are talking about, and they will be prone to misinterpret what is written.

## LITTLE EXPERIENCE OF WHAT THE BIBLICAL WRITERS MEAN

The Book of Acts rests on two solid foundations. Firstly, the words of Jesus in chapter one, and secondly the events which occurred in chapter two. In Acts 1:4–8 Jesus' words are both explicitly clear and vitally crucial. As you read these verses, let me ask you one simple and straightforward question. What did Jesus say would happen to the disciples? His clear and straightforward answer is: *"You shall be baptised with the Holy Spirit not many days from now."* He explained that the promise of the Father was the baptism in the Holy Spirit. Believers today who are not Spirit-baptised easily miss this vital truth, and many sadly proceed to invent a variety of unscriptural theories about the Day of Pentecost, based on their own limited human understanding. Here are some of those theories:

### Theory 1 – Pentecost was the arrival of the Spirit

This sentence is close to the truth but requires further explanation. The Day of Pentecost was not a simple arrival of the Holy Spirit, either into the world or onto the Church. In that sense, the Holy Spirit had already come. In the New Testament there are abundant examples of the Spirit's vital activities prior to the day of Pentecost. John the Baptist is filled with the Spirit from his mother's womb; Mary's conceives by the Holy Spirit; Elizabeth is filled with the Spirit; Zacharias and Simeon are filled with the Spirit and they prophesy; Christ is anointed, filled and led by the Spirit; Jesus returned to Galilee in the Spirit's power and fulfilled prophecy by being filled with the Spirit. Before going to the cross, Jesus told the disciples that the Spirit was already with them, and after His resurrection He breathed the Holy Spirit into the disciples, as described in John 20:19–23. So Pentecost was not a simple arrival of the Spirit, but rather the arrival and first occurrence of the *"baptism in the Spirit"*. Even if the disciples had received the Holy Spirit when Jesus breathed on them, they had not received the "baptism in the Holy Spirit" from Jesus! The interaction of the Holy Spirit when you are saved does not obviate nor counteract a need for Spirit baptism.

### Theory 2 – Pentecost was a complete Church baptism

At Pentecost, Spirit baptism occurred for all the believers who were gathered together, but it says tongues of fire *"separated"* and rested *"on each of them"*, therefore it was primarily an individualistic experience, and not essentially a composite group experience. John the Baptist emphasised the individuality of his baptism in water. When Jerusalem, all Judea, and all the region around the Jordan went out to him and were baptised by him, He baptised them as individuals, not as a conglomerate mass! John explained to each person, one by one, *"I indeed baptise you with water, but*

*He* [Jesus] *will baptise you with the Holy Spirit."* Spirit baptism is essentially an individual experience, although it can occur at the same time to many. This also applies to conversion. A mass of people can be saved together at one time, but essentially it is an individual experience of God's redeeming grace as each person repents and believes in the Lord Jesus.

Those who sidestep the importance of Spirit baptism often propose the idea that the whole Church received the Spirit on the Day of Pentecost. Then they proceed to extend this to mean that it was a once-for-all experience for the Church of all time. They say, since the Spirit has come upon the Church, we are all baptised in the Holy Spirit at the moment of our salvation – it now happens automatically at conversion! We no longer have to ask for the Spirit (or the baptism in the Spirit) because it is ours as a matter of course. Unfortunately, the Bible says no such thing. The poor Brethren elder who accused me of usurping the Scriptures because I said a young girl did not need to cover her head before he spoke in the confines of his own living room, was himself thoroughly usurping the Scripture by using one single verse (1 Corinthians 12:13) to prove his theory that Pentecost was never repeated. From this text incredulously he taught for half an hour that Pentecost was purely a one-off event, even though the Bible shows the opposite! Bible twist has been the demise of many denominations as well as individuals. If we were all automatically baptised in the Spirit at the moment of conversion, then all new converts would by be familiar with prophecy, speaking in tongues and the other manifestations of the Spirit. They would be Pentecostal from the start, but their individual lack of such things disproves this theory!

*Theory 3 – Pentecost was the birthday of the Church, its inauguration and launching*

This seemingly innocent phrase is unsupported by the Scriptures. It was conjured to emphasise that what happened at Pentecost was a one-off happening! It gave validation to a situation which it was hoped need not be repeated. Did the Church have a birthday? The Bible never uses such terminology, and imagining a day when the Church was born is not a Biblical concept. The word *Church* (*ekklesia*) means 'those called out' by God, and the Bible talks about the Church beginning in the Old Testament (Acts 7:38).

*Theory 4 – Pentecost was the descent of the Holy Spirit upon the followers of Jesus*

Here the word *descent* is emphasised because the Holy Spirit was sent from the Father by Jesus (John 15:26), and in that way He may be considered to have descended. But Pentecost was more than a mere descent. It was the descent of the Spirit as the baptismal medium into which Jesus would immerse each individual believer. Dr Luke records the words of Jesus about prayer which concludes with, *"how much more will your heavenly Father give the Holy Spirit to those who ask him!"* Some who disregard Spirit baptism suggest we need never ask for the Holy Spirit, since He has already descended on the Church. The context of Luke 11 shows that Jesus was speaking to His disciples who were already saved, because Jesus had already explained that their names were written in heaven. This was long before the events on the Day of Pentecost, so was Jesus indicating that they alone would be the only individuals who would ask later for the Holy Spirit? Is it true that after Pentecost no one would ever need to ask for the Holy Spirit? Such thinking is foreign to Scripture, and this theory is shattered by the numerous Bible persons who received their personal Spirit baptism long after the Day of Pentecost.

Without the experience of Spirit baptism, we remain perplexed over many incidents recorded in the Book of Acts. Such events are beyond our understanding. We remain bewildered by what we read. How easily we grasp a cop-out thought that such happenings are no more than an historical account of what used to be, rather than the pattern of what should be today! Let's look at some examples of this.

*Lame man healed Acts 3:1–10*

How was this miracle possible? We could ask many questions, such as, "Why didn't Peter and John call the Church together to pray for the man? How did Peter know what was God's will in this case? What enabled Peter to know that his command to the lame man to 'rise up and walk' would be honoured by the Lord?" Such questions serve to endorse our confusion and lack of understanding.

Is it right to treat this miracle as a piece of historic information only? Is it what God did in the early days of the Church, but which He no longer does nor expects His disciples to do today? Such human reasoning overlooks the Scripture where Jesus said, *"Truthfully I say to you, he who believes in Me, the works that I do shall he do also; and greater works than these he will do, because I go to the Father"* (John 14:12). Even here with pernicious alacrity our minds scrabble for some explanation which academically refutes what Jesus said and meant. Did Christ's words apply only to the small band of apostles to whom He was speaking at the time? We cannot overlook the fact that the Bible does not say that the words *"he who believes in Me"* applies only to the eleven; or only to a few early believers! Indeed, *"he who believes in Me"* applies to every born-again believer in the world today, and *"because I go to the Father"* refers to Christ's ascension and the ensuing ascension gift of the baptism in the Holy Spirit. The baptism in the Spirit enables us to receive and to obey the Spirit's instructions. Peter said and did what the Spirit told him. Often the Bible does not deal with specific cases, but the Holy Spirit can!

*Outstanding miracles Acts 5:12–16*

In this passage of Scripture, many signs and wonders are performed, and large numbers of people from the surrounding towns come to Jerusalem, bringing their sick and demonised folk, and it says *"they were all healed"*. Stephen was a deacon, not an apostle, but he was full of grace and power, and did great wonders and signs among the people. He was opposed by certain religious Jews, but they were not able to resist the wisdom and the Spirit with which he spoke. In similar vein, the academic teachers were offended by the blind man whom Jesus healed, because, despite the man's wisdom about his healing, he was considered uneducated. The Spirit's anointing is more important and powerful than secular education! Philip was a deacon, and he preached Christ in Samaria. His audience responded to both his words and his miracles, demons were cast out and many paralysed and lame people were healed. Those who have never witnessed a miraculous healing will find such accounts difficult to appreciate. Others beset by disappointment over the loss of loved ones might also baulk at these Scripture passages. Our consternation indicates our failure to hear what the Spirit says to the churches.

*Peter and Aeneas Acts 9:32–35*

Peter found Aeneas, who had been paralysed for eight years. Here Peter did not pray for him, nor call the believers together to seek God on his behalf. Peter simply spoke the word of command, *"Aeneas, Jesus Christ heals you. Arise and make your bed."* This paralysed man was healed and got up immediately. Listening to the Holy Spirit grants confidence in the Lord Jesus to speak the word of healing, rather than resort to praying for healing. Just like God commanded Moses to speak to the rock, so that water would gush out. Just like Jesus spoke to the fig tree and caused it to whither. The Master later explained that whoever says to this mountain, *"Be removed and be cast into the sea"* without doubting, but believes that what he says will be done, he will have whatever he says. Three times Jesus uses the word *"says"*. Do not foolishly substitute the word, *"prays"*. Praying is talking to God, while "saying" is exercising God-given authoritative words, as directed by the Spirit.

### Peter and Tabitha (Greek: Dorcas) Acts 9:36–43

The name Tabitha is Aramaic for gazelle, which would be translated into Greek as *"Dorcas"*. This industrious and well-loved lady died in Joppa, so they send for Peter who is nearby in Lydda. Naturally everyone is upset, but Peter puts everyone out of the room where Tabitha's body is lying. Instead of an immediate word of command, Peter kneels down to pray. We are not told the reason for this, but could he be asking about God's will on the matter? Having spoken to God and finding the Lord's mind, Peter turns to the body and speaks the command, *"Tabitha, arise."* Immediately she returns to mortal life and sits up when she sees Peter, who takes her hand, helps her up, and presents her alive to the saints and widows. Unlike healing for the sick, there is scant information about bringing the dead back to life. We have only a number of examples scattered through the pages of Scripture. But we should bear in mind the words of instruction that Jesus gave to His twelve apostles in Matthew 10:8, *"Heal the sick, cleanse the lepers, raise the dead, cast out demons. Freely you have received, freely give."* Human reasoning will suggest this was just for them.

### Philip's instructions and transport Acts 8:26–40

Philip receives instructions from the Lord (the Lord is the Spirit, 2 Corinthians 3:17) who instructs him where to go. Then the Spirit instructs Philip what to do. Later something remarkable happens, as the Spirit transports Philip and puts him down in Azotus, a distance of about thirty miles! Those who have never been Spirit-baptised may consider this to be ridiculous – or at best something that happened in the early Church, but not meant to happen today. I disagree, and state that I believe this is normal Christianity. The Greek word used here in Acts 5:39 is *harpazo*, meaning 'to snatch away'! It is used again by Paul who says those Christians who are alive when the Lord Jesus returns to earth will *"be caught up together with them* [that is, with the resurrected bodies of believers who had died] *in the clouds to meet the Lord in the air."* We refer to this as the 'rapture' of the Church.

There are other passages of Scripture in which a snatching away occurs. Enoch, the father of Methuselah, was the first human being to be snatched away to heaven. We read that he walked with God for 300 years, after which God took him and he was seen no more on earth, Genesis 5:22–24. Enoch is the pioneer of those who will be transported by the Lord from earth to heaven. Then Jesus Himself followed the same pattern, when forty days after He rose from the dead He ascended visibly into the heavens, Acts 1:9–11. We also have Paul's testimony where he describes how he was caught up into Paradise and heard unspeakable words. Paul was transported back to earth in order to continue his ministry for God. Others in our own time have experienced this, including myself.

*Peter's sermon Acts 10:36-38*

Peter's message to Cornelius includes a brief description of Christ's ministry, how God anointed Jesus of Nazareth with the Holy Spirit and with power, who went about doing good and healing all who were oppressed by the devil, for God was with

Him. We recall that Jesus was anointed with the Holy Spirit at His water baptism, when John saw the Spirit descend upon Him in the form of a dove. I like the phrase, *"healing all who were oppressed by the devil."* It is the devil who oppresses people with illness and disease. Such oppression can be physical, mental or spiritual, but it is time we pointed in the right direction when we discuss the troubles of this fallen world. It is a grievous error to attribute them to the Lord God, instead of to the devil – the oppressor who is described as the god of this world.

Also, it is a dreadful crime to use the sovereignty of God as an excuse to blame Him for the disasters that beset us all. Though God is the supreme sovereign, it is the opposing forces of evil, stemming from Satan, sin and godless humanity which create havoc in our lives and in our world. God's masterplan of salvation in Christ is effectively saving and empowering individuals in every part of the world, even amidst the sufferings of this present time – a time of tribulation as our world experiences the birth-pangs of a new age. I suggest that God is not only saving people from sin and hell each day, but bringing all things to the place where sin is eradicated for all eternity, so that it can never break out in His creation again.

We rightly see Jesus as the supreme and pre-eminent Son of God, but we dare not suggest that Christ's ministry of preaching, teaching, healing and delivering cannot be perpetuated by His followers until He returns. Christ ordains us, commissions us and He baptises us in the Spirit in order that we can continue His ministry in the world. The Master Himself said that believers in Him would repeat His works and do greater works because Jesus would return to the Father. Dr Luke referred to his Gospel as containing all that Jesus began both to do and teach. What Christ did in the Gospels was only a beginning! Having ascended to the Father in heaven, Jesus continues those same deeds through the power of the Spirit in His followers, through the

Church which is His body on earth, and of which He is the Head (Colossians 1:18).

When Jesus talked about *"greater works"* I believe He was referring to quantity not quality! Jesus raised to life a four-day dead man and nothing could be considered greater in quality than that! Jesus was going back to the Father, allowing the Holy Spirit to come as the One into whom all could be baptised and through whom all could receive power to be Christ's witnesses. Today we have millions of Spirit-filled believers throughout the world witnessing mighty miracles, including marvellous healings and raising the dead. Some argue that the *"greater works"* spoken about by Jesus refer to saving converts, but the context of John's Gospel does not allow such an interpretation. When Jesus spoke about His *works,* He was not referring to the number of His followers, but to His miracles.

The reasoning which dichotomises soul-saving and healing is unjustified as far as the Bible is concerned. Jesus ministered to people holistically; for their body he gave healing and food, and promised drink and clothing; for their soul He gave teaching, truth and blessing; for their spirit He gave salvation and forgiveness. In fact, all these are included in the one great package of eternal life, administered in time and which propels us into eternity. By the way, *salvation* (Greek *sozo*) is an all-inclusive word, embracing every God-given mercy –wholeness for the spirit, soul and body of every person who repents and believes.

## Paul and Elymas Acts 13:6–12

On the island of Cyprus a false prophet named Bar-Jesus (son of Joshua), or Elymas, tries to turn the Roman governor, Sergius Paulus, from the gospel. With indignation Paul, filled with the Holy Spirit, pronounces temporary blindness on Elymas, whom he calls son of the devil. How Satan endeavours to prevent intelligent rulers from embracing the Christian faith. We must be aware of this, and be bold enough to respond to Holy Spirit directives with judgment. Paul's obedience to the Spirit resulted in the proconsul's salvation. There are many more instances recorded in the Acts of the Apostles of miraculous signs and wonders being accomplished through the lives of God's servants. Ministers today, bereft of such experiences, attribute their lack to God, who they falsely claim has changed His procedures. Such dynamics, they say, were for the early Church only. Would it not be better to be honest and to acknowledge and accept their personal shortfall from all that God has promised? Their failure to believe God and to be Spirit-baptised is the root of the problem.

## PRONE TO MISUNDERSTAND MANY NEW TESTAMENT REFERENCES TO THE HOLY SPIRIT

Many New Testament references to the Holy Spirit will not be fully understood by those who have not been baptised by Jesus into the Spirit. Consider some examples below:

**Romans 8:9:** *"If anyone does not have the Spirit of Christ, he is not His."*

This verse is used by some to confirm that a Christian believer has the Holy Spirit, but no distinction is made between having the *Person* of the Holy Spirit and being *baptised* in the Spirit. The fact that a person has been convicted by the Spirit and born again by the Spirit, is no guarantee he has been baptised in the Spirit by Jesus.

**Romans 8:11:** *"If the Spirit of Him who raised Jesus from the dead dwells in you, He who raised Christ from the dead will also give life to your mortal bodies through His Spirit who dwells in you."*

It is all too easy to restrict the fulfilment of this verse to the day of resurrection at the return of Christ. The verse may indeed allude to this, but the words, *"give life to your mortal body through His Spirit who dwells in you"* cannot readily refer to a decayed bag of bones at the end of time! It has a wider and more immediate application, concerning the restorative and healing power of God's Spirit. Those without Spirit baptism fail to consider the implication of God's Spirit actually dwelling in us! They are not cognisant of His presence. In contrast the Spirit-baptised believer is readily aware of His indwelling presence – they know Him, sense Him, feel and experience Him.

**Romans 8:14:** *"As many as are led by the Spirit of God, these are the sons of God."* Interpreting this simplistically and by reversing its logic, some say, those not led by the Spirit of God are not sons of God! This reverse logic could be applied to many people mentioned in the Bible. For example Peter and Barnabas, who failed to be led by the Spirit over the matter of Jewish separatism and circumcision, as recorded in Galatians 2:11–16. Were they not sons of God because they failed to be led by the Spirit? I observe that countless numbers of Christians fail to be led by the Spirit – are they then not sons of God, are they unsaved? Remember, Paul is writing to believers who are Pentecostal by experience, and who indeed are led by the Spirit in their daily lives, although human weakness may prevent their compliance. In this verse Paul simply draws a distinction between these and the unsaved who do not know the leading of the Holy Spirit at all.

**1 Corinthians 12:7–10:** Lists the nine manifestations of the Holy Spirit, which many will relegate to a bygone age. It says the Spirit distributes to each one individually as He wills. The *"as He wills"* phrase is used to blanket over these verses by adversely claiming that an absence of manifestations means the Holy Spirit has not been willing to grant any! May the Lord save us from such insincerity. Granting Spirit gifts is exactly what He desires to do, *"distributing to each one"*. *"As He wills"* is not a restriction on *who* receives His gifts, but on *which* gifts they receive. The text assures us that the Spirit does distribute manifestations of Himself, and that He has not gone out of business!

**1 Corinthians 13:1–13:** This passage is acceptable because it's all about love. In fact, it is all about the gifts of the Spirit being operated in love, which is a different thing. As we know, chapters and verses are a later insertion in the Bible text, therefore 1 Corinthians chapters 12, 13 and 14 are three chapters about spiritual entities. It is inconceivable that part way through his theme the apostle Paul would include a radically different, detached and disconnected subject! The verses about love can be divorced from their context, as can any Bible text, but the best exegesis retains the context, which shows that chapter 13 is about the *"more excellent way"*, namely the gifts of the Spirit operated in love.

**2 Corinthians 1:21–22 and 5:5:** These verses endorse the fact that Spirit baptism includes our *sealing* and that it is a *guarantee* that what we experience now is a foretaste of more to come. Giving us Holy Spirit baptism is the first instalment of everything the Lord has for us.

**Galatians 3:14:** *"That we might receive the promise of the Spirit through faith."* This verse point unmistakably to Spirit baptism, which is the "Promise of the Father". The phrase *"through faith"* must not be interpreted to mean we receive blessings from God without a trace of feeling, evidence or confirmation. *"Through faith"* refers to the process by which we receive, not the lack of tangible effects when receiving. Ephesians 1:13 says, *"In whom also, having believed you were sealed with the Holy Spirit of promise."* The Ephesian converts displayed the outward evidence of their Spirit sealing with speaking in tongues and prophecy.

**Ephesians 2:21–22** says the Church is a dwelling place of God in the Spirit. Dare we substitute the Spirit's dynamic presence with architectural atmosphere, or stylised music, or academic prose, or a score of other human novelties to attract attendance? Even symphonic music without the Spirit can be little more than noise!

**Ephesians 5:18–19:** Spirit-inspired singing, new songs and choruses, are a principal feature of the vibrant Spirit-baptised Church. The Brethren Church banned music, and their singing became dour! They banned musical instruments in church despite the fact that God gifted men with musical ability (Genesis 4:21). God included Psalms (songs) in the Scriptures often complete with musical instructions. David, the great musician of Israel, is described as *"a man after God's own heart"*. Elisha is asked to declare the word of the Lord, but first he calls for a musician to play (2 Kings 3:15), and the music became the vehicle for the Spirit to inspire Elisha, who prophesied. There is an obvious link between music and the dynamics of the Holy Spirit.

**1 Thessalonians 5:19–21:** *"Do not quench the Spirit. Do not despise prophecies. Test all things; hold fast what is good."* (NKJV). Four direct commands which are mostly ignored today by those not Spirit-baptised in the Biblical way.

**Hebrews 2:4:** *"God also bearing witness both with signs and wonders, with various miracles and gifts of the Holy Spirit, according to His own will."* This beautiful verse confirms the presence of dynamic miracles in the early Church. That is history. Today signs and wonders are witnessed worldwide, and they confirm that such phenomena are *"according to His own will"*. God hasn't changed, so His will remains the same. Even dispensationalists must accept that we today live in the same age as the early Church, between the first coming of Christ as Saviour and His second coming as King. Therefore His Being, His Will and His Ways remain the same throughout. Joel endorses the fact that the outpouring of God's Spirit (the baptism in the Spirit) continues as long as people are being saved by calling on the Name of the Lord. Hence Spirit baptism continues up to the time of the Lord's return to earth.

**1 John 2:20–27** John mentions *"the anointing"*. This obviously refers to the action of the Holy Spirit with His baptising and filling power. These verses contain some significant phrases. *"Abides in you"* means the anointing remains and lives in us with a high degree of permanence. Link this with John 14:16 where Jesus says about the Holy Spirit: *"that He may abide with you forever."* John also says, *"You do not need anyone to teach you; but the same anointing teaches you concerning all things."* This text is not dispensing with "teachers" whom Christ has granted to the Church. Rather, it is saying that the believers to whom John was writing had already been well-taught in God's Word, and that their abiding anointing would direct them away from error and steer them into all truth. Also, Jesus says the Spirit would teach, aid our memory, guide into all truth and show us the things of Christ. There is little doubt that the anointing mentioned by John refers specifically to Spirit baptism. Paul mentions the believers being *"anointed"* and *"sealed"* and *"guaranteed"* future blessings – all through the Holy Spirit, and Peter settles the matter by saying that Jesus was *"anointed with the Holy Spirit"*.

# CHAPTER NINE

# DOES THE EARLY CHURCH SET THE PATTERN FOR US?

THIS IS A CRUCIAL QUESTION, AND ITS ANSWER WILL influence our expectations of God and how our Christian life is lived and expressed today. At the outset we should acknowledge that nowhere does the Bible say the early Church sets the pattern for Church order and practice down the centuries to our own day. Equally, nowhere does the Bible say the Church in the Acts of the Apostles does not set the pattern for the Church today. This absence of specific texts could leave us in a quandary difficult to be resolved. If we appeal to Church history for practice and belief, we find we are struggling through unsurmountable obstacles. If we turn to Church traditions and customs, similar hurdles present themselves. For example, the early Church had no church buildings, should we then follow suit? Later they met in the catacombs, should we do the same? If the early Church began without buildings but later moved to catacombs, it would seem acceptable for us also to adopt divergent ways and methods according to the day's demands. If we say the early Church did not set the pattern for the Church down the centuries, then we have no authoritative pattern at all! Without an authentic mode of practice we are left to our own devices, enabling us to do whatever we like. To sort this out, the Lord has provided two definite elements. Firstly, the written Word of God, and secondly, the guidance of the Holy Spirit.

## THE WORD OF GOD

I believe in the plenary verbal inspiration of the Bible – sixty-six volumes which are the out-breathing of God – His Word in the language of men. Doctrine must be based only on the Scriptures, and if it is not, we open the door to anything from false religion to cultist ideas. Church traditions and customs are interesting, but if they remain unsupported by the Bible, then they must not dictate our belief system. Although doctrine must be established from God's written Word only, it is important to realise that some scriptures demand a cultural interpretation. The Bible mentions early Church practices dictated by the circumstances of the day, and which later it altered. An example of modified practices according to expedience and demand concerns meeting in the Temple in Jerusalem. This could not continue after AD 70 because Titus, the Roman general, destroyed the Temple, and the believers were scattered to distant provinces far from Jerusalem.

Another example is the practice of bread and wine that Jesus instituted. This was firstly conducted on a daily basis at meal times in the homes of believers. Later it was practised by the early Church on the first day of the week only. Such examples give credence to adapting Church practice today as best fits our circumstances. Other scriptures contain a definite cultural interpretation, such as not eating blood, and ladies wearing hats, which have only little relevance to our situation in Great Britain. In the Philippines beer is cheaper to buy than water, encouraging drunkenness. For this reason born-again Spirit-filled believers try to set a good example by abstaining from alcoholic beverages. Such adaptations and procedures are well within the limits of scriptural understanding.

## THE HOLY SPIRIT

Because it is so easy to misinterpret the Bible, the Lord has provided us with the guidance of the Holy Spirit who comes to teach us all things. However, that guidance is not fully active until after we are baptised in the Spirit. Consider how Arius (AD 250–AD 336. *Presbyter of Alexandria and founder of the heresy known as Arianism*) decided from the Scriptures that Christ Jesus was not God. He was condemned by a synod at Alexandria in AD 320 or 321, and defeated at the Council of Nicæa in AD 325. The protagonist Athanasius of Alexandria (AD 298–373), known as "a pillar of the Church" and "Father of Orthodoxy", opposed Arius and won his case. Could it be that Arius was not Spirit-baptised, but Athanasius was? Most Spirit-filled believers today accept the Athanasian Creed, except the Pentecostal Oneness group known as "Jesus only". They deny the Threeness of God, which does violence to the meaning of many scriptures. If they are baptised in the Spirit, are they listening to what the Spirit says to the Churches? I wonder.

Since we have the truth of the Bible and the guidance of the Holy Spirit, we return to the question, "Did the early Church set the pattern for us?" The New Testament presents a stark absence of any indication that Christ's early Church would be different from His Church in later centuries. Nothing alludes to the fact that the first believers' experience was exclusive to them. No hint is found that "the Way" was temporary, and that it would be distinctive from all succeeding generations of believers.

**To conclude that the early Church does not set the pattern for us today results in alarming problems.**

1.  It relegates the events in Acts to a mere historic record, at best describing what once was rather than illustrating what should be.

2.  It permits the Church to depart radically from the Scriptures in faith and practice.

3.  It allows the Church today to do what it likes and act how it likes.

4.  It means we no longer embrace "the Way" (as Christianity was first described). We choose a different way, which we might consider to be better, but it will not be Biblical Christianity!

5.  It leaves us without a pattern. The Church is bereft of an authentic record of how it should operate. Historic accounts, other than the Scriptures, describing life in the early Church are clearly inferior to the New Testament record, and therefore cannot be used as the basis for belief or practice today.

**To accept that the early Church set the pattern for all time leads to the following satisfying conclusions.**

1.  We have a divine record of how the Church should operate in all generations.

2.  Our expectations of God and the power of the gospel are heightened.

3.  There is a benchmark, a standard of excellence, by which today's Church can be measured and judged.

4. We will ardently endeavour to remain Biblical in doctrine, belief and practice.

5. Inventing theories why the early Church would be different from the Church in succeeding generations becomes totally unnecessary.

6. Anti-scriptural theories (such as cessationism which declares that miracles and Spirit manifestations ceased with the death of the first apostles and/or after the canon of the New Testament was completed) are confirmed to be spurious human improvisations.

Attempts have been made to show that miracles would cease, by using Paul's statement *"prophecies will fail and tongues will cease and knowledge will vanish away"*. Crucially, when will this be? The Bible says, *"When the perfect has come, that which is in part will be done away, when we see face to face."* Truly that is at the return of the Lord Jesus to earth as King. Theories and ideas endeavouring to convince us that miracles have ceased already simply confirm that part of today's Church is substantially different from the early Church. This is plain and evident to those who have a Bible in one hand, and hold certain sections of the Church in the other. Jesus instructed His disciples to teach converts exactly what He had taught them. The directives and mandate included in the Great Commission applied *"to the end of the age"* and included such factors as believer's water baptism, Holy Spirit baptism and confirmatory signs. The early Church was the 'real thing' which set the pattern for all time.

## WHY DOES TODAY'S CHURCH DIFFER FROM THE EARLY CHURCH?

There are a number of reasons for this. We have departed from the Scriptures, like the Sadducees of whom Jesus said, *"You do not know the Scriptures nor the power of God."* We have failed to wait on God for the baptism in the Spirit and its subsequent fillings. The guidance of the Spirit has been neglected and quenched. Human traditions and procedures have become more acceptable than Biblical statements. We have built churches often on a small piece of textual evidence and fractured the Church into denominations which are adhered to more avidly than Jesus Himself. We have invented theories which are not only unscriptural (not supported by the Bible), but which are anti-scriptural (at variance with what the Bible actually says). False teaching has affected our understanding of the Lord and His ways. We have turned our relationship with God into a religion, and we have preferred churchianity to Christianity. We have compromised life in the Holy Spirit, preferring pleasure to persecution.

Referring to persecution, Paul said, *"None of these things move me."* It seems we lack such tenacity and have moved ourselves further away from the Biblical pattern set by early believers. Another factor is that we live in a modern age, with all its available accoutrements and technological tools for getting the job done. Modern transport, printing, computers, the worldwide web, projectors, recording equipment and the media all contribute to our doing things differently. Our tools may have advanced, but our lives and practice should echo those in Bible days. God's Spirit is just the same, and His power is vitally necessary for us. It will be hopeless to substitute modern equipment for the power of God. The anointing of His Spirit must not be replaced by scholastics! The world today urges academic achievement simply because it experiences no anointing of God's Holy Spirit – mind-knowledge is the world's substitute for spirit-knowledge. But the position is not hopeless because Jesus said He would build His Church and the gates of Hades would not prevail against it! Although the pendulum of

Christianity swung away from its early beginnings, it is now swinging back again. The centuries which saw decline are witnessing a return to "the Way" of Biblical Christianity. As promised, the Lord Jesus Christ continues to build His Church which is waking out of darkness into light.

## WAITING OR NO WAITING

Jesus told His disciples, *"Wait in the city of Jerusalem until you are clothed with power from on high"* (Luke 24:49). Does that instruction apply to us? Does it apply in whole or in part? Was this instruction simply for the first disciples only? It is clearly evident that there is no scripture that applies directly to us. We weren't there when Jesus spoke to people, or when Paul preached, or when the Scriptures were written. Even so, it would be erroneous to consider that nothing in the Bible applies to us. The words of Jesus are *"spirit and life"*. They have an everlasting application. It is through faith that we take the words of God and apply them to ourselves. The Lord said to Joshua, *"As I said to Moses"*, indicating that the Lord's words spoken to Moses applied to Joshua as well! Also the Lord said to Joshua, *"As I was with Moses"*, meaning the Lord would relate to Joshua in the same way He interacted with Moses. Simply Joshua must accept and believe this.

In the same way we take the words of Jesus and by faith accept and believe they are for us. For example, John 10:10: *"I have come to give that you might have life and more abundantly."* If you say such words were not spoken to us, you are quite right, but in faith we accept those words for ourselves. This demonstrates the eternal quality of God's Word, and the essence of faith. We believe what the Lord says is as much for us as for the immediate people to whom He spoke. Jesus also instructed His disciples to teach converts throughout the nations exactly what He had taught them. They were to pass on His every command and instruction so that future converts would know the eternal power of His words! They would believe those words and act on them. They would follow the same practices that Christ had originally taught. What He said to the first disciples applies to us, and for this reason we continue with the Communion of bread and wine, believing that Jesus' words, *"Do this in remembrance of Me"* is as much an instruction for us today as it was for His followers then. Jesus is the immutable, unchanging Word of God and the Bible is His written Word of God which is eternal, unbreakable, having significance throughout time.

The instruction, *"Wait in the city of Jerusalem until you are clothed with power from on high"* at best can apply to us in part only. The specific city of Jerusalem would be totally overwhelmed if every new convert assembled there to receive Spirit baptism! But if *"the city of Jerusalem"* is interpreted as the place where we begin our Christian life, whether Glasgow or Gloucester, it is there we wait to receive power from above. This instruction can be condensed to, *"Wait* [where you are] *until you are clothed with power from on high."* We must keep in mind the context of this instruction. It was spoken to scores of disciples, most of whom had witnessed Christ's ministry of teaching and healing. The Master had sent out many of them to accomplish the very same works. They had witnessed the Lord's death and resurrection, and Jesus had breathed on them to receive the Holy Spirit. I would suggest that they had received far more spiritual input from Jesus Christ than most believers experience today. Despite that, the Lord firmly instructed them not to begin the work of publishing the gospel until they had been baptised in the Holy Spirit.

*"Wait for the Promise of the Father"* is an instruction which applies to us before embarking on our fulfilment of the Great Commission. How many converts today are told to be baptised

in the Holy Spirit before trying to spread the gospel? Generally we have replaced Spirit baptism with other activities, such as Bible study, Bible school attendance or theological seminary courses, missionary training, academic qualifications and the like. Now I am not saying these are unnecessary, but I am saying that none of these can ever be a legitimate substitute for the baptism in the Holy Spirit. After obtaining degrees in the best theological colleges, you will remain less qualified than the disciples who followed Jesus for three years. If the Master commanded them to wait for Spirit baptism before engaging in Christian ministry, how much more should we ensure we are baptised in the Spirit before launching out with the gospel?

It is appalling to witness the number of Church incumbents, preachers, teachers, lecturers, pastors, missionaries and leaders who engage in gospel work without Spirit baptism. The result is that they operate mostly in their own human strength. They often accomplish little, become discouraged and give up on what they thought was their calling. The ineffectiveness of much of the Christian Church today can be traced back to an incomplete salvation. In some cases they have no born again experience, but too many have received no endowment of power through the baptism in the Holy Spirit.

It is pointed out that the first disciples had to wait for their Spirit baptism on the Day of Pentecost because it was necessary first for Jesus to ascend to heaven and to be glorified. It is suggested that since Jesus has done this, and the Spirit has been released as the medium for baptism, we no longer need to wait. To this I would say, yes and no! Truly we do not need to wait for the exultation of Jesus and for Spirit baptism to be activated, but we do need to wait for our personal Spirit baptism before engaging in ministry! Although we do not have to wait logistically for heavenly events to be completed, this does not exonerate us from waiting on God for what the Lord said was essential for spreading the gospel. Rushing ahead in disobedience (and probably in disbelief) is responsible for a feeble and ineffective Church.

Finally, it is deplorable that so many are taught that they were baptised in the Holy Spirit at the moment of their conversion. Such teaching is only possible by twisting Scripture texts, or by taking verses which speak about the Person of the Holy Spirit and applying them to the baptism in the Holy Spirit. Two scriptural arguments defeat this theory.

Firstly, a Biblical Spirit baptism is always accompanied by tangible outward evidences, such as speaking in tongues, prophesying and audibly magnifying the Lord. If, like Cornelius, every new convert exhibited such phenomena we would know they had been saved and also baptised in the Spirit. The fact that most converts have no such experience, and display no such manifestations belies the assumption that they have automatically been baptised in the Holy Spirit. Secondly, time-gaps between conversion and Spirit baptism generally occur. The disciples at Pentecost may have waited over two years for their Spirit baptism. The Samaritan believers waited perhaps a week for their Spirit baptism. Saul waited a number of days for his Spirit baptism. The Ephesians converts waited only an hour or so for their Spirit baptism, after Paul first baptised them in water. Cornelius and his household experienced only moments between their salvation and their Spirit baptism. Time-gaps occurred, and the Bible does not say anyone was baptised in the Holy Spirit at the very moment they were saved!

According to John MacArthur's video blog[6] being born again and being baptised in the Spirit occur at the same time, they are one and the same thing! This means the first 120 followers of Jesus were not saved until the Day of Pentecost! This is absurd because their names were already written in heaven, and Jesus prayed for them (John 17) in terms which could not be applied to unsaved people! For many the way around this is to suggest that the first believers were in fact saved before they were Spirit-baptised at Pentecost, but that their situation was special, not typical, because they lived at an interim stage, so they do not set the pattern for us today. None of these suggestions are scriptural. Both human opinions and non-biblical theories are meaningless when placed alongside Jesus' words that Spirit baptism would provide power to be His witnesses (Acts 1:8).

# CHAPTER TEN

# IT'S ALL IN YOUR HEAD!

CHICKEN RUN WAS A FABULOUS FILM MIRRORING *THE GREAT Escape*. It featured a chicken farm owned by Mr and Mrs Tweedy, in which Mrs Tweedy was both the brains and the brawn behind the whole enterprise. The weedy Mr Tweedy looked at the chickens, scratched his head and somehow knew they were planning mischief. Plucking up courage he began to explain to his wife that he thought the chickens were planning an escape. She scolded him because after all, they were only chickens! With derision she roared at him, "It's all in yer 'ead, Mr Tweedy! It's all in yer 'ead!" In fact, it was all in Mrs Tweedy's head! Her level-headed views had overlooked the intuitions and nuances of the human spirit which in Mr Tweedy sensed that something was wrong in the chicken run. It was all in her head that chickens are only chickens and therefore cannot plan an escape.

The allegation, "It's all in your head" could well be levelled at some believers today. Like Mrs Tweedy, they cling to doctrine and experience which is all in their head. They might pontificate on part of a Bible text such as 2 Timothy 1:7 where Paul mentions *"a sound mind"* but they overlook that God has not given *"a spirit of fear"* but that He has given a spirit of *"power and of love and of a sound mind"*. Their lifestyle and ministry fail to demonstrate they have received *"a spirit of power"* or anything else arranged by God for extending His Kingdom. Like the cultists they may *"draw disciples after them"* (Acts 20:29), including many students, but offering academia rather than God's anointing will prove empty in the long run. The Holy Spirit cannot use anti-Biblical ideas to expand God's rule among people.

Some demonstrate clearly that they do not have a sound mind. An example of this concerns the belief that miracles have ceased. At best it is sickening intransigence, and at worst it is crass lies. But what else can they do? Lacking a Spirit baptism experience, they have no recourse but to *"lean on their own understanding"*. The human mind is their only resource! Their purely human understanding of Bible passages presents a biased, deformed interpretation of Scripture, similar to that of the cults who, by the way, also repudiate the miraculous today. Recall that the Pharisees and the scribes were all *words*. They invented scenarios in an endeavour to trap Jesus, because the human mind is adept at manufacturing objections to anything! Jesus said to the Sadducees, *"You err, not knowing the Scriptures nor the power of God."*

## BLINDNESS

Ah! The unsound human mind blocks itself from the truth which sets us free. The Pharisees suffered with the same problem. They searched the Scriptures but failed to see that those writings pointed them to Jesus Christ (John 5:39–40). Physical blindness can be overcome in many amazing ways, including by divine healing, but spiritual blindness cripples the soul. John chapter 9 records a man born blind, and after explaining that there was no correlation between this man's sin (nor his parents' sins) and his blindness, Jesus proceeds to heal him. From this outstanding miracle came a number of arguments against Jesus, and against the man with restored sight:

## Neighbours and others

1. v.9 Is this truly the man born blind, or someone like him? The man testified, *"I am he!"*

2. v.10 How were your eyes opened?

3. v.11 The man explained, a man called Jesus – *"clay ... wash ... obedience ... sight restored".*

4. v.12 Where is this man? The healed man said, *"I don't know."*

## Pharisees

5. v.13 They bring him to the Pharisees.

6. v.14 It was on the Sabbath that this man was healed.

7. v.15 The Pharisees ask again how he came to see. The man explained again – *"clay ... wash ... can see."*

8. v.16 Pharisees conclude, not of God because this healing took place on the Sabbath!

9. v.16 Other people ask, *"How can a sinner do signs?"* This causes a division.

10. v.17 Pharisees ask the man what he thinks of Him who made him see. Reply, *"He is a prophet."*

11. v.18 Pharisees disbelieve the man had been blind in the first place, so they call his parents.

*Parents*

12. v.19 Pharisees ask parents, "Is this your son, who *you say* was born blind?" *Definitely!*

13. v.19 Pharisees examine further, "How can he now see?"

14. 14. v.20 Parents testify that they know this is their son and that he was born blind.

15. v.21 Parents *say they don't know how, or who, opened his eyes; he is old enough, ask him!*

16. vv.22–23 Parents are afraid of religious repercussions, of being put out of the synagogue.

*The healed man*

17. v.24 Pharisees say Jesus is a sinner, and tell the man to glorify God by admitting the same.

18. v.25 Man doesn't know about Jesus. He knows only one thing – *"he was blind but now he sees"*!

19. v.26 Pharisees ask again how the man came to have sight.

20. v.27 Man replies, *"I've already told you but you did not listen. Do you want to be his disciples?"*

21. v.28 Pharisees revile him: *"You are his disciple, but we are Moses disciples."*

22. v.29 Pharisees have faith in Moses, but they don't even know where this Healer is from.

23. v.30 Man replies, *"Amazing, he's done a great miracle but you still don't know where he is from!"*

24. vv.31–33 Man's explanation: *God hears the godly, without God no miracle could have occurred.*

25. v.34 Pharisees retort, why is this sinner attempting to teach us doctors of the law?

26. v.34 Pharisees cast him out, excommunicating him from the synagogues and all places of worship.

## Jesus

27. vv.35–38 Jesus reveals that He is the Son of God, and the man believes and worships Jesus.

28. v.39 Jesus has come to open blind eyes, but also to blind those who think they see.

29. v.40 Pharisees ask Jesus, *"Are we blind also?"*

30. v.41 Jesus' answer exposes both their blindness and their sin.

## Further repercussions

31. 10:19–21 Further division arises and the people ask, *"Can a demon open blind eyes?"*

32. 10:25 Jesus declares that His works done in His Father's Name bear witness to who He is.

33. 10:31 The Jewish leaders want to stone Jesus to death!

34. 10:32–38 The rulers may not believe who Jesus is, but the works (miracles) are surely from God.

35. 10:39 The rulers try to seize Jesus, but cannot!

Here is a simple story of a man whom Jesus healed of blindness. The incident is straightforward and without complications; it is one of the many healing miracles of the Lord Jesus Christ. It is a sign of His love and compassion, His power, His identity as the Son of God and His ability to save and deliver. Simply accept it and give Him all the praise and glory! But no, in their blindness the elite Pharisees and Jewish rulers were unable to accept this man's healing at face value. They considered there were doctrinal issues involved which had to be challenged – for example, this healing was done on the Sabbath! Thus what was obvious and transparent must be ruthlessly examined and debated. Consider again the thirty-five steps listed above, involved in testing Christ's work, and which culminated in the Jewish leaders wanting their Messiah dead!

## THE ORIGINAL BIBLE TEXT IS INFALLIBLE

We assert that the Bible in its original form is the infallible Word of God. It was *out-breathed* by God Himself, who used human beings to record His words in writing. Today we use translations from ancient copies, and all translations have their weaknesses, and are not infallible! We require thorough research and study, but we need more than that – we need the guidance of the Holy Spirit in order to understand the Scriptures and interpret them correctly.

When the Holy Spirit manifests Himself by means of prophecy, the utterance is not infallible, as 1 Thessalonians 5:20–21 shows. This is simply because it involves the imperfect human element which can prevent it being flawless. Therefore, prophecy must be judged, weighed and measured according to the standard of Scripture so that the good can be accepted and the bad rejected. This was the case in the early Church, and it is the same today. Those judging the utterances should themselves be prophets, or at least persons who manifest prophecy, including ladies who are legitimate purveyors of prophecy. It is important to accept that preaching is not infallible and we are wisely advised to weigh each sermon since some preach their own opinions, and use the Word of God as a launch pad for their own (often insidious) ideas.

# HUMAN BEINGS ARE TRIPARTITE

It is stated in 1 Thessalonians 5:23 that human beings are comprised of *spirit, soul* and *body*. These three parts are integrated; they relate to each other, making a complete and whole human being made originally in *"the image of God"*. However, each of the three parts has a distinct function. Although I cannot see my spirit and soul (only my body), I am perfectly aware that I can think, make decisions and feel sensations. This is because my soul includes my mind, my will and my emotions. Similarly, my human spirit has three functions which although related to the functions of my soul, are also distinct, allowing me to be sensitive spiritually. Unsaved people live physically, with their bodily appetites and desires ruling their lives. They also function in a 'soulish' way resulting in unworthy desires, feelings, and enticements which lead to questionable decisions. They are 'spiritually' dead, because their unsaved spirit is subdued and

| THE HUMAN SPIRIT – GOD CONSCIOUS | | | | |
|---|---|---|---|---|
| INTUITION | CONSCIENCE | | COMMUNION | |
| Intuitive knowledge | Approval or disapproval | | Worship, fellowship, love | |
| THE HUMAN SOUL – SELF-CONSCIOUS | | | | |
| MIND | WILL | | EMOTION | |
| Acquired information | Desires and decisions | | Feelings and sensibilities | |
| THE HUMAN BODY – WORLD-CONSCIOUS | | | | |
| SEEING | HEARING | SMELLING | TASTING | TOUCHING |
| We can see for miles | We can hear distant sounds | We can smell in the air around us | We taste with our tongue | As far as our hands can reach |

mortified by unforgiven sin, with the consequence that they receive very little help from their human spirit. The table above shows the component parts of a human being.

Can you see the relationship between the God-conscious spirit and the soul? Intuitive knowledge relates to acquired knowledge, and it is important to see that both are essential for life in all its fullness. The conscience relates to the will, approving or disapproving what we think, and thereby influencing our decisions. The conscience can be desensitised, leading to harmful decisions. Communion with God is personal and intimate, allowing us to love Him, and to worship Him in Spirit and truth. It is linked with our emotions, so that we sense God's presence. In this way worship should be emotional. Without the influence of godly spirit communion, our feelings remain flat. We sing a hymn by rote but feel and sense very little.

Godly communion enables us to worship the Lord as we sing, which produces a critical difference. A non-Spirit-filled church can imitate the style of music and sing the same songs as Spirit-filled Christians, but the end result can be just noise. The same song leaves people unmoved, rendering the whole 'act of worship' boring and often no more than an act!

Western Christian leaders without Spirit baptism might have accumulated a massive store of head knowledge. That is not wrong in itself, but it is suspect when understanding with the mind replaces knowledge from the spirit. When the human mind is deemed more important than the human spirit we are in trouble. Our mind can rationally deduce and process information, but it cannot 'know'. Even scientists begin with a theory – an intuitive idea that must be proven. No experiments would ever be made if intuitive ideas were entirely absent!

God speaks directly to our human spirit; it is His principal area of communication. We understand with our mind, but we know with our spirit! The same faculties are used by us to know other people. Some are difficult to get to know – you might have much data and information about them, but you seem to never reach them – their spirit is closed down and your receive nothing from them. Others you know in just a few minutes after meeting them; your mind may know nothing about their life, but you know them personally as their spirit relates to yours. Through intuitive knowledge in our spirit, we know who we can trust. It is through our human spirit that we can know God, whom to know is eternal life (John 17:3).

Tom Marshall in his book *Free Indeed!* says that the tragedy is that we have made the Christian faith so much a matter of head knowledge that experiences of the human spirit are almost totally neglected. It's all in our head! Do you recall when Jesus was in a room crammed full with people, He knew exactly what the scribes and the Pharisees were thinking? This wasn't head knowledge. He didn't chat with them and ask for their thoughts! His spirit instinctively and directly knew what was going through their minds. The NKJV says Jesus *perceived* their thoughts (Luke 5:22). The same word is used again when Jesus *perceived* the thoughts of the disciples in Luke 5:22, 9:47. This area of spiritual perception and knowledge is most keenly developed by means of the baptism in the Holy Spirit.

# CHAPTER ELEVEN

# THE FOUNTAINHEAD

THE BAPTISM IN THE HOLY SPIRIT IS THE FOUNTAINHEAD of all other Spirit blessings and experiences. Under the Old Covenant, particular individuals were filled and empowered by the Holy Spirit. This enabled them to perform God's work and execute specific tasks. The Old Testament abounds with such people, like skilled artisans, leaders, judges, rulers, kings, prophets and priests. We also discover that seven out of the nine manifestations of the Holy Spirit operated during that dispensation. The two manifestations which were not witnessed were *"speaking in tongues"* and *"the interpretation of tongues"*, which were reserved for the New Covenant age of the Holy Spirit.

It is not surprising, therefore, that numerous individuals who have not been baptised in the Holy Spirit are seen to display some of the Spirit's gifts and to exhibit being filled with the Spirit. My own mother was miraculously healed as I laid hands on her. We could question whether this was purely a simple answer to prayer, or a manifestation of the *"gifts of healings"*. It was probably a combination of both, but interestingly this occurred long before I was baptised in the Holy Spirit! These incidents happen all the time, everywhere, and they have led many Christians towards some unsound conclusions. The following headings have an element of truth in them, but they are not the whole truth.

*The Holy Spirit operates in the lives of believers who are not baptised in the Spirit.*

This is true! The Holy Spirit did this throughout the Old Covenant era, empowering and filling certain individuals at specific times for particular work. We have no scriptural reason to think He has ceased from such acts, but we must not falsely conclude that the baptism in the Spirit is not essential for ministry today!

*The baptism in the Holy Spirit is not necessary for a miraculous ministry.*

In part this also is true! I experienced miracles before I was baptised in the Holy Spirit. However, such occurrences were fragmentary and scarce. This seems to confirm that no one needs Spirit baptism in order to see miracles. But we surely need the baptism in the Spirit if we are to witness copious numbers of miracles, as in the early Church.

*Tongues (and interpretation) are not required for the work of God today.*

I understand why this is thought to be true. It is a view which exonerates those who have not spoken in tongues, and helps to relieve them of any feelings of inferiority. They are able to cling tightly to the rhetorical question in 1 Corinthians 12:30, *"Do all speak with tongues?"* The obvious answer here is "No!" Despite lack of speaking in tongues, their ministry continues with the hope that it is in the power of God's Spirit. However, since the Lord has devised a new Spirit baptism for this New Covenant age, and new Spirit manifestations of tongues and interpretation, who are we to invalidate His design? Such neglect might not only quench the Holy Spirit, but also grieve Him.

*Forget the baptism in the Spirit, just aim for the gifts of the Spirit.*

It would appear that this is a common stance in some charismatic churches, where a genuine Spirit baptism is neglected, but the gifts are emphasised. This is putting the cart before the horse! Many may well be satisfied with this approach, but it is not the Biblical way and it easily leads to confusion and disappointment. We are more than gifts; we are the people of the living God whose Spirit resides in the temple of our bodies.

Some of the above conclusions have an element of truth in them, but it is now time to return to a Biblical stance. We have already shown that a *complete experience* of salvation incorporates four major elements: 1) Repentance and faith 2) New birth 3) Believer's water baptism 4) Spirit baptism. Regretfully both water baptism and Spirit baptism are sometimes viewed as 'gospel additions', offering a level of blessing, but not essential. The Biblical stance shows that these elements are not mere 'add-ons' or non-essential extras, regarded as nice for those who want them. Such thinking has afflicted the evangelical wing of the Church for too long. The Holy Spirit is active at each stage of the salvation process, none of which should be regarded as inconsequential!

Those not baptised in the Holy Spirit, but who seek miracles and gifts, have inadvertently shifted into reverse gear under the Old Covenant arrangements. Not bad, but nowhere near good enough for a New Covenant ministry and relationship with God. They have taken a backward step. Would they retreat also from the cross of Christ to offer a lamb or goat on their own altar of forgiveness? If it is repugnant to step back from the cross, it is also abhorrent to step back from New Covenant believer's water baptism and Spirit baptism. How can a person say, "Thanks, but no thanks," to some of God's New Covenant provisions? Why treat the blessings of Jesus as superfluous to our lives?

The situation in Christendom today is that about two-thirds of believers are not baptised in the Holy Spirit, and I wonder what proportion are not born again, being only nominal Christians. Concerning those who are saved, many belong to denominations or churches where the baptism in the Holy Spirit is never taught, and possibly never mentioned. The Biblical concept of Spirit baptism on the Day of Pentecost is watered down to a mere arrival of the Holy Spirit. Such a misunderstanding serves to make the subject more obscure and less vital. The devil is happy with this situation, but the Lord is not, and this book is but a small instrument to induce Biblical truth about the baptism in the precious Holy Spirit.

Every Christian believer in the early Church experienced their own individual baptism in the Spirit. This was part of the work of the ascended Christ. It is a promised provision of power which is refused at our peril. What difference does the baptism in the Holy Spirit make in our lives? In the New Testament, Spirit baptism completed a full salvation experience for each convert. Spirit baptism was the fountainhead of all that God had for them throughout the rest of their lives. That pouring out of God's Spirit into them, within them and through them issued in copious torrents of living water, which not only satiated their own lives but also drenched others to whom they ministered. I shall attempt to itemise the benefits of Spirit baptism, but doubtless my list cannot be exhaustive. How can we enumerate multitudes of blessings from Him who is able to do exceedingly above all we can ask or imagine?

From the fountainhead of the baptism in the Holy Spirit pours forth every spiritual blessing in Christ. Each jet of water provides a separate yet unified aspect of the Lord's gifts and grace. All nine manifestations of the Spirit are available so that a person has the potential to exercise any of them *"as the Spirit wills"*. Another jet of water divides into droplets issuing in the nine-fold fruit of the Spirit, confirming that Spirit baptism not only provides power, but also purity. The fountainhead of the baptism in the Holy Spirit provides the filling of the Spirit, and the sealing of the Spirit, and the whole experience becomes a deposited down payment or foretaste of the life to come in eternity. Each stream of life-giving water yields a never-ending supply of signs and wonders – miraculous events which glorify the risen Lord.

Plunged into the Holy Spirit, the disciple is empowered to declare the truth of the gospel and to demonstrate the authority of the Kingdom. Spirit baptism means being Spirit-filled, which means being love-filled, joy-filled and faith-filled. The believer finds that his body is the temple of residence for the Holy Spirit. He easily hears the voice of the Lord, understands His guidance and directives, and is more easily enabled to respond to the Lord's will. Through Spirit baptism, the believer himself becomes the Holy Spirit's treasured possession – a vessel fit for the Master's use. The Spirit-baptised child of God finds he can readily receive many revelations of the reality of Jesus Christ – that which belongs to Christ is unmasked and made real to him.

The Spirit-baptised Christian finds that the Bible becomes a new Book, and that the Spirit's anointing guides him into all truth, making clear the passages that previously were problematic. His mind is renewed and refreshed; it is sharpened and enlivened, and his memory capacity is increased as the Holy Spirit reminds him of truths and incidents that otherwise would have been long forgotten. The Spirit reveals things which are yet to come. Words of wisdom and knowledge, discerning of spirits, the working of miracles, gifts of healings, mighty faith, rivers of prophecy, speaking in tongues and the interpretation of tongues become a present reality, rather than a moribund record of what once was.

With tongues God speaks to the Church, and with tongues the believer edifies himself. His Christian character is changed deep within; he becomes alive in God's love and at last he understands divine compassion – it wells up in him, often at unexpected moments.

Doubts and fears are minimised, if present at all, being replaced by courage and boldness. An audacity flows from him with authority over demons and all the power of the enemy. He learns to pray, rather than 'say prayers'. He finds worshipping the Lord as spontaneous and easy as breathing. His opinion of himself changes; he realises he is nothing compared with the Lord. Yes, he is nothing, but Christ is everything! He better understands God's grace, knowing that he has merited none of heaven's blessings. He appreciates God's mercy towards him, and finds no difficulty in giving all the glory to God. He hungers for Christ, the Living Word, and hungers to know the Bible, God's written Word. He knows he must continue to grow spiritually and reach maturity in Christ and that there is a resurrection to attain and a bema-judgment to face. He longs to see the Lord. He longs for the Lord to return to clear up the mess of this godless world. On some the spirit of apostleship will rest. Others become prophets. Some are clothed with the zeal of an evangelist, with longings for the unsaved to know Christ. Some become teachers, sensitive not only to truth, but also to error. Others become pastors who shepherd and feed God's flock, and who feel responsible for the souls under their care.

Have you grasped something of the greatness of the baptism in the Holy Spirit? It truly is a mighty, heaven-sent, earth-shaking experience which sets in motion incredible utterances, confident attitudes, powerful declarations and convincing demonstrations of the reality of our Lord and Saviour, Jesus Christ. Spirit baptism has also been described as a 'baptism of love' because the *"love of the Spirit"* wells up within the believer and flows out in a mighty stream of compassion. During my pastoral work I have sometimes felt annoyed or even angry with believers, but upon visiting them and meeting them face to face, my annoyance has subsided and my heart has been filled with compassion from the Holy Spirit.

*"Eye has not seen, nor ears heard, neither has it entered the heart what God has prepared for those who love Him. But God has revealed them to us by His Spirit"* says 1 Corinthians 2:9–10. It is through the fountainhead of the baptism in the Spirit that God reveals such wonders to us. This was written by Paul, who was Pentecostal by experience, and he was writing to believers who were the same. Without a Biblical Spirit baptism it is presumptuous to apply this phrase to ourselves, just as it is ridiculous for an unsaved person reading Philippians 3:20 to claim on the strength of that statement alone that his *"citizenship is in heaven"*!

Paul battled constantly against erroneous teaching in the early Church, and I understand why he wrote: *"From now on let no one trouble me"* (Galatians 6:17 NKJV). Truth sets us free, and we must contend earnestly for it, but battling with unbelief in fellow Christians is a wearying experience in the extreme, especially when they refuse to see what the Bible clearly teaches.

Paul was accused of terrifying the believers with his letters. They said his writings were weighty and powerful, but they added that his bodily presence was weak, and his preaching worthless! Whatever he was, he was God's person, filled with the Holy Spirit, just as you and I can be, to the glory of God.

# CHAPTER TWELVE

# THE FOUNDATION OF
# GOD'S WRITTEN WORD

HOW REGRETTABLE THAT SOME WHO WOULD LABEL
themselves 'Christian' question the authority of the Bible.
Just recently a man heard a sermon based on John 3:1–15
entitled, 'Religion is not enough – you must be born again.'
Afterwards he claimed that we do not know what Jesus said –
He may not have said you must be born again – it is merely
recorded that He said it! This stance throws the whole of John's
Gospel into question; indeed, it throws the whole Bible and the
whole of historic literature into question. This idea is an
impossible one since it means that we can no longer accept any
historic statement as true! *"I am a worm and no man"* speaks
prophetically about Messiah, and none of us is greater than He,
therefore we all at best are *worms* in God's sight! The one and
only recourse is to let the Holy Spirit guide us into all truth, as
Jesus said He would. The Spirit will confirm that the Bible is
true indeed and that we can accept its veracity.

Once I gave a Bible study on 'The Authority of the Bible' to a small Methodist group. During a question and answer time at the end, the minister said, "How can you believe the Bible? For example, Genesis chapter 1 about creation disagrees with Genesis chapter 2!" I simply replied, "I have never heard or seen that Genesis chapters 1 and 2 disagree with each other. Chapter 2 takes a closer look at how God made human beings; it exemplifies and elucidates in greater details the broad statements given in chapter 1. There is no disagreement." What seminary produced such doubts and unbelief? What Christ is the minister preaching, I wonder?

It is most alarming to find that an ordained minister of the gospel cannot accept God's Word of Scripture, in spite of the fact that the Lord Jesus and the New Testament writers accepted and attested the veracity of the complete Old Testament![8] Also, many New Testament writers affirm the historic reality of Adam.[9] Since Jesus accepted without question the authenticity of the Old Testament and endorsed the accuracy of the Pentateuch, the Prophets and the Psalms, who has the right to disagree? Can we vaunt our petty minds against Him and win? Another student from a seminary showed great amazement after my teaching sessions on 'The Differences of the Four Gospels'. I showed why there are four, why they differ, and that the differences are divine distinctions, not discrepancies. Part way through my lectures he exclaimed, "Why didn't they teach us this? I lost my faith in that seminary!"

The Bible is its own authority. I am in favour of study, scholarship and critical investigation, but it is by far more important to *"know the Lord"* (John 17:3). True theologians are those who know the Lord and not merely know about Him. Those who have no personal experience of Him (even if they regard themselves as scholars or academics) operate on a much lower authoritative plane than the Bible itself. The Bible is self-authenticating. Simply accept it, believe it and obey it, and the outcome is that you know God is real; you know the Bible is His Word; you personally receive salvation and His glorious Spirit, who takes up residence within your life. You discover that the opinions of scholars and academics are inconsequential by comparison with the anointing of the Spirit of God.

Church history shows that most major doctrines were debated. Protagonists on both sides of an argument gave reasons for their Biblical stance. For example, Arias taught that Jesus Christ is not God, while Athanasius showed from the Scriptures that Jesus Christ is God. In the days of the Reformation, John Calvin's arguments for salvation by election (often quite wrongly described as predestination) were contested by Jacobus Arminius (a successor of Calvin in 1560–1609), and today most born-again Christians follow Arminius. We have to be sensible and brave enough to see that not all men of God in the past got everything right! Much of what Calvin taught is true, but not all, and we need the Holy Spirit's guidance and discernment to see the difference.

Today some of the principal arguments revolve around water baptism – is it for babies (sprinkling) or for believers (immersion)? Secondly, Spirit baptism – was it merely a dynamic for the early Church, or is it for today? This book should leave no one in doubt that a demonstrable Spirit baptism is the Biblical norm for every born-again Christian. But doubts will remain, principally because people prefer to cling to their traditions than objectively accept Bible truth. Perhaps we all find it difficult to read the Scriptures without bias, but sadly many Christians believe what they have been wrongly taught by others, rather than what the Bible actually says.

**Hermeneutics** is from the Greek word *hermēneutikos* which signifies an expert in interpretation. It is the science of

Scripture interpretation; the branch of theology that deals with the principles of Biblical exegesis. It lays down rules to follow, and gives procedures to shun when seeking the meaning of Bible texts. Many ignore the rules because keeping to them would challenge their tradition and beliefs. One rule states that doctrine must be established on the clear statements of Scripture, not on the silences of Scripture. Another rule says that Bible *trends* are more important than Bibles *texts*. This means that one verse of Scripture cannot establish a doctrine. Doctrine is established by numerous Bible passages relating to a particular subject, which together confirm the truth.

**Exegesis** is a noun referring to the critical explanation or interpretation of a text or portion of the Bible, and it specially refers to a correct explanation of the Scriptures. It is drawing from the Scriptures what they actually say.

**Eisegesis** is a noun referring to an interpretation that expresses the interpreter's own ideas, bias, or the like. Eisegesis refers to what we put into the meaning of Scripture. It is common with the cults, since they interpret the meaning of Scripture according to their own ideas. For example, two Latter Day Saints (Mormons) called to see me, and mentioned that the Bible spoke about another Book, namely the Book of Mormon. Since I had never found such an idea in the Bible I asked them to show me the scripture. They turned to Ezekiel 37:15–20, and proceeded to explain that the first stick was in fact the Bible and the second stick was the Book of Mormon. Their eisegetical interpretation rode roughshod over the Lord's explanation where He says the first stick is Joseph (Israel's ten northern tribes) and the other stick is Judah (the southern tribes of Judah and Benjamin). The context of this chapter promises to join together the divided kingdom of Israel under the rulership of one king (David) in the end times.

I am disturbed and saddened by the extent to which the human mind is capable of ignoring the wise rules of hermeneutics and twisting the meaning of the Scriptures. How foolish to champion an isolated text such as 1 Corinthians 12:13 to assert that Spirit baptism was never repeated after the Day of Pentecost – a conclusion which opposes the whole Bible trend on that particular subject. The same mistake was made centuries ago to justify belief in baptismal regeneration, by leaning on one statement found in 1 Peter 3:21 *"baptism that now saves you"*. Wrested from its context, and taken literally in isolation from other texts on the same subject, a verse can be made to mean whatever the human mind (corrupt or otherwise) determines!

## WHAT DOES 1 CORINTHIANS 12:13 MEAN?

1 Corinthians 12:31 is a verse of Scripture which seems to present particular difficulties for translators. A precise translation of this verse is given here in NT Greek (minus the bit about Jews, Greeks, slaves and free) with a literal English translation beneath:

Και γαρ εν ενι πνυματε ημεις παντες εις εω σωμα εβαπτισθημεω

And for in one Spirit we all into one body were baptised

... και παντες εω πνρυμα εποτιαθημεν

...and all one Spirit were given to drink.

Differences primarily revolve around the third word in the Greek sentence, namely εν, which generally means *in* or *by*. In this verse the Greek sentence followed by a dative noun indicates that the word εν should be translated simply as *in*. Translating εν as *by* suggests that the Spirit himself is the One who baptises us into

Christ's body. Diligent study reveals that nowhere else in Scripture is the Spirit said to baptise anyone! Note also the phrase *in one Spirit* follows the same NT Greek construction about being baptised *in Holy Spirit.* (The words *Holy Spirit* are used as a title in John 14:26, but in most verses the word *holy* is an adjective describing the Spirit, and should not be capitalised.)

In 1 Corinthians 12:13 we have the phrase *"into the body"* using the Greek word εισ (into). This preposition is never used for Spirit baptism. Therefore a correct understanding of 1 Corinthians 12:13 is that we are "baptised in one Spirit into one body." "Into one body" is one of the consequences of Spirit baptism.

Results show that ten English versions translate this verse *"IN one Spirit"* and that twenty-seven versions say *"BY one Spirit."*

### IN one Spirit (ten versions)

American Standard Version
Darby (in the power of one Spirit)
Douay-Rheims 1899 American Edition
English Standard Version
Mounce Reverse Interlinear New Testament
New American Bible
New English Translation
Orthodox Jewish Bible
Wycliffe Bible
Young's Literal Translation

### BY one Spirit (twenty-seven versions)

21st Century Bible
Amplified
Common English Bible
Complete Jewish Bible
Contemporary English Version
Disciple's Literal New Testament (uses with, in, by)
Expanded Bible (uses through, by, in)

Geneva Bible
God's Word Translation
Good News Translation
Holman Christian Standard Bible
International Standard Version
J.B. Phillip's New Testament
Jubilee Bible 2000
King James Version
Lexham English Bible
Living Bible
*The Message*
Names of God Bible
New American Standard Bible
New International Reader's Version
New International Version
New King James Version
New Life Version
New Living Translation
Revised Standard Version
Worldwide English New Testament

Such treatment shows why many have been taught that this verse is not speaking about water baptism or Spirit baptism, but a new baptism *by* the Spirit into the body of Christ, the Church. Fortunately our better knowledge of NT Greek enables us to see differently. This verse refers to Spirit baptism, and can be paraphrased as *"We were baptised in one Spirit into one body . . . and were given one Spirit to drink."* Note the past tense of the verbs, *"were baptised"* and *"were given one Spirit to drink"* indicative of that fact that the believers had already received their one Holy Spirit baptism beforehand. The context of chapter 12 is the diversity and unity of Christ's body on earth, and verse 13 emphasises this same unity – one Spirit baptism, one Spirit to drink and one body (the Church) to belong to.

# DOCTRINE FOUNDED ON THE PLAIN
# MEANING OF SCRIPTURE

The golden rule of Bible Interpretation says:

> If the plain meaning of Scripture makes common sense,
> seek no other sense. Therefore take every word at its pri-
> mary, ordinary, usual, literal meaning, unless the facts of
> the immediate context studied in the light of related pas-
> sages and axiomatic and fundamental truths indicate
> clearly otherwise.

I thoroughly recommend a book by Dr Jack Deere to every
minister and student. Deere's book is entitled, *Surprised by the
Power of the Spirit.*[10] He demonstrates that cessationism (believing
that Spirit-gifts and miracles were for the early Church only) is
not based on Scripture and is therefore unbiblical. He says that if
you were to lock a brand-new Christian in a room with a Bible
and tell him to study what the Scripture has to say about healing
and miracles, he would never come out of the room a cessationist.
Jack Deere confesses that he had to be *taught* that the gifts of the
Spirit had passed away, and he says that the reason some
Christians do not believe in the miraculous gifts today is simply
that they have been taught that such things have ceased.

Many Christians have never seen a miracle, and consequently
they are tempted to accept that such displays are not for today.
How easy to fall into the pit of basing doctrine on lack of
experience, rather than on what the Bible says! God is able to do
exceedingly abundantly above all that we ask or think according to
the power that works in us, but in some cases His power is not at
work in us at all! Often our experience of God falls dismally short
of what it should be. When Paul mentions *"the power that works in
us"*, understand that he is writing to those who have been baptised
in the Holy Spirit and who have experienced miraculous gifts.

Dr Deere also tackles the issue of healing, with poignant chapters on 'Why does God heal?' and 'Why God doesn't heal'. He highlights the compassion of Christ and says that when some people say that God no longer heals, or that he only heals rarely, he wants to ask them where the Lord's compassion gone? Does Jesus Christ no longer walk among our churches? Does he no longer notice our pain? Does he no longer care for the families who have loved ones in mental hospitals, or whose babies are born with twisted bodies?

Jack continues that he believes Christ's compassion has not changed at all and that He is just as willing as He was in the first century to touch both our spirits and our bodies. Rather, it is the Church which has changed, not our God who is everlasting perfection, and incapable of being less than that.

The immutability of the Lord (His unchanging Being and character) is a well-established Biblical doctrine. The Lord spoke through Malachi, saying, *"I am the LORD. I do not change; therefore you are not consumed, O sons of Jacob."*(Malachi 3:6 NKJV) Despite Israel's sin and lack of holiness, God remains the same. His compassion never falters, therefore He assures the nation that they will not be consumed. W.H. Monk (1823–89) echoes the eternal truth of God's unchangeability in the second stanza of his beautiful hymn 'Abide With Me'.

> *Change and decay in all around I see:*
> *O Thou who changest not, abide with me.*

## SIGNS AND WONDERS

Quite irrespective of my experience, I believe in signs and wonders because the Bible includes them in the Church. I believe God performs signs and wonders, often through the channel of His Spirit-empowered people, because the Bible demonstrates that He does. The Bible presents a creator God who originated and sustains both the unseen spiritual realm and the visible material realm. The Father sent the Son to show us what God is like, and Christ did only what He saw the Father do. The Bible is clear that the Lord's power operated in both the physical realm and the spiritual realm. Jesus not only forgave sins but healed sick bodies, and supernatural acts were not an interruption in His ministry, but an integral part of it.

Generally, however, the Church has presented a Christ who no longer heals the sick or delivers the oppressed, but whose ministry operates solely in the unseen realm of the spirit. Too long the Church has preached a gospel void of confirmation with mighty signs and wonders. It has made numerous attempts to eradicate from its theology any expectancy in the supernatural. Bathed in its own doubt, the Church has offered a miracle God stripped of His miracles, a compassionate Christ deprived of His compassion, and a doctrine of eternal life having little effect in time!

The miraculous has always been the prime divider of the religious. Christians down the centuries have not firstly been divided over denominationalism or tradition; the real rift has been between those who accept the supernatural and those who reject it. The dominant issue between evangelicals and Pentecostals is not speaking with tongues, but expectancy in the supernatural today. Religious leaders arrayed themselves in bitter hostility against Christ because of His miracle ministry. They realised if He were 'words only' they could in a measure compete with Him for popularity, but they could never match His miracles. His supernatural acts constantly caused division, and ultimately His death.

John 9:16 records, *"Some of the Pharisees said, 'This Man is not from God, because He does not keep the Sabbath.' Others said, 'How can a man who is a sinner do such signs?' And there was a division among them.* "Today those who disbelieve in the supernatural are also divided among themselves, and fall into at least one of the following four categories:

*Group 1: The heretical view – discard every miracle recorded in the Bible*

Such adherents conclude that all Biblically recorded miracles are spurious prefabrications of the truth. In which case the Bible cannot be regarded as divine revelation, which means it has no offer of life eternal. At best it can only take its place alongside Shakespeare or Dickens, with little more value than those!

*Group 2: The liberal modernist view – reinvent every miracle recorded in the Bible*

These folk advocate that miracles did not take place literally, but accept their inclusion as parables, having spiritual, moral and ethical value. This strange twist of Bible interpretation directly conflicts with Christ's view of Scripture. Jesus accepted the miracles of the Old Testament as solid facts of history, even if they were signs pointing to deeper truths. Jesus said, *"As Jonah was three days and nights in the belly of the great fish . . ."* It could be argued that Jesus was just using an invented story to illustrate His own death, but this is valueless human presumption. Nowhere does Jesus refute any Old Testament miracle – if they were good enough for Him to accept, they are acceptable to me!

*Group 3: The cessationist view – admit Bible miracles actually happened then, but not today*

This view accepts the miracles of the Bible as legitimate happenings, but states that such miracle signs were for the early Church only, and that miracles do not happen today in the same way as they did in the early Church. We will appraise their arguments later in this book.

*Group 4: The evangelical view – accept that Bible miracles were real, and sometimes occur today*

This view is running close to Bible truth, but sadly too many in this category believe that the place of miracles is secondary to the real work of the gospel. We agree it is more important for a person to be saved from sin than to remain unsaved after being healed from sickness. However, this dissecting of the Good News into which parts are more vital than other parts does not follow the Biblical stance. The gospel is Christ in all His fullness – He is the Saviour, the Healer, the Baptiser in the Holy Spirit and the Coming King. The Redeemer who offers a holistic salvation. Those who purposely de-emphasise the miraculous, often do so to cover their own lack of faith. How regrettable that some daub those who do have positive faith as members of that *"evil and adulterous, sign-seeking generation"* mentioned by Jesus. However, Jesus spoke such words to the religious Pharisees and scribes, who did not believe in the multitude of miracle-signs He had personally performed! To His followers, Christ spoke very different words of promise. He said, *"These signs shall follow those who believe."*

People with the differing views mentioned above are all in the same boat to a greater or lesser degree. They all defame or belittle the supernatural and shy away from the miraculous. But the God of the Bible is a miracle God who pervades all realms and whose influence affects all historic periods and beyond. Jesus Christ forgives sins and heals sick bodies; His salvation caters for the whole person – healing for the body, teaching for the mind, regeneration for the spirit, deliverance for the complete person. We might admit that it is easier to preach *"All things work together for good"* than to preach *"The prayer of faith shall save the sick, and the Lord will raise him up"*, but shall we stagger at the promises of God through unbelief? Abraham didn't, and we have less reason to waiver than he.

We should be surprised today at the absence of miracles, not the performing of them. God's routine ministry is active in the material realm of flesh and blood, and miracles are normal for Him. The New Testament clearly portrays how the early Church operated. We have no other authoritative record of what Christ's Church should be like, and how it should operate, and what God accomplishes through its members. The early Church is the only legitimate model we have, and the only guide to its shape and content in every century until Jesus returns.

## DOES SPIRIT BAPTISM OCCUR AT CONVERSION?

There is no scripture which says we are baptised in the Holy Spirit at the time of our conversion. The Bible trend on this subject shows that Spirit baptism takes place after we are converted believers, and that the time-gap between these two should be minimal. Cornelius experienced Spirit baptism moments after his conversion, but it is important to see that his Spirit baptism was not without powerful physical evidences. The idea that Spirit baptism occurs unnoticed, in a silent way, does not accord with Scripture. It is Biblically unsound to assert that we are baptised in the Holy Spirit in an unfelt, unseen manner. Every instance of the baptism in the Spirit in the New Testament shows it is accompanied by physical manifestations, such as tongues, prophecy and magnifying the Lord. Simon the sorcerer was prepared to pay for the power to baptise people in the Holy Spirit because it was accompanied by outward physical effects.

A silent, unnoticed, inner Spirit baptism is not a Biblical one! Such a thing would be:

> An assumed Spirit baptism, not an actual one.
> A barren Spirit baptism, in place of a beneficial one.
> A bogus Spirit baptism, not a Biblical one.
> A conjectured Spirit baptism, rather than a concrete one.
> A symbolic Spirit baptism, as opposed to a substantial one.
> A theoretical Spirit baptism, distinct from a theological one.
> A vestigial Spirit baptism, instead of a valid one.

An unfelt Spirit baptism is no baptism at all, it is merely wishful thinking! If, like Cornelius and his household, everyone was automatically Spirit-baptised at the moment of their conversion, they would all become vocal like Cornelius, since Jesus said, *"out of the abundance of the heart the mouth speaks."* They would all be Pentecostal by experience, and from that moment on they would know and understand much about the manifestations of the Spirit. Marvelously there would be little difference between the varied denominational groups who believe in being born again, since all would experience the same power of the same Holy Spirit in the same Biblical way.

The fact that this is not the case endorses the view that Spirit baptism does not occur at the point of conversion. A Biblical Spirit baptism is augmented, amplified, intensified and reinforced by physical sensations and manifestations of praise to God, by prophecy, by speaking in unlearned languages, and by magnifying the Lord. It contains a unique vivacity; a vigor and verve, distinct from any other experience. It is bigger and more powerful and satisfying than any adrenalin rush. It puts sparkle into the Christian's life which cannot be adequately imitated by anything else. Why are there physical effects? Because *"your body is the temple of the Holy Spirit"*, as stated in 1 Corinthians 6:19. Speaking about Spirit baptism, Jesus said, *"Out of your belly* [innermost being] *will flow rivers of living water."* Not merely the human soul is baptised in the Holy Spirit, but the whole person.

Some shy away from talking about the baptism in the Holy Spirit. They prefer to talk about the filling of the Spirit. One reason is that they assume the filling is an ongoing, unnoticed, purely spiritual experience which fails to affect the human sensibilities, and not accompanied by physical effects. So let's ask a question: "When were the first Christians filled with the Spirit?" They were first filled with the Spirit when they were baptised in the Spirit on the Day of Pentecost. The second time we read that they were filled with the Holy Spirit was when they met together and prayed earnestly for miracles to happen and for boldness to speak, with the effect that the house was shaken by the Holy Spirit. Is that the kind of filling you desire?

Opting for the word *filling* in place of the word *baptism* is made on grounds that no miracle signs, wonders, gifts (including tongues) need to be witnessed. Unfortunately, that kind of filling with the Spirit is unknown in Scripture. Reducing the baptism or filling of the Holy Spirit to an undetectable inner event flies in the face of all that the Scriptures teach, when it says that they were filled with the Spirit and spoke in languages, as the Spirit enabled them (Acts 2:4). Also we are exhorted to *"be filled with the Spirit, speaking to one another in psalms and hymns and spiritual songs, singing and making melody in your heart to the Lord"* (Ephesians 5:18–19 NKJV).

## IS BEING BORN AGAIN AND BAPTISED IN THE SPIRIT THE SAME THING?

An alarming view has been offered to me that baptism in the Spirit refers to being born again (regenerated) in the Bible! This view balances precariously on twisted interpretations of various texts. It rides roughshod over the rules of hermeneutics and relies almost exclusively on eisegesis (what we want the Scripture to say, or what we think it says) rather than exegesis (what the Scriptures actually say). It begins with an assumed idea, followed by the effort to find Bible verses to confirm the theory!

It is said that in Matthew 3:11, John Baptist uses the phrase "baptism in the Spirit" in the context of salvation not of empowerment, but John doesn't qualify what he means. The immediate context in Matthew must not be used to radically alter John's statement about baptism in the Spirit. John does not say that his phrase *"baptise in the Holy Spirit"* refers to salvation! That is an eisegetical assumption. The context of the Gospels of Mark and John will not support this idea, and in fact, what John Baptist meant by the phrase *"baptise with the Holy Spirit"* can be legitimately understood only in the context of the whole Bible. In other words, it is necessary to examine all the Bible texts and trend on this subject to ascertain what it means.

It is also said that Cornelius "believed and the Spirit was poured out upon him at the same instant. It was at this time that Cornelius was regenerated". Firstly, the text does not say the Spirit was poured out on Cornelius *at the same instant* that he believed – it could have been a few, or many, moments after his regeneration that he was Spirit-baptised while Peter continued to preach.

It is further suggested that in the Old Testament salvation/ regeneration and empowerment of the Jewish life went hand in hand; they were not seen as two distinct experiences. But what the Old Testament remains unclear about, the New Testament explains and elucidates. Being saved and being Spirit-baptised are seen as two distinct experiences in the New Testament. The Old Testament saints could at best be filled with the Spirit, but none were ever baptised in the Spirit – that was a New Covenant experience reserved for New Covenant converts to Christ. It is asserted, "Salvation can be positional and regenerational." Starkly, the Bible doesn't say that. This theory is neither stated nor explained anywhere in the Old or New Testaments, and if it is not in the Book, throw it out!

He continues, "The Bible never once commands us to pray for the Baptism of the Holy Spirit." This argument follows John MacArthur's suggestion that we are not told to seek for the baptism in the Holy Spirit! We can add that neither are we told to ask/pray/seek for the filling of the Spirit. However, we must not negate the words of Jesus, who said, *"How much more will your heavenly Father give the Holy Spirit to those who ask Him!"* Asking God is prayer. The Lord would not have told us to ask/pray for the Spirit if He is automatically administered when we are born again. Jesus indicated that we should *"ask"* (Luke 11:13) and also that we should *"wait"* (Luke 24:49) to be baptised in the Spirit, which is the Promise of the Father offered to *"as many as the Lord our God shall call"* (Acts 2:38–39). By the way, the reason the New Testament writers do not exhort members of the early Church to be baptised in the Holy Spirit is because they already have been Spirit-baptised! All were Pentecostal by experience and, like water baptism, Spirit baptism is a one-off phenomenon, not a repeated experience.

## THE SECOND BLESSING MISNOMER

The baptism in the Holy Spirit is often thought of as a second blessing – an event which takes place after conversion, and which sees the new Christian leaping forward in spirituality, in understanding and in obedience to God. A *second blessing* was first preached by John Wesley, truly a man of God. Without detracting from the amazing work that John did, we do have to realise that he didn't get everything right! For example, he retained infant baptism in the Methodist movement founded by him. He did this despite the clear teaching of the New Testament about believer's water baptism, and despite the rise and teaching of the Anabaptists long before Wesley was born.

After his mission work in Savannah, Georgia, John returned to England and attended a Moravian meeting in Aldersgate Street, London on 24 May 1738. His experience there caused him to pen the now famous lines, *"I felt my heart strangely warmed."* Whatever this experience was, it revolutionised the character and method of his ministry. Some believe he was born again and genuinely converted in the Aldersgate meeting, while others see the event as a new experience of sanctification. It appears that this was Wesley's view of it, causing him to consider that there was a second blessing available to believers.

Consequently he preached and taught two distinct works of grace. In the first work, a person is saved; in the second, he is sanctified. Wesley claimed that the second work of grace significantly helps believers to deal with sin in their personal lives and to walk in new power. In retrospect we can see that Wesley formed his beliefs from his experience, rather than from the Bible, and unfortunately he failed to identify his own experience with the Scriptures, as well as the experience of many Methodist converts who often manifested gifts of the Holy Spirit – they remained unsure of what was happening to them! Truly many of Wesley's converts were baptised in the Holy Spirit, many speaking in tongues, but without seeing these things from a scriptural perspective, they were derided and as a result many formed their own branch of the Methodist Church known as 'Ranters'.

Charles Finney, the American evangelist, further developed the idea of a second blessing after experiencing the baptism in the Holy Spirit himself, which he describes like this:

> The Holy Spirit descended upon me in a manner that seemed to go through me, body and soul. I could feel the impression, like a wave of electricity, going through and through me. Indeed it seemed to come in waves of liquid love . . . It seemed like the very breath of God. I wept aloud with joy and love; and I do not know, but I should say, I literally bellowed out the unutterable gushings of my heart. The waves came over me, and over me, and over me, one after the other, until I recollect I cried out, "I shall die if these waves continue to pass over me." I said, "Lord, I cannot bear any more."[11]

That is a most accurate record of how a person is affected by the baptism in the Spirit. No one can be baptised by Jesus Christ into God the Holy Spirit and say, "I felt nothing; it was an inner, unnoticed experience!" A *second blessing* was also advocated by D.L. Moody, who basically taught that there is a second experience after the new birth, which empowers the child of God. People are taught that they need to seek this second experience to give them assurance, power, and victory in their Christian life – this is Biblically identified as the baptism in the Holy Spirit.

A believer not Spirit-baptised is justified before God (saved) but there is more to experience. Similarly a person who has been sprinkled as a baby, but never been through believer's baptism in water, finds he has more to experience.

I do not see those not yet baptised in the Holy Spirit as second-class Christians. Such terminology is all wrong; it is unbiblical. Also the terms 'second blessing' and 'second work of grace' prove to be a stumbling block to many leaders and believers who deep in their hearts long for more of God, but whose inadequate theological views insist there is no more to come, until after they are physically dead! Their creeds assert that the initial experience of conversion includes all that God has for them. But behind this façade is a nagging honest truth from the pages of Holy Writ. Thank God for men in the past who sometime after they were saved experienced a new dynamic in Christ. They shifted Bible understanding a small step nearer to the heart of God. Spirit baptism is an integral part of salvation which completes the new birth package, and which allows a believer to develop in Christ, to become mature in understanding and in character.

## OBEDIENCE AND NEARNESS TO GOD

We cannot overlook the sanctifying power of God's Spirit, who constantly encourages us to live a holy life. Paul tells believers that they were saved through the sanctifying work of the Holy Spirit and through believing the truth of the gospel (2 Thessalonians 2:13). That sanctifying process progresses through our Christian lives, but it specially begins when we are baptised in the Holy Spirit. Today we better understand that responsibility rests on us to be the best we can be for God, so that He has maximum resources available for His Kingdom work. The illustration opposite details how we can be better temples of the Spirit.

| BEING OUR BEST FOR GOD | | | |
|---|---|---|---|
| NOT BAPTISED IN HOLY SPIRIT | BAPTISED IN HOLY SPIRIT | NOT BAPTISED IN HOLY SPIRIT | BAPTISED IN HOLY SPIRIT |
| LEVEL OF FAITH AND PRACTICE | | | |
| NO BIBLE STUDY WEAK FAITH | NO BIBLE STUDY WEAK FAITH | STUDIES BIBLE BELIEVES GOD | STUDIES BIBLE BELIEVES GOD |
| This person attends church but they are not baptised in the Holy Spirit. They rarely study or prepare for God's service. God is restricted by their lack of dedication | This person is baptised in water and baptised in the Holy Spirit. They rely on the Spirit for guidance, but rarely study the Bible, and the Spirit finds difficulty in using them | This person is saved, but not baptised in the Holy Spirit. Continually they study the Bible and pray for God to use them. They are better material for the Spirit's ministry | This person is saved, baptised in water and in the Holy Spirit. They seek God daily to be filled. They avidly study the Bible, pray and trust God to use them powerfully for His glory |
| EFFECTIVENESS 20% | EFFECTIVENESS 40% | EFFECTIVENESS 70% | EFFECTIVENESS 100% |

# CHAPTER THIRTEEN

# GOD, THE PROVIDER OF GIFTS

The wide variety of gifts listed in the New Testament can be divided into three groups:

**GRACE GIFTS from the FATHER GOD** – Romans 12:6 *charismata*

**MINISTRY GIFTS from the LORD JESUS** – Ephesians 4:11 *domata*

**SPIRITUAL GIFTS from the HOLY SPIRIT** – 1 Corinthians 12:7 *phanerosis*

Here we see the triune God at work, distributing different classes of gifts according to His will. Consider the following facts which apply to each category of gifts:

They are not rewards and cannot be earned – Romans 12:6; Acts 8:18–20

They are appointed by the Lord – 1 Corinthians 12:11,28; Ephesians 4:11

They can be imparted by leaders – Romans 1:11; 2 Timothy 1:6

They are to be recognised and accepted by us – 1 Corinthians 12:1

They are to be desired by us – 1 Corinthians 12:31, 14:1,39

They are to be fanned into flame by us – 2 Timothy 1:6

They are to make us humble, not proud – Romans 12:3; 1 Corinthians 4:6–7

They are to be exercised by all – 1 Corinthians 12:7,11; 14:31

They are to be operated in love – 1 Corinthians 13:1–3;

They are to edify (build up) the Church – 1 Corinthians 12:7; 14:12,17,26

## GRACE GIFTS from the FATHER GOD – charismata

*Gifts which ENCOURAGE*

Here is a list of *charismata* (meaning 'grace gifts') recorded in the New Testament:

1. **Unnamed** – Romans 1:11–12, encouraging and strengthening

2. **Eternal life** – Romans 6:23, confirming that salvation is a free gift

3. **Prophecy** – Romans 12:6, but not all who prophesy are prophets

4. **Ministry** – Romans 12:7, serving; 1 Corinthians 4:1; 1 Peter 4:10, stewarding

5. **Teaching** – Romans 12:7, remember not all who teach are teachers

6. **Exhortation** – Romans 12:8, the Barnabas ministry of encouragement

7. **Giving** – Romans 12:8, God loves a hilarious giver! 2 Corinthians 9:7

8. **Leading** – Romans 8:12, having initiative and willingness to go first

9. **Mercy** – Romans 8:12, ability to discern sin and forgive the sinner

10. **Marriage** – 1 Corinthians 7:7, your spouse is a grace gift from God Himself

11. **Celibacy** – 1 Corinthians 7:7, the ability to remain contentedly single

12. **Spiritual gifts** – 1 Corinthians 12:4,7–11, nine manifestations of the Spirit

13. **Helps** – 1 Corinthians 12:28, an indispensable, wide-ranging ministry

14. **Administration** – 1 Corinthians 12:28, to guide, pilot, steer others

15. **Extended life** – 2 Corinthians 1:10 *"If the Lord will we shall live ..."* James 4:15

16. **Preaching** – 1 Timothy 4:14; 2 Timothy 1:6, see context for Timothy's gift

17. **Hospitality** – 1 Peter 4:9, *"If you give a cup of cold water ..."* Matthew 10:42

18. **Speaking** – 1 Peter 4:11, declaring the truth of God's word

Gifts from God the Father are of a different character from those granted by the Lord Jesus and the Holy Spirit. The list of eighteen given above is taken from the New Testament only, and it can be extended considerably if we include Old Testament texts, such as musical ability (for example Jubal, in Genesis 4:21 and others in 2 Chronicles 5:13, 34:12). Father's gifts sometimes come to us as natural talents and abilities, including artistic ability in craftsmen as mentioned in 1 Chronicles 29:5.

## MINISTRY GIFTS from the LORD JESUS – domata

*Gifts which EQUIP*

Ephesians 4:8: *"He gave gifts to men."* Here the Greek word for gifts is *domata* and it stresses the concrete character of the gift, which in this case is *people* as Ephesians 4:7–16 shows. There five ministry gifts:

1. Apostles – Ministry of pioneering and establishing churches with God's word

2. Prophets – Ministry of revelation and declaration to the Church of God's word

3. Evangelists – Ministry of reaching and winning unbelievers through God's word

4. Pastors – Ministry of leading and feeding the Church with the truth of God's word

5. Teachers – Ministry of interpreting and explaining the truth of God's word

It is evident that the five ministry gifts from the Lord Jesus differ greatly from those granted by Father God. Christ's ministry gifts are linked with His ascension, and could be called 'Ascension Gifts'. Christ Jesus equips men and women whom He has called to the high office of leadership. In turn, they equip the believers to do God's work, enabling us to come into a mature knowledge of Christ.

# SPIRITUAL GIFTS from the HOLY SPIRIT – phanerosis

*Gifts which EDIFY*

Nine gifts are listed in 1 Corinthians 12:7–11. It is important to emphasise that these gifts are unique. They are imparted to individuals directly by the Holy Spirit *"as He wills"*. They cannot be acquired through education or practice, and they differ immensely from the many natural talents and abilities bestowed by Father God.

It is important to see that the word *gift* or *gifts* is found only *twice* in chapters 12, 13 and 14 of 1 Corinthians. Firstly, 1 Corinthians 12:4 says *"There many different gifts [charismata], but the same Spirit."* Secondly, it is used in 1 Corinthians 12:31: *"Covet earnestly the greater gifts [charismata]."* The significance of this means that what the Spirit imparts to individuals are indeed *grace gifts* (*charismata*), but they are *special* grace gifts which cannot be earned or learned by human practice. They differ from those eighteen which come from the Father. What a pity that many English translations have included the word *gift* in so many places where it is not found in the Greek text. The New King James Version uses italics to indicate the word's absence from the Greek manuscripts, but the New International Version frequently uses the word *gifts* in these chapters, and flagrantly uses it twice in 1 Corinthians 14:12, where in fact it is not included at all! You may well ask, "Does this matter?" According to Jesus, not the smallest part of a Hebrew letter would go missing from the Old Testament, until it was fulfilled. If that is so, then including extra words in the New Testament can easily lead to misinterpretation, false ideas and error.

Consider the following points:

Firstly, in 1 Corinthians 12:1 and 14:1,12, what has been translated *"gifts"* is the Greek word *pneumatikon*, meaning 'spirituals' or 'spiritual matters'. So 1 Corinthians 12:1 should read, *"Now concerning spiritual matters, I don't want you to be ignorant."* Secondly, 1 Corinthians 12:8–10 lists nine different impartations by the Holy Spirit, and only once does it use the word *gifts*, namely, *"gifts of healings"* in verse 9, where a double plural is used and will be explained below. Notice it does not say that the Spirit gives the *gift of* prophecy or the *gift of* faith or the *gift of the* gifts of healing, or the *gift of* tongues etc. Such expressions are a mistranslation and although they are in common usage today, they tend to cloud the issue and detract from what the Spirit actually gives!

## BEWARE OF IGNORANCE

In 1 Corinthians 12:1 Paul desires the believers in Corinth to be free from ignorance about spiritual matters. The diagram below shows a large circle which includes all spiritual entities. It includes the Father's grace gifts, the Son's ministry gifts and the Spirit's manifestations. The four differing NT Greek words connected with this subject are:

1. **Spirituals** – *pneumatikon*
2. **Grace gifts** – *charismata*
3. **Ministry gifts** – *domata*
4. **Manifestations of the Spirit** – *phanerosis*

The diagram below illustrates that s*piritual matters (pneumatikon)* include all things spiritual. They cover the whole gamut of salvation, from conviction to completeness. It includes grace gifts from the Father, ministry gifts from the Son and manifestations of the Spirit (commonly termed 'the gifts of the Spirit').

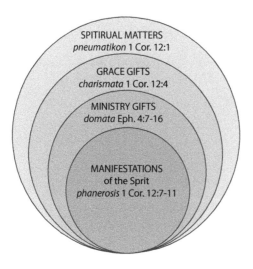

**Grace gifts for encouragement** *(charismata)* include natural talents as well as specific spiritual endowments such as eternal life, prophecy and teaching, but all are given by God's grace, James 1:17–18.

**Ministry gifts for equipping** *(domata)* are anointed and appointed people who equip and direct the Church, enabling its members to serve. Ephesians 4:12 says these offices are *"for the equipping of the saints for the work of the ministry, for the edifying of the body of Christ"*.

**Manifestation gifts for edifying** *(phanerosis)* are for our edification, the building up of the Church. It is common usage today to call the *"manifestations of the Holy Spirit"* the "gifts of the Spirit" or "spiritual gifts", and indeed they are gifts *(charismata)*, but they are special gifts by which the Holy Spirit can reveal His presence and power. For this reason we will refer to them as *"manifestations of the Spirit"*. In the next chapter we shall see why the word *manifestation* is used.

# CHAPTER FOURTEEN

# THE NINE MANIFESTATIONS OF THE HOLY SPIRIT

I WANT TO ASK SPECIFICALLY, "WHAT ARE THE MANIFESTATIONS (gifts) of the Spirit? What is it the Spirit actually gives?" The answer is found in 1 Corinthians 12:7–11 which says, *"The manifestation of the Spirit is given to each one . . . for to one is given the word of wisdom."* The English word *manifestation* is translated from the Greek word *phanerosis*, which means 'to reveal' or 'to show forth' and includes the idea of 'shining'.

The manifestations of the Spirit are nine special ways in which the Holy Spirit reveals Himself. Each one confirms His presence and power. What we often call a 'gift of the Spirit' is in fact the Holy Spirit expressing Himself in various ways through His anointed people, and by this means He declares His presence in the Church. Now we can understand why Paul says, *"Do not quench the spirit. Do not despise prophecies."* When a believer prophesies, it is the Holy Spirit revealing Himself in that extraordinary way! Through each of the nine manifestations, the

Holy Spirit divulges and exposes His actual presence. This is marvellous! It is far more powerful and exciting than little me receiving a gift and then scattering it about at my own discretion or when I feel blessed! The nine manifestations of the Holy Spirit can be grouped into three sections:

| REVELATION MANIFESTATIONS | POWER MANIFESTATIONS | VOCAL MANIFESTATIONS |
|---|---|---|
| Word of wisdom | Faith | Prophecy |
| Word of knowledge | Gifts of healings | Speaking in tongues |
| Discerning of spirits | Working of miracles | Interpretation of tongues |

### The character of the manifestations of the Spirit

They are supernatural, not natural (unlike some of the *charismata*), 1 Corinthians 12:7

They are the Spirit of God revealing Himself as he chooses, 1 Corinthians 12:11

The Holy Spirit works through human vessels, with human cooperation, 1 Corinthians 14:32

### The purpose of the manifestations of the Spirit

To continue Christ's work, Acts 1:1 (*began*), John 14:12 (*greater* = quantity not quality)

To enable us to work with God, 1 Corinthians 3:9; 2 Corinthians 6:1

To glorify only the Lord Jesus, 1 Corinthians 1:26–31, 2:1–5, 4:7; 2 Corinthians 4:7

To confirm the truth of God's word, Mark 16:17–20; Romans 15:18–19; Hebrews 2:3–4

To edify the Church, 1 Corinthians 12:7, 14:5,12

To benefit unbelievers, 1 Corinthians 14:21–22

To enable every believer to serve God, 1 Corinthians 12:7,11

*The importance of the manifestations of the Spirit*

Earnestly desire, 1 Corinthians 12:31, 14:1,39; Psalm 37:4

Despise not, 1 Thessalonians 5:20

Neglect not, 1 Timothy 4:14; Hebrews 2:3-4

Stir up, 2 Timothy 1:6

Don't be ignorant, 1 Corinthians 12:1, 14:37–38

Exercise and use them, Romans 12:6; Matthew 25:15,28–30; 1 Peter 4:10

There is one Holy Spirit, but nine special ways in which He reveals Himself in the Church. We will now look at each of the nine manifestations of the Holy Spirit in turn.

## WORD OF WISDOM

**NT Greek: Λογος σωφιας** – *Logos sophias*

This manifestation gives the divine answer to a problem or situation.

It is not natural wisdom acquired from experience, neither a natural sagacity which some might possess (1 Corinthians 1:20, 2:6). Neither is it spiritual wisdom which is available to every believer from God and His Word (Proverbs 9:10; James 1:5), but it is a word of supernatural wisdom imparted by the Holy Spirit in a moment of time to instruct and grant insight to God's people.

Words of wisdom are frequently given when *preaching, decision-making, counselling* or just in *conversation*. They occur spontaneously as the Spirit gives them. He can impart them through an inner voice, or with an audible voice, through Scripture, or by means of a picture, dream, vision, or an angel. Believers may not always be aware that it is a word of wisdom at the moment it is given, but when it is spoken out it bears a supernatural characteristic which confirms it is a word from the Lord.

Some examples from Scripture:

1.  Solomon's judgment in 1 Kings 3:16–28

2.  Jesus opposed by the chief priests and elders, Matthew 21:23–27

3.  Jesus confounding the Pharisees and the Herodians, Matthew 22:15–22

4.  Jesus confronting the Sadducees, Matthew 22:23–33

5.  Answering persecutors, Mark 13:11; Luke 21:15; Acts 6:10

6.  Resolving a Church problem, Acts 6:1–5

7.  Peter guided by the Lord about Gentiles, Acts 10:15

8.  Church leaders and Church rules, Acts 15:19–22

9.  Paul speaking to the ship's crew, Acts 27:33–36

10. Paul's preaching, 1 Corinthians 2:4; 1 Thessalonians 1:5

In modern times many who oppose the truth have tried to entangle men of God in arguments, but the divine wisdom of their answers has completely confounded such opponents! My friend Derrick and I often talked about the Lord with a young lady, Julie, from the Brethren Church, Ebenezer Hall in King's Square, Gloucester. One day a Brethren elder called Julie and me to his home, where he spoke from the Scriptures for over half an hour, to show that what happened on the Day of Pentecost was never repeated. His champion verse was 1 Corinthians 12:13

*"For by one Spirit we were all baptised into one body."* He explained meticulously that when the disciples received the Holy Spirit on the Day of Pentecost, it was for the whole Church for all time, and I was included in that! I went away troubled and unsure. The next evening I attended the Bible study at the Gloucester Elim church, and spoke to the minister, Rev. George Canty, about the elder's teaching. George's answer was a word of wisdom from God. Firstly he chuckled, then said, "1 Corinthians 12:13 is speaking about being baptised into the body of Christ by the Holy Spirit, not about being baptised into the Holy Spirit by Jesus." Immediately I saw the distinction, and my fears were completely allayed.

When a young minister, I was sent to pastor a small Pentecostal church in Romford, Essex. After my first Sunday, a lady asked me to visit her because she and her friend wanted to speak to me. On arrival at the house, I saw two middle-aged ladies who appeared to be stalwarts; they had been in that little church for many years and were considered to be leading lights. They said to me, "We are leaving the Pentecostal church since we both want more mature ministry, so we propose to attend the large Baptist church in Romford." I was disturbed and felt deflated, and I asked them if they would miss the gifts of the Spirit in another church nearby (where none were used or expected in those days).

They replied along the lines that the gifts of the Spirit were not so important to them. Then God spoke immediately into my soul, saying, "Let them go with your blessing, and I will give you two persons for each one who leaves." That was a word of wisdom for me, and I told them, "I will let you go with my blessing!" Then I prayed for them positively and lovingly, trusting they would find all that they sought from God. On hearing what had happened, the deacons said I was not to let them go, since they had been the mainstay of that little congregation. "I can't stop them," I said, "but I am happy for you to see them and persuade them to remain." They never returned; no others left, however, and we doubled our congregation to about ninety members in the first year.

In the same church, a believer came to see me one day, challenging the use of singing in church and claiming that hymns and songs should be spoken "silently to oneself". He deduced this from Ephesians 5:19 and showed me in the Authorised Version where it says, *"Speaking to yourselves in psalms and hymns and spiritual songs . . ."* Immediately I received a swift answer from the Lord, and replied, "Ah! It doesn't say speaking to *yourself* (singular), but speaking to *yourselves* (plural)!" He saw the wisdom of this immediately, backed down and acknowledged that what we were doing was right! This verse is correctly translated in modern English versions with *"speaking to one another"*. What a blessing that we don't need to *"lean on our own understanding"* but rather *"trust the Lord with all our hearts"* as Proverbs 3:5 says, then His wisdom will be imparted to us as required! Praise the Lord!

Later on in my evangelistic work I was conducting a crusade in Broadstairs, Kent. A lady came forward for prayer in one of the meetings, hoping that her locked arm could be healed. The Spirit told me she needed to be saved, and I talked to her about something even more important than being able to use her arm, namely knowing her soul was healed, that her sins were forgiven and that she was saved from judgment and hell. The next day she again attended the crusade meeting and came forward for prayer. This time, the Spirit told me, she needed healing from fears and inner stress, so I questioned her and she told me she had not slept properly for years. We prayed for inner healing and for peace to flood over her life. The next evening she came again to the meeting, and there was a bright sparkle in her eye. She told me she had just had the most perfect night's sleep she could remember! Now the Lord told me she was ready for physical healing. I saw the faith in her eyes, and as I prayed, immediately her locked arm was released and she could lift it up, wave it about and move it in almost any direction.

Through gentle words of wisdom, the Holy Spirit guided me how to bring her to salvation, then to spiritual healing and finally to a miracle of physical healing. She had found the abundant life Jesus had promised. This incident definitely included words of wisdom, allowing me to know how to proceed with this dear lady; but it is possible that words of knowledge were also operating here, informing me of the lady's difficulties and needs.

## WORD OF KNOWLEDGE

**NT Greek: Λογος γνωσκω –** *Logos gnosko*

This manifestation of the Spirit imparts facts, describes details and grants information previously hidden. The Spirit enables you to know the person you are ministering to: whether unsaved or saved, sinful or forgiven, sanctified or suffering, sensible or suicidal, true or false. Particular sins, sicknesses, motives, ambitions and circumstances can be revealed.

Here are some examples from Scripture:

1.  Samuel knows that Saul will be king, 1 Samuel 9:15–16,20

2.  Nathan knows what David did, 2 Samuel 12:1–15

3.  Elisha knows what Gehazi did, 2 Kings 5:20–27

4.  Elisha knows the war plans of the king of Syria, 2 Kings 6:8–12

5.  Daniel knows what King Nebuchadnezzar had dreamt, Daniel 2:19–47

6.  Jesus knows what the scribes are thinking, Matthew 9:3–4

7. Jesus knows Peter's challenge about paying tax, Matthew 17:24–27

8. Jesus knows that Peter will deny Him, Mark 14:29–31

9. Jesus knows all about Nathanael, John 1:46–49

10. Jesus knows details about the life of the Samaritan woman, John 4:16–19

11. Peter knows what Ananias and Sapphira did, Acts 5:3–11

12. Ananias knows about Saul and his Damascus Road experience, Acts 9:10–19

13. Agabus knows about a coming famine, Acts 11:27–30

14. Agabus knows what will happen to Paul, Acts 21:10–14

15. Paul knows that he and the crew will be safe, Acts 27:22–26

Numerous modern examples of the word of knowledge flowing through believers could be cited. When we are successful in God, the enemy often attempts to raise up opposition against us, and this is what happened to me. The leader of a small church contacted one of my respected members who was a medical doctor, and accused me of serious misconduct. I was summoned to the doctor's house, where the church leader harangued me for about half an hour. His attitude indicated that he wanted me out of the Christian ministry!

After a while, the Lord dropped a word of knowledge into my heart about this man. I had not met him previously, nor heard of him before, but I now had knowledge of what he had done. I spoke the word of knowledge and suggested we call his wife to be present with us. His response amazed me! He quickly ended our discussion, stating that he was sure the matter had been cleared up satisfactorily. Then he got up and left! I knew he was sweating over the next few days, thinking I might spill the beans to his wife, which, of course, I never did.

The Spirit gave a word of knowledge to our pastor about an injured big toe, and he mentioned this in the Sunday service, but no one responded nor came forward for prayer. It was a couple of days later that the church pianist telephoned the pastor and confessed that she was the person with the bruised and painful toe. She said she was completely taken aback that anyone should know about it, and embarrassment had prevented her coming forward for prayer in the church service. The pastor prayed for her over the telephone, and she was healed there and then!

I once heard a testimony from a well-known businessman, named John (name changed for anonymity). He resisted anything to do with church, even though his wife was an avid believer. He developed a serious heart condition but refused any prayer. After a long battle with only partly successful operations, his wife persuaded him to attend a nearby evangelistic service. In trepidation he went with her and they sat in what he felt was an inconspicuous seat in the balcony. Part way through the meeting the evangelist paused, and said, "The Lord has told me that there is a man here with a chronic heart condition," and he asked him to make his way to the platform. Nobody responded. The evangelist warned, "You are in a serious condition and the Lord wants to heal you, please come for prayer." The man sank further into his seat. Then the evangelist said, "The Lord tells me the person's name is John!" With that his wife helped him to his feet and along to the platform, where he was not only prayed for, but miraculously healed and wonderfully saved. Here a forgiven sinner was redeemed, and a reluctant person was healed and blessed through the challenge of a word of knowledge. Praise the Lord!

# DISCERNING OF SPIRITS

**NT Greek: Διακρισις πνευμα – *Diakrisis pneuma***

This manifestation of the Spirit distinguishes between different kinds of spirit. The NT Greek word *pneuma* (from which we derive *pneumatic, pneumonia* etc.) refers to many things in the Bible: wind, John 3:8; breath, 2 Thessalonians 2:8; the invisible human spirit, Luke 8:55; the Holy Spirit, Matthew 4:1; angels, Hebrews 1:13–14; demons, Matthew 8:16; character, Luke 1:17, 9:55; Numbers 14:24.

W.E. Vine lists another twelve uses of *pneuma* in the New Testament.[12] Importantly we must understand that there are three principal spirit realms:

| SUPERNATURAL SPIRITS | NATURAL SPIRITS | SUBNATURAL SPIRITS |
|---|---|---|
| The realm of God<br><br>The Holy Spirit<br><br>Cherubim & seraphim<br><br>Good & righteous<br><br>angels of God | The realm of humankind<br><br>The human spirit –<br><br>Fallen, sinful<br><br>and deceitful | The realm of satan<br><br>The devil<br><br>Evil & occult<br><br>Psychic and<br><br>demonic powers |

Notice I use the word *subnatural* to describe the satanic realm. The world advertises the occult as supernatural, but it is the complete opposite of anything which is super! Discerning of spirits allows a believer to identify and determine which spirit realm is influencing a person's words or life. It can reveal the carnal nature behind a person's actions; it can disclose the activity of the Holy Spirit; it can affirm the presence of holy angels, but also it can expose the activity of demonic spirits. Distinguishing between spirits is a supernatural manifestation which allows a believer to identify the spiritual forces behind a person's attitude or actions, behind a natural event, or initiating and influencing a particular circumstance.

Some examples from the Bible:

1. Jesus heals people by casting out demonic spirits from a woman who had been crippled for eighteen years, Luke 13:10–17. From a mute man, Matthew 9:32 and from a blind and mute man, Matthew 12:22.

2. Jesus rebukes the storm, Luke 8:24. The same word *rebuke* is used when Jesus cast out a demon in Matthew 17:18.

3. James and John wanted to bring retribution on a Samaritan village because they would not receive the Lord Jesus, but Jesus said, *"You know not what kind of spirit you are of"* (Luke 9:51–56).

4. Jesus rebuked Peter, saying *"Get behind Me, Satan"* (Mark 8:33), indicating where Peter's ideas had come from!

5. Paul identifies and casts out a demon, Acts 16:16–18.

We must point out that not all illnesses are demon-induced, but some are, and it is important to know the difference, which is where discerning of spirits is required. A lady in her mid-twenties and not long married came to our Sunday services in Birmingham. However, she always seemed to be under a cloud of despair. There was a dark heaviness that appeared to rest upon her. I asked her about her husband and their relationship, but it was not that. I asked her about her work, but it was not that either. One Sunday evening we invited her back to the manse where we could counsel her further. I recall that as I was talking with her, the Lord spoke into my heart saying, "It is a demon!" I looked at her and told her the Lord had just shown me the root cause of her distress.

As she sat back on the sofa, I said to her, "There is a mountain which must be removed, so I want you to just relax and keep your spiritual eyes on the Lord Jesus." Then, without touching her, I commanded the mountain to be cast into the sea. With immediate effect she slumped down limply, then after a few seconds she sat up and looked at me, this time with the biggest smile imaginable on her face. She was free through Jesus' Name! This is a clear instance of the discerning of spirits in operation, leading to an effective exorcism.

Many people may be stressed, morose or depressed, but these things may not necessarily be from direct demonic activity. Discerning of spirits allows us to know the root cause behind a variety of ailments, like Paul in Acts 16:16–18. Here, the demonised girl followed Paul and his companions, crying out what was basically true, and we read that *"this she did for many days"*. Why didn't Paul cast out the demon on day one? No explanation is given in Scripture for Paul delaying to cast out the demon until many days had passed. However, the best explanation is that until discerning of spirits revealed information to Paul, he refused to act on his own initiative. How easy to have assumed that this girl was controlled by a demon, by falling back on experience or other factors, such as the knowledge of how demons operate.

We are not meant to act on mere human knowledge and experience, rationally thinking we know what is happening! We are Spirit-filled members of Jesus Christ, into whom God invests His power and abilities to make us effective and true. Human wisdom, knowledge and intuition are no substitutes for the guidance of the Holy Spirit. I sometimes think that the Holy Spirit says, "Why won't you listen to Me? Why continue to act presumptuously?"

Assuming a demon is active in a person's life, when it isn't, has led to unacceptable excesses which cause confusion to a hurting person. Neither does it bring healing or wholeness, and doubtless it grieves the Holy Spirit, who cannot bless or use anything which is untrue. I have met some who assume everything is a demon!

A friend of mine went to a Saturday meeting in Birmingham with a painful wrist. The person who attended to her said, "It is a demon which is causing this," and they began to cast out the imaginary demon! Now, my friend had been a Christian for many years. She was baptised in the Holy Spirit; she was also an exceptional musician who had published Christian albums, led worship weekly in her local Pentecostal church, and sung the gospel on the streets and in many venues. She knew that the person supposedly ministering to her was in error, and as far as that church in Birmingham was concerned, like the famous Dr Foster in Gloucester, she never went there again!

Later we discovered this church leader was teaching his people wrongly. He maintained that the Western world view was erroneous, since it rarely included God or demons, and that we needed to embrace the Eastern world view, where spirits are attributed to all things, including trees and rocks, as well as people. Having worked many years in the Orient I knew much about the Eastern world view, and saw that it was just as flawed as the Western world view. Both were seriously in error, and the Lord whispered into my heart, "The only true world view is the Biblical one." Thank You, Lord! I told this to my friend and it eased her mind, and very shortly she was healed. That church in Birmingham has now closed – the Lord Jesus has removed the candlestick. One reason why discerning of spirits is granted by the Holy Spirit is simply because not every sin, sickness or calamity is demon-motivated, and this gift enables us to know the difference.

Discerning of spirits provides:

## a) A defence against human and satanic counterfeit

Exodus 7:8–13 records how Aaron's rod became a serpent, and shows that the Egyptian sorcerers did the same, illustrating Satan's power to imitate miracles! On the outside everything looked identical, but one was divinely orchestrated and the other satanically induced! Discerning of spirits shows the difference – and don't forget that Moses' snake ate up the magicians' snakes! In no way is Satan a match for the living God! Jeremiah 14:14 and 23:16 mentions false prophets. Outwardly their activity was similar to that of Jeremiah, but they operated from the opposite ends of the spirit spectrum. Ezekiel 13:1–10 deals with the same matter. 2 Corinthians 11:13–15 deals with false prophets in New Testament times who operate as ministers of Satan! 2 Peter 2:1–3 talks about false prophets and false teachers who reap havoc in the Church.

## b) An offence against satanic activity

Luke 4:33–36 tells about a man with an unclean demon, which Jesus rebuked and cast out of the man. Luke 13:11–17 describes a woman who had a *"spirit of infirmity"* which had caused a woman to be bent over for eighteen years. Jesus said that Satan had bound her, then He released the woman and healed her. What do the medics make of such cases today? We need discerning of spirits to reveal the demonic forces behind a physical malady. Sometimes medical practice deals only with the symptoms, not with the root cause of an illness.

## c) An encouragement from angel presence

In 2 Kings 6:8–18 we read about hostile Syrian forces surrounding Elisha in order to capture him. Elisha's servant is vexed, but his eyes are opened in answer to Elisha's prayer, and he sees *"the mountain full of horses and chariots of fire all around Elisha"*. Here is angel protection, which discerning of spirits allows us to see. Luke 2:9–15 and 24:23 show angelic beings revealing themselves. In John 1:51 Jesus says that Nathanael would see angels of God ascending and descending upon Him. Paul in dire straits is visited by an angel, Acts 27:23–24.

At seventeen years of age I got into enormous and dangerous difficulties driving a van. Before the engine had warmed up to a suitable running temperature, I went to overtake an empty long logging vehicle on the road from Gloucester to Tewkesbury. Traffic came toward me before I could pass, and I called on the Lord for help, who immediately sent angel assistance. I was starkly conscious of a divine being steering and controlling the speed, position and direction of my vehicle. The angel allowed my van to be placed between the front and rear bogies of the logger as it sped along, and I remember looking up into the logger's side mirror in which I could see the driver's face. Immediately I prayed, asking the Lord to prevent him looking into his side mirror when he would have panicked and braked. The angel eventually guided me to safety, but without his help I would have surely perished.

## FAITH

### NT Greek: Πιστος – *Pistos*

Hebrews 10:38 shows that without faith we cannot live, we only exist! Without faith we cannot be saved, Ephesians 2:8; we cannot please God, Hebrews 11:6; we cannot overcome this dark world, 1 John 5:4.

**A description of faith:** Hebrews 11:1 shows faith is tangible concrete evidence and a certainty of spiritual realities.

**A definition of faith:** Hebrews 11:6 shows faith is believing and relying on a good God who rewards us.

**An explanation of faith:** In Mark 5:36 Jesus said, *"only believe"*, as though it is a most simple and accessible faculty. Indeed, faith is not struggling effort, but rest and repose in an omnipotent and omniloving God. I lie back in His arms as He carries me through!

There are many kinds and degrees of faith:

1. **Natural faith** – the ability to trust when we post a letter, sit on a chair or turn a key.

2. **Saving faith** – a gift from God, Ephesians 2:8, as we hear His Word, Romans 10:17.

3. **The Faith** – the whole body of Bible teaching, Acts 14:22, 16:5; Romans 1:5; Galatians 1:23; Jude 3.

4. **The fruit of faith** – the Spirit produces faithfulness which grows and develops, Galatians 5:22.

5. **The manifestation of faith** – imparted by the Holy Spirit, 1 Corinthians 12:9.

The manifestation of faith differs from all others in the following ways:

*It is given to selective individuals at the Spirit's discretion: 1 Corinthians 12:9–11*

The manifestation of faith is not based on human experience, like natural faith. Neither is it a quality which grows and develops within us as we serve the Lord, like the fruit of faith. We cannot earn it, train hard to acquire it, or develop it through practice. It is a supernatural and divine impartation, dispensed at God's will. Consider also that this special faith often flies in the face of contrary physical evidence. It allows us to believe God's promise, His word and His goodness, despite dissentient outward indicators.

*It is given at a specific time for a special task – 1 Corinthians 12:7–9*

The manifestation of faith has been described as a spontaneous upsurge of the Holy Spirit's power, given at a special time for a special task to promote the will of God or to frustrate the purposes of the devil. Paul on board ship with sailors and companions reached a place where *"all hope for their survival had gone"* (Acts 27:20)! After that, Paul is told by the Lord that everyone would be saved and Paul believed God despite all the raging outward evidence to the contrary. This surely was a manifestation of faith in an extreme circumstance.

Consider raising the dead to life. I believe God can raise the dead back to life. He has done so many, many times, and I have met people to whom this has happened. But without the manifestation of faith, personally I would find it difficult to believe that God would raise a particular and specific person from the dead. I need this impartation of faith to enable me to believe God for such a miracle.

*It is the most powerful form of faith – Mark 11:22–24*

*The New Testament in Modern Speech*[13] by R.F. Weymouth (1822–1902) translates 1 Corinthians 12:9 as *"special faith"*. Donald Gee[14] says, "It is a little bit of that faith which is an attribute of the Almighty, dropped into the soul of man." It is the *"all faith"* which moves mountains, 1 Corinthians 13:2, and which Jesus described as *"the faith of God"* in Mark 11:22–24 (literal translation). There are abundant examples of manifested faith in Scripture:

Romans 4:17–21: Abraham and Sarah were well past procreation age, but despite contrary physical evidence,

Abraham believed God's promise that He would grant them a son through Sarah in their extremely old age.

Hebrews 11:17–19: Abraham was tested by God when He asked him to sacrifice his son Isaac, Abraham concluded that God would no doubt raise Isaac from the dead, to fulfil God's earlier promise that his progeny would continue through Isaac.

1 Kings 18:20–40 Elijah believes God will demonstrate His power by sending fire on Mount Carmel. Elijah believed and obeyed saying, *"I have done all these things at Your word."* Indeed, the fire fell!

Daniel 3:8–30: Shadrach, Meshach and Abednego are threatened with death by being thrown into the furnace of fire. They replied to the king that their God was able to deliver them from the fiery furnace, and to deliver them from the king's hand! Only the impartation of special faith could have evoked such a confident reply. Hebrews 11:34 speaks of those who by faith quenched the violence of fire, and may well be a reference to those three Hebrew men.

2 Kings 6:4–7: Elisha causes an axe-head to float, which required a manifestation of both faith and the working of a miracle.

Daniel 6:10–24: Darius the Persian king could find no way out of preventing Daniel being cast into the lions' den. The writer of Hebrews may well have recalled Daniel when he writes the prophets: who through faith *"stopped the mouths of lions"* (Hebrews 11:33). Also, it could be that Darius himself was given faith to believe for Daniel's deliverance, since he says to Daniel, *"Your God, whom you serve continually, He will deliver you."*

Acts 3:1–10: Peter and John pronounced healing upon a man born lame. Peter didn't pray for the man and then hope he would improve! Rather, in the Name of Jesus Christ he commanded the man to get up and walk. That took faith. In this instance the manifestation of faith was given along with a gift of healing.

Often one or two gifts work together like that, just as tongues and interpretation work together.

Acts 6:5–8: Stephen was *"a man full of faith and the Holy Spirit"*. He even had faith to die for the Lord if necessary, Acts 7:59–60. Many others cited in Hebrews 11:35b–40 were tortured, killed, suffered a variety of abuses, were destitute and homeless, they were 'heroes of faith' *"of whom the world was not worthy"*.

Acts 27:9–25: Paul has already been cited above where in the face of contrary evidence, he believed God for the safety of every person on board the tempest-driven ship.

## GIFTS OF HEALINGS

### NT Greek: Χαρισματα ιαματων – *Charismata hiamaton*

This is the only manifestation of the Spirit which incorporates the word "gifts" *(charismata)* as shown by the Greek text of 1Corinthians 12:9 and 28. In each verse it is a double plural— *gifts of healings*, which significantly indicates that the Holy Spirit grants such gifts to the sick folk themselves, at His discretion. Such manifestations of the Spirit are released *through* a Christian *to* a sick person. This eliminates the concept that a believer is given "the gift of healing" so that he can administer healing to any sick person, where and when he chooses. Were this so, hospitals could be emptied and the NHS disbanded! The term "gift of healing" is not found in the Bible but has been appropriated by spiritualist healers and other psychics, who perceive that certain people seem to be endowed with the ability to induce healing. In such cases people look to others who "have the gift" rather than to the Lord Jesus Christ, as the Scripture exhorts.

Physical illnesses affect us all, including ageing and eventually death. Illness is debilitating and generally painful and has prompted many avenues of healing down the centuries to our own day. Back in history the English Church lacked faith in God's word that a modern miracle of healing was possible. Therefore, it was considered that illness must be God's will, and prayers were said for the sick person to patiently endure! Meanwhile it was non-Christian herbalists who sought remedies from plants and potions, and the days came when the Church accused such people of being witches who devised magic cures and who deserved to be burned! Amazingly the attitude of the Church made God the ally of illness decreed by His will, and the devil the advocate of healing through magic potions!

The doctrine of divine healing is clearly included in the Bible, but human opinions abound which cannot be ratified by Scripture. The overzealous may condemn any form of medical healing on the grounds that it denies faith in God. Others endeavour unconvincingly to show from Scripture that we should never be sick, if we are in right standing with God. At the opposite end of the spectrum, some Christians disbelieve in divine healing, taking the cessationist view that miracles ceased at the close of the apostolic era and/or when the canon of Scripture was complete. This view cannot be substantiated by Scripture, of course, and is clearly refuted by the unchanging faithfulness and character of God and by His many declarations in His Word.

What is termed 'alternative healing' (or in its more politically correct form, 'complementary healing') is mostly suspect, and Christians need not avail themselves of any of these means, because we have ample promises concerning divine healing in the Bible. It is a telling fact that complementary healing embraces a wide variety of methods, except divine healing which ironically is omitted!

Whilst the Lord can use some very suspect and ungodly channels, in general only those saved, set apart for God and filled with Holy Spirit are fit channels for the manifestations of the Spirit. Success in the ministry of divine healing rests solidly upon the depth of a believer's relationship with God, because a shallow relationship will *"quench the Holy Spirit"* (1 Thessalonians 5:19).

Concerning the formation of a doctrine of divine healing, the believer must beware of the following pitfalls:

1. Basing the doctrine of divine healing on experience (or lack of experience) instead of God's word.

2. Allowing human ego, desire and sign-seeking to run ahead of the Holy Spirit's directives.

3. Putting psychological methods before faith in the Lord.

4. Pride in oneself, by using healing success as an accreditation of one's spirituality.

5. Shouting at the devil, rather than listening to the Holy Spirit (the time to shout is when God prompts you to do so!).

6. Trying to establish a routine or formula for the ministry of healing.

7. Blaming sick believers for being ill, and accusing them of lack of faith.

8. Ignoring natural healing remedies.

9. Condemning medical healing practice.

The chart below shows three principal areas of healing under which all healing methods can be applied. The lists are by no means exhaustive, but a cursory glance will reveal that the godly, supernatural means of healing prominently outnumber other means. Whilst the whole subject of healing is vast and beyond the remit of this book, it is important to emphasise that we embrace all forms of both divine healing and medical healing. We do not subscribe to nor recommend any form of occult healing, no matter how innocent it may appear to be on the surface; results have been documented but often people are left with severe psychological problems or other maladies after seeking occult remedies.

| MEANS OF HEALING |
|---|
| **SUPERNATURAL MEANS – DIVINE HEALING** |

1. Prayer to God – Luke 11:9–10; 1 John 3:22; James 5:13,15,16

2. Trusting God's word and the cross – Ps. 107:20; Isaiah 53:4; Matt. 8:16–17; Mark 5:25–34

3. God's covenant of healing – Exodus 15:26; Mark 1:41

4. Breaking Bread (communion) – 1 Corinthians 11:23–30 (consider also Exodus 12:8–10)

5. Laying on hands – Mark 16:18; Luke 13:13; Acts 9:17

6. Anointing with oil – Mark 6:13; James 5:14

7. Forgiveness/confession of sin – Mark 2:5–12; James 5:16

8. Gifts of healings – 1 Corinthians 12:9,28,30

9. Speaking a word of wisdom/faith/instruction – 1 Kings 5:10; John 5:8; Acts 3:6–8

10. Casting out demons – Mark 9:17–27; Luke 4:31–37; 10:17–20

11. Anointing with oil – James 5:14–16

| **NATURAL MEANS – MEDICAL HEALING** |
|---|

1. God-given natural defence systems and bodily healing processes – John 11:12

2. Nursing care providing practical and emotional comfort – Luke 10:33–35

3. Medicine, pain relief, antibiotics, vaccines, tests and scans – Isaiah 38:21, 1 Timothy 5:23

4. Surgical procedures – resetting bones, repairing or eliminating bad parts

| SUBNATURAL MEANS – OCCULT HEALING |
|---|
| 1. Alternative (complementary) healing, hypnotism, yoga, transcendental meditation, homeopathy, charms, cultist rights etc. |
| 2. Faith healing, psychic methods, new age practices, pantheistic approach, spells |
| 3. Spiritist healing, mediums, séances, clairvoyance, witchcraft, satanism |

Examples of the gifts of healings in Scripture are really too numerous to catalogue. Later we shall discuss this subject more in a separate chapter, but here are a few examples:

1. Numbers 21:5–9: Moses made a bronze serpent on the pole, and all who looked at it were healed from fatal snake bites. This was a Biblical type of the cross, and all who look to the cross of Jesus are made whole!

2. 2 Kings 5:9–14: Naaman, the Syrian commander, is healed of leprosy through Elisha's ministry.

3. Isaiah 38:1–5: Hezekiah seeks the Lord and is healed from a fatal illness.

4. Matthew 4:23–25, 8:16–17: Jesus heals and delivers from demons countless numbers of people.

5. John 5:1–15: Jesus heals a man with a chronic illness, who does not recognise the Lord nor have faith in Him.

6. Acts 3:1–10: Peter and John pronounce healing on a man born crippled.

7. Acts 9:32–35: Peter ministers healing to a paralytic.

8. Acts 28:8: Paul ministers healing to the father of Publius.

# WORKING OF MIRACLES

## NT Greek: Ενεργηματα δυναμεων – *Energymata dunamion*

A miracle is a performance or act which issues from God Himself and is impossible for mere human beings to produce. We use the word *intervention* or *invading* when referring to one foreign power meddling with or assaulting another country. However, it is wrong to say that a miracle is the *invasion* of God into earthly life. The Lord God is not a foreigner or alien on earth, as though this planet were not His territory. Psalm 24:1 states, *"The earth is the Lord's, and its fullness; the world and those who live in it."* When I return home from work I do not invade my own property. When driving the car, I may change direction, but it would be ridiculous to suggest that I have intervened in my own life! To describe a miracle as invading the fixed order is misleading. It assumes our universe is a fixed order, but the only entity which is fixed and unchanging is the Being of God Himself! Malachi 3:6: *"I am the Lord, I change not."* Neither can we rightly say a miracle is the violation of natural laws. Easton lucidly illustrates this by saying:

> When a man raises a weight from the ground, the law of gravity is neither suspended nor violated, but counteracted by a stronger force. The same is true as to the walking of Christ on the water and the swimming of iron at the command of the prophet. The universe is not under the exclusive control of physical forces, but everywhere and always there is superior to all else, an infinite personal will, not superseding, but directing and controlling all physical causes, acting with or without them.[15]

Similarly, an aircraft heavier than atmosphere can defeat the law of gravity by operating with the higher law of aerodynamics. In the same way with the Christian life: the law of the Spirit of life in Christ Jesus makes us free from the law of sin and death (Romans 8:2). Those who are not born again know only *the law of sin and death* operating in their lives. They have no experience of *the law of the Spirit of life in Christ Jesus*!

The Bible is full of miracles, from Genesis to Revelation. They occur every day, since our continued existence hinges on the miracle of the sustaining power of Christ, who enables universal coherence despite the ravages of sin, and the works of the devil. In the New Testament, *energymata dunamion* means 'workings of powers' and Paul says he became a minister of Christ through the *working power* of God, and sees the same *powers at work* in the Christians at Ephesus (Ephesians 3:7, 20). This leads me to maintain that a born-again conversion to Christ is one of the greatest miracles we may experience. Bible miracles are also termed *signs* because they point to a deeper truth, such as evidence of the Divine Presence, or confirmation that the message preached is true. Our Lord Jesus appealed to miracles as conclusive proof of His Messiahship and mission (John 5:20,36; 10:25,38).

Throughout Scripture some miracles are wrought by God alone – for example, creation. Some are executed by angels – for example, Herod is killed, Acts 12:20–23. Some are performed through human agencies as when Paul delivers a demonised woman, Acts 16:16–18. The manifestation of the Spirit called *working of miracles* refers to miracles wrought by God through human beings.

Here are a few examples of the *working of miracles* in the Bible:

*The physical realm: demonstrating God's sovereignty*

The miracles in Egypt (Exodus chapters 5–12). The bronze serpent (Numbers 21:4–9). The overthrow of Jericho (Joshua

6:1–27). Samson's strength (Judges chapters 13–16). Elisha's floating axe-head (2 Kings 6:5–7). Jesus turning water into wine (John 2:1–11). Jesus walking on water (Mark 6: 45–52).

## The provisional realm: destitution erased

Water from the rock (Exodus 17:5–7; Numbers 20:10–12). Bitter water made drinkable (Exodus 15:22–26; 2 Kings 2:19–22). Manna and quail (Exodus 16:13–19; Numbers 11:31–33). Elijah fed (1 Kings 17:6,8–16). The widow's oil (2 Kings 4:1–7). Stew made edible (2 Kings 4:38–41). Feeding 100 men (2 Kings 4:42–44). Jesus feeding thousands (Mark 6:35–44, 8:1–9). Catching fish (Luke 5:4–10; John 21:6).

## The protective realm: delivering from danger

Red Sea crossing (Exodus 14:21–31). Enemies slain (2 Kings 19:35–37). Angelic protectors (2 Kings 6:8–19). Saved from fire (Daniel 3:19–30). Saved from lions (Daniel 6:18–23). Tempest stilled (Matthew 8:23–27). Peter saved from prison and death (Acts 12:5–19). Paul and Silas saved from prison (Acts 16:25–34). Paul unharmed by a snake bite (Acts 28:3–6).

## The people's realm: death and decay averted

Elijah raises widow's son to life (1 Kings 17:17–24). Elisha raises boy to life (2 Kings 4:18–37). Elisha's dead bones raise a man to life (2 Kings 13:20–21). Jesus raises a widow's son to life (Luke 7:11–17). Jesus raises to life a young girl (Luke 8:49–56). Jesus raises Lazarus to life (John 11:17–44). Abraham heals Abimelech (Genesis 20:17–18). Naaman healed of leprosy (2 Kings 5:1–15). Jesus heals many (Matthew 4:23–25; 8:16–17; Mark 6:53–56). Jesus heals the maimed and crippled (Matthew

15:30–31; see KJV). Peter and John heal a cripple (Acts 3:1–10). Paul heals Publius (Acts 28:7–8).

### The productive realm: declaring life

Abraham and Sarah have a son (Genesis 21:1–7). Barren Rachel gives birth to Joseph (Genesis 30:22–24). Hannah gives birth to Samuel (1 Samuel 1:8–28). Elizabeth gives birth to John the Baptist (Luke 1:5–25,57–58). Mary gives birth to Jesus (Luke 1:26–38, 2:1–7).

### The principal realm: destroying demonic power

Fire from heaven defeating false prophets (1 Kings 18:20–40). Jesus delivers a demoniac (Mark 5:1–20). Jesus delivers the Greek Syrophoenician woman's daughter (Mark 7:24–30). Jesus releases a boy from a demon (Mark 9:14–29). Seventy disciples cast out demons (Luke 10:1–9,17–20). Jesus promised His followers would *"cast out demons"* (Mark 16:17); Paul delivers a demonised woman (Acts 16:16–18).

### The punitive realm: divine reproof

Er and Onan killed by the Lord (Genesis 38:7–10). First-born Egyptians killed (Exodus 12:12, 29-30). Korah, Dathan and Abiram, plus 250 men slain by God (Numbers 16:1–5,31–35). Achan killed (Joshua 7:24–26). Gideon slays the Midianites (Judges 7:1–25). Haman hanged (Esther 7:1–10). Elisha rebukes young people (2 Kings 2:23–25). Gehazi made leprous (2 Kings 5:20–27). Elisha blinds the Syrians (2 Kings 6:18). Sennacherib defeated and 185,000 Assyrian soldiers killed (Isaiah chapters 36–38). Nebuchadnezzar humiliated (Daniel 4:28–33). Jesus curses a fig tree (Mark 11:12–14,20–24). Ananias and Sapphira die (Acts 5:1–11). Herod is killed (Acts 12:20–23). Elymas blinded (Acts 13:6–12).

# PROPHECY

## NT Greek: Προφητεια – *Propheteia*

*Prophecy promised for today*

Joel 2:28–32: *"It shall come to pass afterward that I will pour out My Spirit on all flesh; your sons and your daughters shall prophesy . . . and I will show wonders in the heavens and in the earth . . . before the great and terrible day of the Lord comes."* This text shows that prophecy continues until the Lord's return, and that fact is also confirmed by the apostle Paul, who says, *"prophecies will fail . . . For we know in part and we prophesy in part. But when that which is perfect (complete) is come, then that which is in part will be done away . . . For now we see dimly in a mirror, but then face to face. Now I know in part, but then I shall know even as also I am known"* (1 Corinthians 13:8–13). Regretfully, these same words of Paul have been misconstrued by some to show that the gifts of the Spirit would cease long before the return of the Lord!

Cessationism teaches that all the miraculous gifts of the Spirit ceased with the death of the first apostles, or when the New Testament canon was finalised. This is a stance totally unsupported by Scripture, and embraced to justify the lack of Holy Spirit manifestations in some branches of the Christian Church in more modern times. It seems easier for such persons to invent a manufactured theory than to believe the Scriptures and seek God for His gifts in their lives! How absurd to suggest that *"the perfect has come"* refers to the death of the last of the twelve apostles! Nor is there the slightest hint in Scripture that *"the perfect has come"* refers to the completion of the New Testament canon! The time will come when *"prophecies will cease"* but as Paul explains, it will be at the return of Christ as King, when at last we *"see face to face"*!

The purpose of New Testament prophecy is clearly stated in 1 Corinthians 14:3 and 31. Prophecy edifies, exhorts and comforts. It also teaches and encourages.

### Edification – the constructive aspect of prophecy

To edify is to 'build up', to 'enlighten', to 'teach' and to 'enrich'. Ephesians 4:11–16 refers to the five-fold ministry gifts from the Lord Jesus, namely apostles, prophets, evangelists, pastors and teachers, who equip and edify (build up) the Church. Edification is emphasised in 1 Corinthians 14:4,5,12,17,26. The manifestations of the Spirit are not for breaking down, or splitting up churches, but for building up the churches in the Lord Jesus Christ.

### Exhortation – the provocative aspect of prophecy

To exhort is to support and encourage, but it also has a sharp edge, which is used to provoke others to love, and not to anger. Hebrews 10:24–25 says, *"Let us consider one another in order to stir up love and good works, not forsaking the assembling of ourselves together, as is the manner of some, but exhorting one another, and so much the more as you see the Day approaching."* Prophetic words can stir up believers to action; they encourage resolve and instil determination in our walk and work for Christ.

### Comfort – the consolative aspect of prophecy

In trials we need comfort. 2 Corinthians 1:3–7 says, *"the Father of mercies and God of all comfort, who comforts us in all our tribulation, that we may be able to comfort those who are in any trouble, with the comfort with which we ourselves are comforted of God. For as the sufferings of Christ abound in us, so our consolation also abounds through Christ . . . If we are comforted it is for your consolation and salvation."* The New Testament Greek words used here for both *comfort* and *consolation* are the noun *parakaleo* and the verb *parakleisis*, which mean 'a calling to one's side' (*para* beside, and *kaleo* to call). The word used in 1 Corinthians 14:3 is *paramuthia*, which means 'speaking closely' (*para* beside, near, and *muthos* speech). This indicates that prophecy speaks closely to those needing comfort. It is both an encouragement and a tender consoling, especially for those experiencing trials.

We can see how prophecy is needed today, where in our Western culture people are bullied, bruised and broken, and where dark spiritual forces grip them in bondage, stress and spiritual blindness. 1 Corinthians 14:31 says, *"For you can all prophesy one by one, that all may learn and all may be encouraged."* This verse expands the purpose of prophecy, which is seen to provide instruction, enabling others to learn more about the Lord and about themselves.

*Prophecy is not preaching*

Prophecy *(prophateuo)* is not the same as preaching *(euangelizo, kerruso, katangello)*, or teaching *(didasko)*. Different words are used in the New Testament to describe each of these. But both preaching and teaching often contain prophecy! When the Spirit is flowing freely through a speaker, He can impart prophetic insights and utterances as the Spirit dictates, and the speaker's words will have a mighty impact on the hearers. Under the powerful anointing of the Holy Spirit, preaching often contains words of wisdom and knowledge, as well as prophecy, and also tongues and interpretation, all of which greatly raises the inspirational level of the discourse. Spirit-filled preaching rarely, if ever, will be boring, pedantic, academic, tedious, tiresome, monotonous, dull, dry or dusty! The words of Jesus were, *"spirit and life"* (John 6:63).

## Prophecy and prophets

Not all are prophets; that is, not everyone will hold the office of a prophet as listed in Ephesians 4:11. But *"all may prophesy"* as Paul states in 1 Corinthians 14:31. So we can rightly say, "All prophets prophesy, but not all who prophesy are prophets!" For example, I am a teacher (not a prophet), but I can prophesy just as I can speak in tongues. The fact that I prophesy does not mean I hold the office of a prophet. But those who do hold the office of a prophet will all surely prophesy, freely and often.

Prophecy comes in many ways—through visions, dreams, pictures, songs, poetry and illuminated words. It is often a *forth-telling* of past or present events or situations. It can also be a *fore-telling* of the future. Jesus foretold His death and resurrection, Mark 8:31, 10:33–34. He foretold Peter's denial, Mark 14:29–31, and His return to earth in power and glory, Mark 13:1–37. Agabus prophesied about a coming famine, Acts 11:28, and about Paul's demise in Jerusalem, Acts 21:10–11. By the way, I do not see that Agabus got his prophecy wrong, as some suggest, since there is no discrepancy between Acts 21:10–11 and Acts 21:27–36. When Agabus demonstrated what would happen to Paul in Jerusalem, he did not prophetically say Paul should not go, he simply relayed what would take place if he did go. Acts 21:12–14 describes a natural human reaction and the words cannot be pressed into a prophetic utterance.

Isaiah foretold Israel's restoration through Cyrus, a Persian king, about 150 years before Cyrus was born, Isaiah 44:28, 45:1–4. Those disbelieving in prophecy have invented other authors for the latter part of Isaiah, claiming that Isaiah himself could not have specifically named him and described what he would do. But that is precisely the nature of prophecy, and Biblical examples are too numerous to catalogue. When God wants you to prophesy, He often gives only a few words, or a sentence. You must take a step of faith and speak these words before God gives you more. Jeannie Morgan says it can be "like taking a bungee jump into the unknown".[2] This is an apt description of how many manifestations of the Holy Spirit operate. Another method by which God imparts prophecy is by showing you a whole picture to describe and explain.

*Should prophecies be written down or recorded for future use?*

Sermons are, so why not revelations from God? Whilst sermons and prophecies never reach the level of authority attributed to the written Scriptures, they nonetheless teach, interpret and explain the written Word, making it active and applicable to our lives. Of course, prophecy, like preaching, is meant to be spoken, and its power is not only in the words, but in the manner and bearing of the speaker – the flashing eye, the waving hand, the very deportment conveyed by the speaker, of which none are a distraction from the message. All these enhancements are absent from the printed page, although many, like myself, remain blessed reading sermons by Spurgeon, Alexander Whyte and others. Personally I have no objection to prophecies being recorded, replayed and reviewed; in fact, I see many advantages, such as an aid to memory and understanding. On numerous occasions people have come to me asking me to repeat or further explain what a prophetic utterance or an interpretation of tongues was saying. Often I cannot remember verbatim, and a recording would be helpful.

*Prophecy guidelines*

A consideration of all that Paul writes in 1 Corinthians chapters 12 to 14 leads to specific guidelines in chapter 14 verses 29–33, *"Let two or three prophets speak, and let the others judge. If anything is revealed to another sitting by, let the first hold his peace. For you may all prophesy one by one, that all may learn and all may be encouraged. And the spirits of the prophets are subject to the prophets."* From these verses we see that no more than two or three prophets should speak once in each service, and the other prophets should judge. Space and opportunity should be given to other prophets, by the first prophet keeping quiet. In Corinth all the Christians could prophesy, but two or three only are permitted to do so in one meeting. The Bible says, *"The spirit of the prophets is subject to the prophets."* No prophet is forced out of control by the Spirit. This guidance is especially for those holding the office of prophet, but the principles apply to others who may prophesy from time to time. All the prophets in Corinth could prophesy one by one, but in a meeting the restriction of only two or three prophets speaking is applied. The first speaker should finish if a revelation comes to another prophet who sits near.

Sometimes it is thought that when the Holy Spirit imparts a revelation of truth, that the person has no option but to speak out; or that the person has no control over what the Spirit requires. This is patently untrue because *"the spirit of the prophets is subject to the prophets".* Which means the person himself is able to control his actions – whether he speaks or not, how he speaks and his attitude and demeanour at the time. It has been said that the Holy Spirit is a perfect gentleman, so His ministry into our own spirit is not compulsive. We are not robotic automatons with actions controlled by some outside influence which overrides our own active intelligence. The Spirit's anointing upon our lives does not afflict us with an obsessive mode of conduct from which we are unable to extricate ourselves. Rather, the Holy Spirit interacts with our own human spirit, seeking our compliance. His enabling, anointing and guidance work together with our acceptance, submission and our willingness to be used by Him.

199

*Proving prophecy*

1 Thessalonians 5:19–22: *"Do not quench the Spirit. Do not despise prophecies. Test all things; hold fast what is good. Abstain from every form of evil."* These injunctions may be considered separately, but they may also be connected, showing a progression from *quenching the Spirit* through to *abstaining from evil*. In other words, one way to quench the Spirit is to despise prophecies! Prophecies are easily despised by people who don't prophesy, just as tongues are despised by people who don't speak in tongues. The reason for this can be jealousy, resulting in the one who prophesies being labelled elitist, proud or superior. But rather than despise prophesies, we are told to test all things.

There are two important tests for prophesies and other Spirit manifestations. Firstly, is it in accord with Scripture? The Bible is the benchmark of truth, and any utterance which conflicts with God's written Word should be considered suspect, and rejected. If a prophecy by a plebe or by a Pope is deemed unscriptural, or unable to be confirmed by Scripture texts, let it be discarded. Secondly, what is the level of inspiration? The percentage of Spirit input, however, can only be assessed by others who prophesy or are prophets. It is inappropriate for those who have none of the gifts of the Spirit to criticise or judge those through whom the gifts are exercised. Just as it is unacceptable for me to judge how a cake is made when I personally do not know how to bake! If you test all things, you can hold fast to what is good. This simply means keep the good and dump the bad. We should hold fast to the good by abstaining from all evil. In God's eyes it is evil to quench His Spirit, to despise His gifts and to fail to discern what is good from what is bad. Some people will believe anything, like miracles don't happen, but such thinking is an evil from which we must abstain.

*Pursuing prophecy*

> 1 Corinthians 14:1: *"Pursue love and eagerly desire spirituals, especially that you may prophesy."*

> 1 Corinthians 14:5: *"I wish you all spoke in tongues, but rather that you prophesied."*

> 1 Corinthians 14:4,12: *"He who prophesies edifies the Church."*

> 1 Corinthians 14:39: *"So my brothers be eager (zealous) to prophesy."*

These verses emphasise that the Christian's primary desire should be to prophesy. Are you zealous and eager to prophesy? Do you desire prophecy in the Church? Failing in this area puts a serious doubt on the genuineness of your Christian attitude – is Jesus really your Lord? Are you truly filled with the Spirit? Or is your New Testament shredded and discarded like Jeremiah's scroll, and stripped of any desire for the miraculous for today?

## SPEAKING IN TONGUES

**NT Greek: Γλοσσαλαλια** *– Glossalalia*

This manifestation of the Spirit's presence is perhaps the most arresting, but it is also the most harangued by opponents of spiritual gifts. The New Testament has more to say about this spectacular manifestation than any other. *Tongues* simply mean 'languages'. It is malicious to add unnecessary mystery to this particular manifestation of the Holy Spirit, but regretfully some speak of *tongues of ecstasy* or *ecstatic speech*, whereas the words *ecstasy* and *ecstatic* are not found in the Greek texts of the New Testament. Not only does this amount to profanely adding to God's Word, it is also extremely misleading. The word *ecstatic* implies an overpowering emotion or exaltation or a state of sudden, intense feeling, and it has been explained as *"the frenzy of poetic inspiration"*. All this enshrouds tongues in a mist of unreality which the Holy Spirit neither desires nor promulgates.

When the Holy Spirit enables us to speak in tongues, our mental alertness is most often heightened (although our mind is not involved in any utterance, 1 Corinthians 14:14). Our spirits are blessed by speaking in tongues, and that is normal Christianity! Use of unscriptural words to describe tongues often reveals the inherent lack of knowledge and experience of this manifestation in a person's life. Genesis 11:1–9 shows that God engineered different languages, causing the dispersion of humankind to other parts of the world. In this Holy Spirit dispensation we taste *"the powers of the age to come"*, so is it unthinkable that the Lord can create a partial reversal of what happened at Babel? Enabling men to speak languages that they have never learned seems just the sort of thing our Lord would do.

1 Corinthians 12:10 introduces the phrase, *"different kinds of tongues"*, meaning different kinds of languages, not merely different languages. Jesus spoke about *"new languages"* in Mark 16:17, implying a language not previously learned by the speaker; but could Jesus have meant more than that? Could He be referring to languages from a totally different sphere? Is it a reference to heavenly languages? Indeed, Paul says he speaks with the *"tongues of men and of angels"* which suggests the use of human spoken languages and heavenly languages not spoken by mortals on earth.

There are many answers in the Bible about the purpose of tongues, so we will list and explain them now.

*Evidence of the baptism in the Holy Spirit*

In all three Biblical instances describing the effects of the baptism in the Spirit there is one consistent sign: speaking in tongues. Those who are baptised in the Spirit will speak in tongues in the majority of cases. They may do other things as well, and some may not speak in tongues until a little later, but in my experience, not too long afterwards. On the Day of Pentecost in Acts 2:1–39, they were all baptised in the Spirit, all filled with the Spirit and all spoke in tongues. Cornelius and his household in Acts 10:34–48 were converted and baptised in the Spirit while Peter was preaching – what a holy interruption! Peter knew this thing had happened because they all spoke with tongues and magnified God. After the Ephesians in Acts 19:1–6 were baptised in water, Paul laid his hands on them to impart the baptism in the Spirit, and the Bible records that they all spoke in tongues and prophesied.

## God speaking to His people

Isaiah 28:11–12 says, *"With stammering lips and other languages God will speak to this people, to whom He said, 'This is the rest enabling the weary to rest,' and 'This is the refreshing,' but they would not listen."* This prophecy is quoted in 1 Corinthians 14:21: *"With men of other tongues and other lips I will speak to My people; and yet they will not listen to Me, says the Lord."* When the New Testament quotes Isaiah it confirms that the subject here is what we commonly term 'speaking in tongues'. It is clear that these verses are not referring to a scenario on a purely human level, where a foreigner methodically learns the language of people from a different country. The context of 1 Corinthians chapters 12 to 14 is spiritual matters, including the supernatural manifestations of the Holy Spirit.

## Speaking in tongues can be a message from God to His people

This message can be spoken or sung, but it emphasises that the Lord wants to speak to the gathered Church, and does so through the twin manifestations of speaking in tongues and interpretation. Interpretation allows people to understand with their mind, rather than remaining purely blessed in their spirit.

*Although God speaks to the Church, regretfully "they will not listen"*

1 Corinthians 14:21 does not mean that no one in the Church ever listens to God when He speaks through the manifestations of the Spirit – that would be absurdly untrue. We read in John 1:11–12: *"He came to His own, but His own did not receive Him."* This cannot be forced to mean that no one received Him, because it continues, *"but as many as received Him"* and we see that many Jews did in fact receive Him, such as His twelve apostles, and the early Church in Acts comprising 5,000 members who were all Jews! *"They will not listen"* indicates that speaking in tongues will be unacceptable to many, which is exactly the situation in the Church today. Tongues are demonised; they are argued against; they are ignored; they are criticised; they are defamed; they are neither sought nor used by so many denominations and churches. The New Tribes Mission incorporated into its mandate that their missionaries were forbidden to speak in tongues, in direct contradiction of the Scriptures, 1 Corinthians 14:39! When the Church refuses to pay attention, God will use speaking in tongues to gain the attention of unbelievers. This leads us to another use of tongues.

*A sign to unbelievers*

In 1 Corinthians 14:22 it states, *"Tongues are a sign, not for believers, but for unbelievers."* The two important words here are *"sign"* and *"unbeliever"*. The NT Greek word for sign is *semeion* – σηειον, meaning "confirmatory supernatural operations . . . such as the gift of tongues".[15] Hence speaking in tongues becomes confirmation of a supernatural phenomenon for unbelievers. The most obvious example of this is what occurred on the Day of Pentecost, when about 120 persons spoke in different languages. The tongues they used were new to the speakers, but clearly understood by the people around them, Acts 2:5–12. This sign of speaking in tongues not only caused the unbelievers to be amazed and perplexed, but it drew the crowd around the disciples, and gave opportunity for an explanation, in which Peter said, *"This is what was spoken by the prophet Joel."*

There is an abundance of modern instances where the sign of tongues is used. For example, the Armenian gentleman who came to my home city in the England, but on the first Sunday found he was too late for the service at the church he wished to attend. So he slipped into a Pentecostal church nearby, and was delighted to hear a man speak out in his own native tongue during the service. On leaving the church he spoke to the pastor, remarking how wonderful it was that someone spoke in his native language, and added how beautifully the pastor had interpreted it! The speaker in tongues did not know he been speaking pure Armenian until this incident took place.

Fred Cooper was baptised in the Holy Spirit and believed passionately in divine healing. One evening he fell ill and was in great pain. He went early to bed, but could not sleep, and as the pain increased he got out of bed and drove himself to the Gloucester general hospital. They diagnosed an appendix ready to burst, and performed an emergency operation there and then.

In the morning Fred was lying in a ward and next to him the curtains were drawn around a man who appeared to be praying in a language that Fred did not know or recognise. This happened at regular intervals throughout the day. Fred asked the nurse why the man was in hospital, but she explained that he could not speak English and they were waiting for the visit of his brother, who spoke some English, to find out more. Fred knew this man was a Muslim, and after the curtains were drawn back, he tried to witness with gestures, pointing to the sky and saying, "You love God and I love God!"

Little was understood, until Fred noticed that the man's voice sounded similar to the way Fred himself spoke in tongues. Knowing he had nothing to lose, Fred began speaking in tongues to the man, who being surprised, grabbed hold of him, then scrambled for paper and pen, and wrote down words as Fred spoke. Later that evening the man's brother arrived, and he spoke to Fred saying that it was wonderful that Fred could speak Arabic, and that he had been talking about Abraham, Isaac and Jacob, and the power and goodness of God's Kingdom. Now Fred knew what language he had spoken. Personally I always wondered if Fred's tongues-speaking was real. The language and articulation sounded so strange, with Fred's tongue seeming to waggle about through his open lips as he spoke. Hearing his hospital story caused me to feel ashamed that I had doubted that Fred's speaking in tongues was genuinely a manifestation of the Holy Spirit. I repented and apologised to the Lord, and have been very careful not to criticise the Spirit's manifestations again, no matter how odd or different they might seem to be.

The Bible college I attended allowed students to visit patients in hospital, and during one of those occasions Fran prayed in tongues for a sick lady. The lady was so surprised, telling Fran she had spoken in her native language. An English missionary prayed for converts to receive the baptism in the Spirit, and was amazed to hear an African boy speak out in tongues using excellent English – which language humanly he did not know. In these instances, speaking in tongues becomes a sign, especially to those who are not yet born-again Christians. Each manifestation of the sign of tongues comprises a legitimate language spoken elsewhere in the world, sometimes by a nation or by a smaller tribe. Acts 2:1–13 is the only Biblical account of speaking in tongues as a *sign*.

*Praying in the spirit*

1 Corinthians 14:14 *"If I pray in a tongue, my spirit prays."* I humbly suggest that the human spirit offers prayer on a considerably higher plane than the human mind. Our minds are affected by many thoughts, some spurious and some noble, but our human spirit is the core of our personalities and it is the essential part which is born again when we come to faith in Christ Jesus. Our minds continue with a need to be *"renewed"* (Romans 12:2) but our spirit is free (John 8:36).

Praying in tongues elevates the prayer-life to new heights. Due to human weakness of mind, often we do not know what to pray for, but when we pray in the spirit (that is, in tongues) the Holy Spirit assists us and prays through us. Since tongues are the Holy Spirit revealing Himself in that particular manner, then He personally is initiating our prayers. Prayer tongues are the Spirit praying through us, and so our prayers are according to the will of God. Now when a person prays in tongues, they will not have a word-for-word realisation of what they are saying, hence their *"understanding is unfruitful"* as 1 Corinthians 14:14 explains. This is not a disadvantage. In fact, Paul concludes, *"I will pray with the spirit, and I will also pray with the understanding"* (1 Corinthians 14:15). Let us be clear about the fact that it is not a question of praying with tongues *or* praying with the understanding. There is no choice offered here! It is a question of doing *both*, since both are needed. The Scriptures say we must *"pray in the Spirit on all occasions with all kinds of prayers and requests"* (Ephesians 6:18).

When praying and speaking in tongues, the speaker is often well aware of his intentions, or even to whom his words are directed. For example, he may be conscious that he is indeed directing his words to God; or he may know that he is addressing the devil, or a demon during exorcism. It is not difficult to see that the type and tenor of the tongue will differ widely in each of these two cases. Prayer tongues are a powerful instrument in spiritual warfare and exorcism – when an oppressive sense of evil is present, or a dear soul is demonised. After describing the Christian's spiritual armour in Ephesians chapter 6, Paul adds *"pray at all times in the Spirit"*. Praying in the Holy Spirit will include praying in tongues and praying with the understanding.

## Singing in the spirit

1 Corinthians 14:15: *"I will sing with the spirit, and I will also sing with the understanding."* This statement further enlarges the territory of speaking in tongues. How marvellous that my spirit can sing! Note once again that singing both in the spirit and with the understanding is advocated here. Once more there is no choice given between these two. Every church should experience prayer in the spirit and singing in the spirit, along with doing both of these with the understanding. Singing in the spirit is often praise to God. It is a high level of worship directed to the Lord. However, just as God speaks to His people through speaking in tongues, He can speak to us just as well through His faithful servant singing in tongues.

## Blessing (giving thanks) with the spirit

1 Corinthians 14:16: *"When you bless with the spirit, how will the uninformed say 'Amen' at your giving of thanks?"* Here *"blessing"* someone, or eulogising over a person, is linked with thankfulness. When we are grateful to another person for their godly aid, we may speak in tongues over them, and transmit a thankful blessing, which will rest in power over their lives.

In 1 Corinthians 14:16–17, the reference to *"how will the uninformed say 'Amen' at your giving of thanks, since he does not understand what you say? You give thanks well, but the other is not edified"* requires clarification.

This reference is not belittling, demeaning or laying aside *blessing in tongues*, as though it is unnecessary or unworthy. The scriptures throughout this chapter emphasise the necessity of edifying (building up spiritually) the Church, and for this to be done it is necessary to speak, pray, sing, bless and give thanks both in the spirit (with tongues) and with the mind (with understanding). Opting for just one of these will not accomplish the edification process. Wonderfully, the Holy Spirit will often reveal Himself through the operation of the *"interpretation of tongues"*. This can result in an utterance in tongues being interpreted in the native language of the gathered Church, to ensure that all understand and are built up. If the Scriptures were demeaning tongues the Holy Spirit would have said so, and He surely would not have provided a manifestation of Himself in the form of *"interpretation of tongues"*.

## A refreshing place of rest

Isaiah 28:11–12: *"With stammering lips and other languages God will speak to this people, to whom He said, 'This is the rest enabling the weary to rest,' and 'This is the refreshing,' but they would not listen."* Paul quotes Isaiah's words and places them squarely in the context of the Holy Spirit's manifestations and associates them particularly with *"speaking in tongues"*. What is Isaiah saying? He is saying that speaking in tongues are the *"resting place for the weary"* and that speaking in tongues by the power of the Holy Spirit is the *"refreshing"* promised and provided by God!

Oh! How surely we need speaking in tongues! Many are physically weary – a condition which a session of praying in the spirit can alleviate so easily. Many are psychologically weary, mentally and emotionally stressed from the pressures of life, particularly so in the Western world. This can be remedied by speaking in tongues – a spiritual transportation to the place of refreshment in God. Many are spiritually weary, and through lack of knowledge *"fall backward and are broken, snared and caught"* (Isaiah 28:13) in a faithless trap of disappointment with God. How easily they lean on their own understanding and draw back wearily from fellowship with the Lord – missing entirely the refreshment and rest that God has for all who are weary pilgrims passing through the wilderness of earthly life.

How is it that so many neglect the manifestations of the Holy Spirit? Indeed, they neglect the Holy Spirit Himself! Of all the nine gifts, for many, speaking in tongues is the big no-no! *"An enemy has done this"*, as Jesus remarked in Matthew 13:28.

Many leave the Church, no longer gathering with the people of God, because they are weary. They are tired of balancing family life with work life and church life. But what did Jesus say to the weary? *"Come to Me, all you who are weary and burdened, and I will give you rest . . . For you will find rest for your souls"* (Matthew 11:28–29). Some will be relieved that Jesus instructed the weary to go to Him and not to the Holy Spirit! But what does Jesus our Saviour do for us? He saves us; forgives us; makes us children of God; heals us; restores us, blesses us and baptises us in the Holy Spirit! Jesus personally leads us to the place of rest and refreshment via the baptism in the Holy Spirit, which includes the Spirit's accompanying manifestation of speaking with tongues, and that is normal Christianity!

*A seeming contradiction? 1 Corinthians 14:22–25:*

> Tongues are a sign, not to believers but for unbelievers; but prophecy is for believers, not for unbelievers. If the whole church comes together in one place and everyone

speaks in tongues, and some who do not understand or some unbelievers come in, will they not say you are mad? But if all prophesy and unbelievers or one who does not understand comes in, he will be convinced by all that he is a sinner and will be judged by all as the secrets of his heart are revealed. So he will fall face down and worship God, exclaiming "God is really with you!"

A surface reading of the above verses might lead some to see an apparent contradiction. First we read that *"Tongues are a sign for unbelievers"* and that *"prophecy is for believers."* Then it continues to say that if all speak in tongues, an unbeliever (or enquirer) will think you are out of your minds, and then conversely, if everyone prophesies, an unbeliever will be convicted and know that God is truly present!

Tongues are a sign for unbelievers, when the unbeliever understands the unlearned language being spoken. But *"if everyone speaks in tongues"* at the same time, unbelievers might be totally confused and consider the whole group to be out of their minds, or drunk, as they concluded on the Day of Pentecost! But two or three speaking in tongues in turn together with the accompanying interpretations (1 Corinthians 14:27) will arrest the attention of unbelievers indeed. It was precisely a 'message in tongues' with its interpretation which spoke to Aston Villa footballer Mike Tindall during his first visit to a Baptist church, and which led to his salvation.

Paul states that *"prophecy is for believers"* because it builds up, encourages and comforts them. But if *"everybody is prophesying"*, unbelievers will readily see that God is truly present and that it is He who enables such torrents of inspirational truth to pour out. They will be convicted by the Holy Spirit, who will have revealed His presence through prophetic utterances. There is no contradiction or confusion here. The matter hinges on the words, *"everyone"* and *"everybody"*. If all speak in tongues at once, there is confusion from an unbeliever's point of view; but if all prophesy at the same time, the Spirit is able to bring conviction to the hearts of unbelievers.

These verses are a divine paradox where the same Spirit manifestation can help or hinder, depending on the number of persons speaking, and the mode of utterance given. This makes sense and justifies the advice in 1 Corinthians 14:27–33 about the extent and use of tongues and prophecy in the Church.

## INTERPRETATION OF TONGUES

### NT Greek: Ἑμηνία λωσσων – *Hermenia glossone*

The Greek word ἑμηνία means *"to explain"* or to give *"an intelligible explanation"* and refers especially to the meaning of words in a different language. From it, our English word *hermeneutics* (which deals with the principles of Biblical interpretation) is derived. In 1 Corinthians 12:10 this word describes the ninth listed manifestation of the Spirit. Note, therefore, it does not rest on academia or human insight, but it is a supernatural manifestation of the Holy Spirit, without whom the interpretation of a message in tongues would be near impossible.

Various Bible instances show that dreams, written words and symbols were interpreted to provide a fuller meaning. But none of these are examples of this manifestation of the Spirit, because this particular manifestation is designated *"the interpretation of tongues"*, not the interpretation of God's word, dreams, written words, symbols or of anything else. This is the only manifestation of the Spirit which operates in conjunction with another – it is dependent on *tongues,* while a message in tongues spoken in the church relies on someone interpreting the message so that all may understand. Tongues together with interpretation are twin gifts, allied and mutually operative.

## Interpretation, not translation

The import of this is that we do not expect a word-for-word translation of speaking in tongues. Indeed, word-for-word translation (known as *formal-equivalence*) is often impossible when translating the Scriptures themselves, as many Bible translators have discovered. Rather, a thought-for-thought translation (called *dynamic-equivalence*) will render the meaning more accurately and present a more understandable interpretation. The Holy Spirit is not restricted in any way, as we may well acknowledge. A tongue can be sung, and the interpretation spoken, and vice versa. A tongue can be specific, but the interpretation can be holistic. A tongue can be spoken to God, while the interpretation can be God addressing His people. A tongue may be in prose, but the interpretation poetic. A tongue may be a straightforward narrative, but the interpretation pictorial and descriptive. Harold Horton writes that an interpretation can be "*pictorial, parabolic, descriptive or literal, according to the urge of the Spirit*".[17]

When we consider New Testament quotations of Old Testament verses, we discover the Holy Spirit often gives a fuller interpretation of His original words. For example, compare Isaiah 6:9–10 with Matthew 13:14–15. The Hebrew contains about twenty-two words, while the Greek about forty-nine words, and in English sixty-eight words. Again compare Haggai 2:6 with Hebrews 12:26–27, where the Spirit directs the writer to the Hebrews to use a free interpretation which adds many other words, but without altering the meaning and sense that Haggai gave originally. This explains why a message in tongues can be appreciably longer, or shorter, than its accompanying interpretation. The Holy Spirit can, of course, grant an exact translation if He so desires, and often this is the case when the tongue that is given is recognised by someone present in the congregation. In this instance both the message in tongues and the interpretation is used by the Holy Spirit to bring conviction and challenge.

*Do prayers or praises in tongues need to be interpreted?*

This depends on the circumstances and the mode of prayer or praise in the church.

Extemporaneous prayer and praise in the spirit, where all (or a large number of the congregation) are praying and praising together at the same time, does not need interpreters! I love spontaneous outbursts of adoration and acclamation of the Lord, perhaps at the end of a hymn or song, or as a conclusion to a time of prayer. Such dynamic worship in the spirit by believers together at the same time does not require interpretation. A single prayer or praise utterance in tongues, when others quietly listen, will be interpreted and the accompanying interpretation will generally follow suit, by likewise taking the form of prayer or praise.

*How does interpretation of tongues function?*

An interpretation of tongues is given in a similar way to prophecy. When a message in tongues is heard, often the person who is meant to give the interpretation will sense a prompting in their spirit by the Lord. The interpreter could receive a vision or mental image; or the entire subject could be impressed on the consciousness. Often just the subject is given, or the first remarks are impressed upon the mind, then as the first words are spoken out, the next line is added and so on – the phrases are like stepping stones which must be crossed one at a time. This naturally requires faith that the Holy Spirit will impart the words to be spoken, that the words will continue to flow until the message is complete. Invariably there will be an anointing upon the person who speaks out in tongues and on the person who gives the interpretation. The anointing provides an inner assurance and confirmation that it is right to speak.

Faith is necessary in almost all that we do for the Lord, and this is certainly so when operating the manifestations of the Spirit. The Spirit will prompt us, but we have to trust Him and believe He will reveal Himself through us in the way He chooses. The adversary can accuse us of 'making it up' and place this thought not only in the mind of the speakers, but in the minds of those who hear! Against such an allegation the shield of faith is required, to counteract the devil's negative attempts to stifle the operations of the Holy Spirit. Many more in our congregations should operate these gifts, but through fear and faithlessness have become slothful, like the servant who buried his talent (Matthew 25:25; Luke 19:20). Even Pastor Timothy needed the apostolic injunction: *"Stir up the gift of God which is in you through the laying on of my hands. For God has not given us a spirit of fear, but of power and of love and a sound mind"* (2 Timothy 1:6–7). Notice the phrase *"which is in you"*.

Since our bodies are the temple of the Holy Spirit, He who dwells in us is resident with all His powers, manifestations and operations which He can utilise at any given moment, as He desires. But we must be willing, full of faith in Him, and careful to eject all aspects of fear and cowardice. Human pride is a pitfall indeed, and many fail to use God's gifts through thinking they will look a fool, or that others will not approve, or that they will be censored in some way. It was that apostle of the Word, Rev. George Canty, who in his inimitable way pointed out that regarding the use of spiritual gifts, *"some are as unstoppable as Halley's comet, while others are stuck like barges on a mud-bank"*.

*Ask God for the manifestation of interpretation*

The advice in 1 Corinthians 14:13 given to all who speak in tongues is *"Let him . . . pray that he may interpret"*. An onus rests upon those who speak in tongues to seek God and ask for the power of the

Holy Spirit to enable them to interpret. This applies to their own messages in tongues, as well as those spoken by others.

The first reason for this is the *edification* of the Church – the positive building-up spiritually of all believers. Tongues without an interpretation will succeed in blessing the human spirit, but leave the mind questioning: "What did that mean? What is God saying? What does the Holy Spirit wish to accomplish?" Tongues without interpretation can produce perplexity in the mind, but tongues with accompanying interpretation are of equal value with prophecy (1 Corinthians 14:5), in which not only are spirits blessed but also minds are illuminated and fruitful, leading to spiritual strength.

The second reason is that a message in tongues lays a responsibility on others to interpret, but if the speaker in tongues is also able to interpret it lifts some of the burden from others. Also, if there is no other interpreter present, then the speaker in tongues may proceed with his message, knowing that he has the right to trust the Lord to grant the interpretation afterwards.

*Someone should interpret*

1 Corinthians 14:27 says, *"Let someone interpret."* The King James Version translated the Greek text *"and let one interpret"*, which caused many to conclude that one and the same person must interpret all messages in tongues in one meeting. However, the Greek word can simply be translated *"someone"* and it does not restrict the use of this gift to one single person in the meeting. Pentecostal pioneers had only the King James Authorised Version of the Bible to hand – very few other translations were readily available at that time. Later, the Knox New Testament, Phillips New Testament, the Twentieth Century Bible, Moffatt's Bible and the New English Bible translated 1 Corinthians 14:27 as *"let someone interpret"*. Even

so, early Pentecostal leaders (such as Harold Horton and Charles Kingston) sensed that this text was not imposing so definite a procedure, and the Elim president said, *"We are often too rigid and literal and need to be more flexible in our outlook, and while it is better for the same person to interpret all messages in tongues in one service, where this is not so we should not worry, but learn to be blessed just the same."* It is plainly evident that the wisdom of Pentecostal pioneers was inspired by the Holy Spirit who leads into all truth.

### A procedure for messages in tongues and interpretation

There are specific guidelines about the operation of tongues in 1 Corinthians 14:27–28. For example, speaking out in tongues for the whole church to hear is restricted to two or three in one service. They are to speak in turn, as opposed to speaking together at the same time.

Someone is required to interpret each tongues message. If no interpreter is present, the tongues speaker should speak quietly to himself and to the Lord.

# CHAPTER FIFTEEN

# GOD, THE PRODUCER OF FRUIT

THE GIFTS AND THE FRUIT ARE BOTH NINE-FOLD, AND ARE supernatural products of the Holy Spirit. They cannot be humanly manufactured, although to some extent they can be pathetically imitated. The gifts (plural) are many, while the fruit (singular) is one. Galatians 5:22–23 describes this single fruit as having a nine-fold property or a nine-fold attribute or flavour! What does this mean? Simply, it means that the Spirit produces the nine-fold qualities within the believer in equal proportions. For example, a person may naturally exhibit a large amount of joy, yet lack kindness or self-control. But when the Holy Spirit produces His fruit within us, each of the nine-fold qualities occurs in equal amounts, because they are combined in one fruit. Therefore the Spirit will not give large amounts of love to one person, and large amounts of faithfulness to another. Out of the nine-fold aspects of the Spirit's fruit, the one we consider to be weakest best indicates the measured amount of the whole fruit which we have allowed the Spirit to produce in us!

## PRINCIPLES OF FRUIT-BEARING

Natural fruit-bearing concerns the production of plant life *"according to its kind"* as designed by God, Genesis 1:11. Hence an apple tree will produced apples, and each apple will contain seeds which if planted will produce more apple trees of the same variety.

Spiritual fruit-bearing concerns the production of godly character. In Matthew 3:8,10, John the Baptist challenged the Jewish leaders to *"bear fruits worthy of repentance"*. He continued to say, *"Every tree which does not bear good fruit is cut down and thrown into the fire."* Jesus continued John's theme in Matthew 7:15–20, stating, *"By their fruits you shall know them"*, referring to false prophets, and explaining that *"a bad tree bears bad fruit"* but *"a good tree cannot bear bad fruit"*.

All this concerns good or bad character; however, God's way is not that we should try to be good people by sheer dint of human effort, because in reality, the more we try the more we fail! Jeremiah says, *"The heart is deceitful above all things and desperately wicked; who can know it?"* (Jeremiah 17:9). Rather, God's plan is that we first repent of (turn away from) our sins and then receive from Him a new heart! Ezekiel promised this very thing, that God would replace the old, godless, hardened heart with a new, sensitive one which could yield good fruit, Ezekiel 11:19–20, 18:31. We may think that the Lord Jesus was uncharacteristically harsh against the Jewish leaders when He said, *"Either make the tree good, and its fruit good, or else make the tree bad and its fruit bad; for a tree is known by its fruit. O generation of vipers! How can you being evil, speak good things? For out of the abundance of the heart the mouth speaks. A good man out of the good treasure of his heart brings forth good things, and an evil man out of the evil treasure brings forth evil things"* (Matthew 12:33–35). Just as a bad tree cannot produce good fruit, so a person who is unsaved and unredeemed in heart cannot display good character in the way God desires. At best he can only offer a poor humanistic imitation.

### The unsaved old nature

The old, sinful nature referred to in Ephesians 4:22 produces fruit called *"the works of the flesh"*, some of which are enumerated in Galatians 5:19: *"Adultery, fornication, impurity, lustfulness, idolatry, witchcraft, hatred, quarrelling, jealousy, anger, selfish ambition, divisions, heresies, envy, murder, drunkenness, wild partyings and similar things."* Paul asks a question in Romans 6:20–21: *"When you were slaves of sin . . . what fruit did you then have in the things of which you are now ashamed?"* Then he states in Romans 7:5: *"When we were in the flesh [old nature], the sinful passions . . . were at work in our members to bear fruit to death."* On a positive note he asks, in Romans 6:22, *"Now being set free from sin, and being slaves of God, you have your fruit unto holiness, and the end, everlasting life."*

### The saved new nature

Those saved by Jesus Christ, have been given a new heart which is able to bear the fruit of the Spirit. 2 Corinthians 5:17 says, *"If anyone is in Christ, he is a new creation; old things have passed away; behold, all things have become new."* Christians become new persons. They are not the same anymore, the old has gone and a new life has begun! But this is not always immediately apparent, so it is often asked, "Does a Christian have two natures?" Or "Is a Christian a Jekyll and Hyde character?" This concept is wrong, and Tom Marshall sees the old and new natures as two alternative computer programmes.[18] By an act of our will we have the ability to discard the old programme, and to accept the new programme. The table below shows the world of difference between the old and new natures:

| OLD NATURE PROGRAMME | NEW NATURE PROGRAMME |
| --- | --- |
| Lost in sin – Matthew 18:11 | Found and saved – Luke 19:10; John 17:12 |
| Hostile to God – Romans 8:7–8 | Loves the Lord – John 14:15 |
| Works of the flesh – Galatians 5:19 | Produces fruit of the Spirit – Galatians 5:22–23 |
| Results in death – Romans 8:6,13; Galatians 5:21 | Results in life – Romans 8:6,13; Galatians 6:8 |

Delete the old programme, don't leave it on the hard disk of your life, where inadvertently it can be read, or where temptation can incite you to consider it again. The New Testament uses decisive words about destroying the old nature programme: We crucify it (Galatians 5:24); we put it to death (Colossians 3:5); we take it off and throw it away, like a filthy garment (Ephesians 4:22; Colossians 3:8–9); we reckon ourselves dead to sin (Romans 6:11); we do not let sin reign, nor obey it, nor let it have power over us (Romans 6:12–14); we do not live out the sinful nature (Romans 8:1,4); we keep our bodies under control (1 Corinthians 9:27).

If the old nature was no longer available, Christians would rarely, if ever, sin; but experience and Scripture shows that we do sin (1 John 1:8, 10). However, if we concentrate on *fighting* the old nature, we shall become preoccupied with it, and we shall never win! Rather, if we concentrate on *"walking in the Spirit"* then we shall *"not fulfil the lust of the flesh"* (Galatians 5:16; Romans 8:13).

# THE PRODUCTION OF FRUIT

What a relief to find that Scripture nowhere says that we must produce fruit! The expression *"fruit of the Spirit"* means the fruit which the Spirit produces. Jesus explained it in John 15:1–8. He states that He personally is the true vine, and His Father is the vine-dresser (gardener), and that we believers are the branches. He emphasised the need for the branches to remain attached to the vine, which makes indisputable sense. If a branch is broken off it will never show fruit, or what fruit may have partially grown will wither and die. Now the crunch! Six times Jesus refers to branches that bear fruit. The NT word for *bear* is *phero* (φερω) which simply means 'carry'. Our responsibility is to remain in Christ, and to carry the fruit He produces in us.

*Our purification – pruning*

Jesus also explained that the vine will produce more fruit if the branches are pruned by Father God. Just as there is a season for pruning in the natural world, so there is a time when the Father cuts back our growth with the purpose that our branch will grow stronger and bear more the fruit of godly character. Can you recall events in your life which suggest the Lord was curtailing your activities, or reducing your influence, or cutting you down to size? The wise king in Proverbs warns us to *"keep little in our own eyes"*. God's desire is not that we should be magnified in the sight of others, but that the Spirit's fruit should be most evident in our lives. Expressed differently, the Lord desires that the first thing others see in us is Christ.

We read in Proverbs 3:11–12: *"Do not despise the chastening of the Lord, nor grow weary of His correction, for whom the Lord loves He corrects."* Pruning is part of the Lord's disciplinary action, which occurs even if we have done nothing wrong. Hebrews

12:3–11 deals with this and teaches that God disciplines us because He loves us.

Discipline, chastening, correction and pruning by God are *"for our profit that we may be partakers of His holiness"*. We dislike discipline, it is often hard to bear and appears to put a restriction on our joy, but *"afterward it yields the peaceable fruit of righteousness"*. Paul's testimony in Romans 5:3–5 may be hard for us to identify with, when he says, *"We boast in afflictions, knowing that afflictions produce patience . . ."* James endorses this by declaring, *"Count it all joy when you fall into various trials, knowing that the testing of your faith produces patience."* Peter covers a similar theme, emphasising that trials come to ensure our faith is genuine.

### Our position – in Christ

In John 15 Jesus said, *"Remain in Me, and I will remain in you."* The Amplified Bible, Classic Edition translates 2 Corinthians 5:17 as *"Therefore if any person is [ingrafted] in Christ…"* *Ingrafted* means 'to be attached as part of" and the word is derived from the art of grafting a branch into a stem or root stock. So when we were saved we were grafted into Christ, and emphasis on the word *in* is demonstrated clearly in Ephesians chapter 1: *"in Christ"* verse 1, *"in the heavenly places in Christ"* verse 3, *"in Him"* verse 4, *"in the Beloved"* verse 6, *"in Him"* verse 7, *"in Christ, in Him"* verse 10, *"in Him"* verse 11, *"in Christ"* verse 12, *"in Him"* verse 13.

### Our productiveness – Christ in us

Not only have we been grafted into Christ, Jesus Himself resides in us. Colossians 1:27 speaks about a mystery, *"which is Christ in you, the hope of glory"*. Jesus told His followers, *"you will know that I am in the Father, and you in Me, and I in you."* Jesus prayed for this union in John 17 by using the phrase, *"I in them."* So fruit production hinges on the Christian being in Christ, and Christ being in the Christian! Divine sap flowing through the vine keeps the branches alive and causes them to be fruitful.

## THE PURPOSE OF FRUIT

Jesus said that God is glorified when we bear much fruit. Holy living magnifies the greatness and goodness of God. Christlike character cannot be imitated by an unsaved person or by the devil. Amazingly, some kind of miracles can be imitated by the ungodly, and deceive many, but Christlikeness is possible only for those indwelt by the living Christ and filled with the Holy Spirit. Another purpose of the Spirit's fruit in us is to demonstrate that we are the Lord's followers. Love for each other enables everyone to know we belong to Christ. Love becomes the distinguishing mark between Christians and others. *Agape* love cannot be humanly imitated, and although a meagre show might be made, in a very short time the absence of love will reveal itself.

# CHAPTER SIXTEEN

# THE NINE-FOLD FRUIT OF THE SPIRIT

HERE IS A CHART ITEMISING THE NINE-FOLD FRUIT OF THE Spirit as listed in Galatians 5:22–23.

| THE NINE-FOLD FRUIT OF THE HOLY SPIRIT | | | |
|---|---|---|---|
| UPWARD – in relation to God | love | joy | peace |
| OUTWARD – in relation to others | patience | kindness | goodness |
| INWARD – in relation to self | faithfulness | meekness | self-control |

## LOVE

**NT Greek:** *agape* (αγαπη)

In the New Testament a variety of words are used to describe the different characteristics and depths of what our one English word translates as *"love"*.

**a) Phileo** (φιλεω), which can be translated best as *"brotherly love"* or *"true friendship"* of the deepest kind. It is used by the apostle Peter in John 21:15–17, where Jesus asks Peter if he *agape* loves Him, and in each instance Peter replies that he *phileo* loves Jesus. Then Jesus asks the third time, *"Simon, do you phileo love me?"* Peter was grieved because Jesus came down to Peter's level and questioned his *phileo* love. Peter replied, *"Lord, You know all things. You know I phileo love You."* It would be literalistic, too harsh and far too simplistic to say, "Jesus asks Peter if he loves Him, and Peter replies that he is His friend"! The problem is that our English language, for all its diversity, does not have sufficient words to describe the many different levels of love. In 2 Peter 1:7 the apostle uses the word *philadelphos* (φιλαδελπος) where it is translated as *"brotherly friendship"* or *"brotherly kindness."*

Note an absolute truth here: the depth of brotherly love experienced between men and the Lord Jesus, or indeed between men and men (such as David and Jonathan), or between women and Jesus, does not overlap into sexuality. It is a modern concept to homogenise the various grades of love into one nefarious sexual mess, where lust and love become indistinguishable! The Bible says such a state is reached when God gives people up to vile affections and to a debased mind because they are filled with all unrighteousness and sexual immorality. These people not only do such things but also approve of those practising them! The falling in love type of emotion (which homosexuals often profess) is from the Greek word *eros* (ερος), from which we derive the English word *erotic*. The Greek word for sexual activity is *venus* (ϖενυς). Neither *eros* nor *venus* is found in the New Testament, indicating that *"brotherly love"* contains nothing erotic, sexual or homosexual.

**b) Storgos** (στοργος) describes natural affection, and **philostorgos** (φιλωστοργος) means tender or kindly affection.

This word is suitable for describing family love between parents and children, or indeed between human beings and animals, such as their pet dogs, cats, horses etc. The negative word *astorgos* is used in Romans 1:31 and 2 Timothy 3:3 and is translated *"without natural affection"* by the King James Version.

c) **Agape** (αγαπη) best describes God's love. It is used in 1 John 4:8 and 16, where it says, *"God is love."* *Agape* love describes the attitude of God towards His Son (John 17:26), and for the human race generally (John 3:16; Romans 5:8), and for believers especially (John 14:21). Thus it is best understood as the kind of love which God is, and the kind of love which pours from Him towards others. This is the highest and purest kind of love, which is *"poured into our hearts by the Holy Spirit"* (Romans 5:5) and which the Holy Spirit seeks to instil in us as His precious fruit, *"The fruit of the Spirit is love . . ."* (Galatians 5:22).

Jesus issued a new commandment, that a*gape* love should be the type of love that Christians have for one another (John 13:34). According to 1 Thessalonians 3:12, *agape* love should be shown by Christians to all people! Paul says that all we do should be done with *agape* love.

1 Corinthians 13:4–8 is the familiar chapter which cites many characteristics of love. Paul states that love is greater than faith or hope – because love is eternal; faith will no longer be required one day, when we see the Lord face to face, and hope will no longer exist when all our desires are realised. But love is eternal and will prompt us to serve the Lord throughout time and eternity.

*Agape* love comes from God, as the Holy Spirit pours it into our lives. It is intended to flow from us in three directions:

**Vertically** – towards the Lord, *"we love Him because He first loved us"* (1 John 4:19). But remember the real test of our love for God is our obedience to Him (John 14:15,21–24).

**Horizontally** – towards others, *"Beloved, let us love one another"* (1 John 4:7). The Holy Spirit makes this possible, providing a love deep within that reaches not only to our friends, but also to our enemies (Matthew 5:44). The baptism in the Holy Spirit is sometimes described as a baptism of love, because through it God's love flows from us as a river of blessing for all.

**Inwardly** – towards ourselves, *"love your neighbour as yourself"* says Matthew 19:19, 22:39. The admonition in Ephesians 5:28–29 is that husbands should love their wives as their own bodies because he who loves his wife loves himself. For no one ever hated his own flesh. Similarly, if we do not love ourselves, how can we love others?

## JOY

### NT Greek: *chara* (χαρα)

Joy is part of God's divine nature; it is not merely something the Lord gives. *"In Your presence is fullness of joy"* (Psalm 16:11). *"I will go . . . to God my exceeding joy"* (Psalm 43:4). *"The joy of the Lord is your strength"* (Nehemiah 8:10). *"The kingdom of God is not eating and drinking, but righteousness, peace and joy in the Holy Spirit"* (Romans 14:17). *"Believing, you rejoice with joy inexpressible and full of glory"* (1 Peter 1:8). Jesus said to His disciples, *"These things I have spoken to you, that My joy may remain in you, and that your joy might be full"* (John 15:11), and the apostle John wrote, *"These things we write to you that your joy may be full"* (1 John 1:4).

How is it that so many arrive at church, and leave again, with faces as long as a wet week? When a young lad, John Moore met with a conundrum, that his earliest recollections of church-going concerned his bewilderment that although he might be happy, he had to pretend to be sad! How can this be, when the Scriptures continually exhort us to *"Rejoice in the Lord"*? *"Clap your hands all you peoples! Shout to God with the voice of triumph!"* (Psalm 47:1). When did we last have a good shout in church? Is the Lord surrounded by a seventeenth-century atmosphere of austerity and morbidity? I felt consternation when I first saw a Pentecostal minister and his assistant smiling as they sat on the church platform. Such alarm was falsely imparted to me by the contrived atmosphere of more formal church services, where human dignity replaced the joy of the Lord. In those days we falsely called it reverence! Looking back I see clearly that reverence was another word for deadness.

The enemies of Christ accused Him of many disdainful things, but not one ever said He was boring or that He was depressing. To accuse the Almighty of bleak and daunting dreariness flies in the face of Biblical facts about God. Referring to His creation of planet Earth, we read, *"the morning stars sang together, and all the sons of God shouted for joy"* (Job 38:7). Later, God asks in Jeremiah 2:31, *"Have I been a wilderness to Israel?"* Is the Lord responsible for the mantle of grey sin which covers the earth? Gripped by disease and despair, Job's condition was no laughing matter, but knowing the justice of God, his friend Bildad promised that God would yet *"fill your mouth with laughter and your lips with shouts of joy"*. How can this be? It is simply because God is the fountain source of happiness and joy. The scenario of the whole Bible, from creation and humanity's fall into sin to the revelation of Christ restoring Paradise is ably summed up in Psalm 30:5 which says, *"Weeping may endure for a night, but joy comes in the morning."* The table below illustrates this truth in cosmic terms:

Morbid religion is engineered by the devil; it is the lie about God Himself that has stuck like superglue to the susceptibility of the human psyche. Leaders often rush to justify their own spiritual deadness by exclaiming, "It is not recorded in the Bible that Jesus ever laughed!" Technically that is true, but we find that many

| MORNING OF JOY | NIGHT OF SORROW | MORNING OF JOY |
|---|---|---|
| Creation – Job 38:7 | Fall into sin, losing God's glory Romans 3:23 | Paradise restored Revelation 21:3–4 |

things about Jesus are not recorded in the Bible, which doesn't mean He didn't do them! For example, it is not stated that Jesus ate with His fingers, hugged anyone, or went to the toilet, but to assume He never did any of these things because they are not recorded is begging the question and renders the argument futile.

The Scriptures state that *"Jesus rejoiced in spirit"* (Luke 10:21). Laughter is but the outward expression of inward joy and delight, and the phrase *rejoicing in spirit* indicates a deep well of inner exuberance – the exhilarating zest of the heart.

Spirit-baptised people can experience *"laughing in the spirit"*, when they are filled up so much with the joy of the Lord that it can only be expressed in laughter. I thank God for the experience of a deep persistent bubbling stream of delight in the Lord which at times seems too much to bear! Sarah said, *"God has made me laugh, and everyone who hears about this will laugh with me"* (Genesis 21:6). Psalm 2:4 says, *"He who sits in the heavens shall laugh"* at the petty defiance of humankind.

*Is laughing in the Spirit legitimate?*

A closer look at this subject illustrates how prone we are to lose our scriptural balance, and to offer baloney in place of Bible truth! This example will also illustrate the need for studying the Bible trend on the subject of laughter. Although it is correct to say, "It is not recorded in the Bible that Jesus laughed", it is not correct to say, "Jesus never laughed." The truth of the matter is that we simply don't know if Jesus laughed while He was on earth, and no doctrine can be established from such silence.

However, the Bible does tell us that God laughs! Psalm 2:4: *"The One enthroned in heaven laughs."* Psalm 37:13: *"The Lord laughs at the wicked."* See also Psalm 59:8. He caused Sarah to laugh contagiously (Genesis 21:6). Jesus promised we would laugh, saying, *"Blessed are you who weep now, for you shall laugh"* (Luke 6:21). When Psalm 2 says the *"One enthroned in heaven laughs"*, does it refer solely to Father God, or could it refer to Jesus, the Son of God who sits at the right hand of the majesty on high? Jesus said, *"I and my Father are one"*, so it could be argued reasonably that if God the Father laughs, so does the Jesus the Son. If Father God makes people laugh, then He could very well make Jesus, the perfect Man, laugh too.

The true motive for emphasising that it is not recorded that Jesus laughed is to wrongly implant the idea that laughter is unacceptable. Then, if it is unacceptable, there is no such thing as 'laughing in the Spirit' because it is argued that the Holy Spirit would not encourage an undesirable effect! Some claim that laughing in the Spirit is not induced by the Holy Spirit, but by a worldly or devilish lack of self-control! Observe the following graphic downward slide of some people's reasoning:

1.  It is not recorded that Jesus laughed

2.  Therefore laughing is bad (Ecclesiastes 2:2, 7:3)

3.  Introduce a word to demean the subject – *uncontrollable* laughter

4.  In Galatians 5:22 the fruit of the Spirit includes self-control, not lack of it

5.  Therefore "uncontrollable laughing in the Spirit" cannot be of God

Like an algebraic equation, the logic is fool-proof, except for one thing – the Bible states that God laughs! Surely He who is thrice holy would never engage in something nefarious and which induces lack of control! See how surreptitiously the word *uncontrollable* is introduced to disparage laughing in the Spirit, but since it is God who causes us to laugh, where is the evidence that it is uncontrollable? Why do people think such laughter is uncontrollable? They simply assumes it is, and then proceeds to set against each other two aspects of the Holy Spirit's fruit: *joy* and *self-control*. Unwittingly they set the Holy Spirit against Himself, by polarising two aspects of His fruit! Does the fruit of self-control suppress the other parts of the Spirit's fruit? This type of *"leaning on your own understanding"* has beleaguered the Church for centuries, and does the devil's work for him. Rather, a true Biblical understanding and a more accurate logical slide is this:

1. The Bible says God laughs

2. The Bible says God makes people laugh

3. So laughter is not intrinsically bad

4. We are *"followers of God as dear children"* Ephesians 5:1

5. Therefore we should laugh more often

The character of God's Kingdom is not eating and drinking, but *"righteousness and peace and joy in the Holy Spirit"*. Joy in the Holy Spirit means it is God Himself who administers His joy within us, and what will be the outcome? *"Out of the abundance of the heart the mouth speaks"* and the Lord's implanted joy will lead to various expressions, which includes praise to God, and the ultimate joy indicator – laughter!

Did Jesus lack self-control when He rejoiced in spirit? Does the Lord lack self-control when He sings with the Church, as it says in Hebrews 2:12? Will the Almighty lack self-control when He rejoices over you with gladness and singing, as declared by Zephaniah 3:17? The Hebrew word *rejoice* in this verse is *rinnah*, meaning 'a loud cry'. I can hear S. Michael Houdman advising God, 'Please use self-control, Lord!' His gripe is akin to that of Michal, daughter of Saul and David's wife, who saw King David leaping and dancing before the Lord and despised him in her heart. David's acceptable explanation was, *"It was before the Lord."* The Lord's judgment was that Michal had no children to the day of her death. Barrenness can be a spiritual condition too, Mr Houdman!

Some years ago, I preached a series of messages on the subject of salvation. Each sermon title began with the letter 'F', allowing such subjects as Salvation – The Fall, The Foe, The Favour, The Freedom, The Faith, The Father, and so on. Twenty titles in all, and number ten was 'The Fun', in which I spoke about the pursuit of happiness, quoting Richard Whately who said, "Happiness is no laughing matter!" I mentioned that Christianity includes the serious matter of our eternal destiny, but most of the message examined the joy of the Lord and we concluded that Rev. George Canty summed it up best when he wrote,

> That cold aloofness called for as proper in religion is the product of "the spirit that now works in the children of disobedience." It is the culture of the world, not of Christ. A sober-sided religion is a surrender to the Devil. Pentecost is a challenge to it. Christianity emerged from the Upper Room, not from the top office, Whitehall.[19]

*Joy indicators*

**A glowing face** – Proverbs 15:13: *"A happy heart makes the face cheerful."* 2 Corinthians 3:18: *"And we, with unveiled faces, all reflect the Lord's glory."*

**A singing heart** – Psalm 149:1–6: *"Sing to the Lord a new song . . . sing praises . . . Let them sing aloud on their beds. Let the high praises of God be in their mouth."* Ephesians 5:18–19:

*"Be filled with the Spirit, speaking to one another in psalms and hymns and spiritual songs, singing and making melody in your heart to the Lord."* James 5:13: *"Is anyone cheerful? Let him sing psalms."*

**A divine strength** – Nehemiah 8:10: *"Do not sorrow, for the joy of the Lord is your strength."* Psalm 84:5: *"How happy are those whose strength is in You."*

**A holy laughter** – Genesis 21:6: *"God has made me laugh, and everyone who hears about this will laugh with me."* Luke 6:21: *"Blessed are you who weep now, for you will laugh."*

Tom Marshall writes, "The Bible reveals quite clearly that for man, transcendent joy comes from one experience alone: the experience of a personal encounter with the living God."[20] Tom continues to describe the night he was baptised in the Holy Spirit, "In the depth of my spirit, as I was being prayed for, I touched God the Holy Spirit and there burst up from within me a gushing of pure, ineffable joy ... I laughed for joy, I shouted for joy." Tom states, "Joy, by its very nature, has to be expressed," and he points out the plethora of words found in the Bible, such as *joy, rejoice, gladness, sing, shout, dance, leap, clap, music.* After their Pentecostal experience of the baptism in the Holy Spirit, the early disciples were *"continually filled with joy and with the Holy Spirit"* (Acts 13:52).

*Joy hindrances*

**Forgetfulness** – Deuteronomy 6:12: *"Be careful that you do not forget the Lord."* Psalm 78:11: *"They forgot what He had done, and the wonders he had shown them."* Psalm 103:2: *"Praise the Lord, O my soul, and forget not all His benefits."*

**Discouragement** – doubts and disbelief wreck joy. Ten out of the twelve spies, sent out to report on the Canaan situation, gave an evil report! The report was intrinsically true, but it lacked faith in God. Their report was bathed in doubts and discouragement which made God angry, and their later vain attempt to obey brought defeat, Numbers 13:26–14:25. Consider the disciples on the Emmaus Road, Luke 24:13–27. They had loved the Lord Jesus; they had placed their faith in Him. Now He is dead, although some far-fetched tales of seeing Him alive had been told! When Jesus appeared incognito to them, He asked why they were sad. Doubts and disbelief had discouraged them.

**Unforgiven sin** – In Psalm 32:1–5 the psalmist says how happy is the person whose sins are forgiven; but failing to confess and repent brings spiritual and physical problems. Seeking God's forgiveness enables the Lord to protect His people and surround them *"with songs of deliverance"*. James 5:15–16 says, *"If he has sinned, he will be forgiven. Therefore confess your sins to each other and pray for each other so that you may be healed."*

## PEACE

**NT Greek:** *eirênê* (ειρηνη)

*"The God of peace"* is a title used in Romans 15:33, 16:20; Philippians 4:9; 1 Thessalonians 5:23, and in other places. The phrase *"the Lord of peace"* in 2 Thessalonians 3:16 doubtless refers to the Lord Jesus. Peace describes harmonious relationships between: a) People, Romans 14:19; b) Nations, Luke 14:32; c) Churches, 1 Corinthians 14:33; d) God and people, Acts 10:36; Ephesians 2:17.

*Peace with God*

Romans 5:1: *"Being justified by faith, we have peace with God through our Lord Jesus Christ."* Ephesians 2:14–18: *"He is our peace, who has made both one, and has broken down the middle wall of separation . . . That He might reconcile them both to God in one body through the cross, having putting to death the enmity. And He came and preached peace to those who were afar off and to those who were near. For through Him we both have access by one Spirit to the Father."*

The Lord Jesus Himself is our peace, since by His death He took the blow of separation from God which should have been ours. Isaiah 53:5: *"The punishment that brought us peace was upon Him"* enabling us to enjoy *"peace with God"*. Hence Jesus is the Prince of Peace.

## Peace from God

John 14:27: *"Peace I leave with you. My peace I give to you."* Ephesians 1:2 and Philippians 1:2: *"Grace to you and peace from God our Father and the Lord Jesus Christ."* Colossians 3:15: *"Let the peace of God rule in your hearts, to which also you are called in one body; and be thankful."*

The angel choir sang significant words at the birth of Christ our Saviour, Luke 2:14: *"Glory to God in the highest, and on earth peace, goodwill toward men!"* Here was a declaration of peace flowing from God to the world, and which would become *"peace with God"* to all who received Christ as Lord and Saviour.

## Peace with men

### Peace with other Christians

The Scriptures show how Christians should live in peace with each other. We are told to pursue peace with everyone (Hebrews 12:14). We are told to pursue peace with others (2 Timothy 2:22). 1 Peter 3:11 quotes the Old Testament scripture from Psalm 34:14: *"Seek peace and pursue it."* In three of the above verses, the word *pursue* is used – we should chase after peace and hunt it down.

## Peace with unsaved people

Romans 12:18: *"If it is possible, as much as depends on you, live peaceably with all men."* This verse instructs us to do our part towards peace. Those who know the Lord may well live peaceably with each other, but those who do not have faith are often influenced by belligerent and bellicose spirits which can render peace impossible between you and them. In His Sermon on the Mount, recorded by Matthew, Jesus said: *"Blessed are the peacemakers, for they shall be called sons of God."*

Just as the joy which the Spirit produces is not dependent on congenial outer circumstances, so the Spirit's peace *"passes all understanding"*, being produced in us often in direct contra-distinction with outward events. It is especially present in the midst of trials and troubles.

### *Tranquillity*

The fruit of the Spirit called peace conveys the meaning of tranquillity. Great calmness and the assurance of safety is expressed by King David in Psalm 4:8 who says, *"I will lie down in peace and sleep, for only you Lord, make me dwell safely."* The Hebrew word for *peace* is Shalom – an all-inclusive word meaning complete wholeness or the total well-being of a person. Jesus uses the word *peace* (NT Greek: *eirênê*) when greeting the disciples after His resurrection. They were bewildered by Mary Magdalene's testimony that she had seen the Lord alive and heard Him speak. They were fearful of the Jewish authorities who caused their leader to be killed, and who may now be planning to arrest them, so they met together secretly behind locked doors. But locked doors could not prevent the Lord's presence, and appearing to them, Jesus allays their fears and doubts with the greeting, *"Peace to you."*

## Harmony

Harmony is the maintenance of unity and agreement as used by Paul in 1 Thessalonians 5:13: *"Be at peace among yourselves."* Christian believers today often take a more lax approach to the subject of agreement, stating, "We may not all agree, but we can agree to differ!" Such human wisdom makes good sense, but it can be used as a cop-out when it refers to Biblical doctrine. Nonetheless, the Bible exhorts believers to be at peace, even if they do disagree. Lack of harmony among Christians arises from concentrating on ourselves, or on our viewpoint, rather than on the Lord Himself. Isaiah 26:3 says, *"You will keep him in perfect peace whose mind is steadfast, because he trusts in You."*

## Security

Feeling safe issues from a relaxing trust in the Lord, who is the *"author of peace"*, as we are told in 1 Corinthians 14:33. Significantly this verse follows on from a discourse about tongues and prophecies in the Church – it reassures us that such manifestations of the Spirit are granted by the *"God of peace"*, with the intention of bringing and sustaining peace in the Church. The prayer of Saint Francis of Assisi is remarkable in that the first line is laid as the foundation on which all the other lines are built:

> Lord, make me an instrument of your peace.
> Where there is hatred, let me sow love;
> where there is injury, pardon;
> where there is doubt, faith;
> where there is despair, hope;
> where there is darkness, light;
> and where there is sadness, joy.
>
> O Divine Master, grant that I
> may not so much seek to be consoled as to console;

to be understood as to understand;

to be loved as to love.

For it is in giving that we receive;

it is in pardoning that we are pardoned;

and it is in dying that we are born to eternal life. Amen.

## Symbols of peace

a.  Father God is a LOVING Person, John 3:16–17

b.  Jesus is a LAMB, John 1:29. The NT Greek word is *probaton*, a strong male lamb

c.  Holy Spirit is a DOVE, Matthew 3:16

d.  Believers are LITTLE LAMBS, Luke 10:3. The NT Greek word is *arnion*, which are new-born lambs

# LONGSUFFERING

## NT Greek: *makrothumia* (μακροθυμια)

This is the fourth characteristic of the fruit of the Spirit. The New King James Version rightly translates the NT Greek word *makrothumia* as *longsuffering* – *Makros* = *long* and *thumos* = *temper*, denoting *patient endurance;* the ability to endure persecution and withstand ill-treatment. Some translators use the modern word *patience* in place of longsuffering, but we need to understand that the NT Greek word for *patience* is *hupomone* (υπομοɯη), as used in 2 Thessalonians 3:5 where *"the patience of Christ"* is mentioned. Interestingly, the New International Version translates this text as *"Christ's perseverance."* This alters the meaning radically. *"The patience of Christ"* refers to His waiting until all evil is subdued at His return to earth, while *"Christ's perseverance"* only makes sense if it refers to His earthly life in withstanding the opposition of sinners. At least you can see that using different English words can be helpful, but also it can lead us further away from the meaning of the Greek text. To make the subject clearer, when *makrothumia* is used in the Scriptures below, we include it in bold type as *longsuffering*.

### Longsuffering of God

Romans 2:4: *"do you despise the riches of His . . . **longsuffering**?"* The longsuffering of God speaks of how He endures the sinful wickedness of humankind through countless centuries. Would you despise this?

### Longsuffering of Abraham

Hebrews 6:15 says: *"After he had **long suffered**, Abraham obtained what was promised."* The use here of *makrothumia* indicates that Abraham struggled to cope with the many childless years of his life.

### Longsuffering in trials

Hebrews 6:12 mentions those who through faith and ***longsuffering*** inherit the promises. Waiting for the promised purposes of God to be fulfilled in our lives, or in the world generally, is not just a matter of patience, but of persevering through the difficult days of trial spawned by godless people. James 5:7 says, *"Be **longsuffering** therefore brothers until the presence of the Lord. Behold the farmer awaits the precious fruit of the earth, **suffering long** over it until he receives the early and latter rain."* James also calls us to consider *"the afflictions and **longsuffering** of the prophets"*. Jeremiah suffered long the insults and abuse of his hearers, but he didn't give up heralding God's word to the nation.

### Longsuffering others

The NIV translates 1 Thessalonians 5:14 as, *"be patient with everyone"*, but it is more accurately *"be longsuffering with all"*. In other words, endure others who are difficult; put up with their animosities or other annoying traits. Patience can be waiting for something wonderful, but longsuffering is connected with things unpleasant. It enables us to put up with difficult people, harsh trials, distressing pressures and the devil himself! But it is the Holy Spirit who produces this fruit within us. It is the Holy Spirit who enables us to suffer long those conditions which normally we would shun. Without the Holy Spirit's input we would rarely display longsuffering; rather we would say, "Enough is enough," and with indignation we would endeavour to change the situation or to remove ourselves from it!

There is a connection between longsuffering and bearing our cross. It is repeatedly recorded that Jesus said, *"He who does not take his cross and follow Me, is not worthy of Me."* We can be guilty of wanting the crown but not the cross! Appreciate that the Holy Spirit, our Comforter, provides us with the fruit of longsuffering which enables us to bear our cross daily. James 1:2 says, *"Count it all joy when you fall into various trials, knowing that your faith is approved by endurance."* We generally agree that faith is easy when all is well, but more difficult to maintain in the midst of trials. But it is right at that point that the Spirit's fruit of longsuffering allows us to endure through the tough times; to accept them joyfully and even boast about them, just as Paul and his companions boasted in afflictions, knowing that they produce patience. The latter part of Colossians 1:10–11 says, *"empowered by His mighty glory to all endurance and longsuffering with joy."* Once again *endurance* and *longsuffering* is linked with *joy!* Such traits are possible only by the fruit of the Spirit: *"Love, joy, peace, longsuffering . . ."* The many facets of this single fruit work together in glorious harmony, enabling the Christian's character to develop more and more into Christlikeness.

Before we leave this particular fruit of the Spirit, a point of clarification about Job is required. James 5:11 is often translated *"the patience of Job"* but the NT word is *hupomeno*, meaning 'endurance'. *Hupomeno* is not patience or longsuffering. The text should better read, *"You have heard of the endurance of Job."* Many have pointed out that Job wasn't very patient, as probably no one would be in his situation; but he did bear all the pains, both mental and physical, without losing his faith in God – that's endurance!

## KINDNESS

**NT Greek:** *chrestotes* (χρηστοτας)

This word is rendered *gentleness* in the Authorised Version, but this is a mistake which has been corrected in most modern translations, including the NKJV, NIV and NLT. This Greek word is used as a noun, a verb and an adjective, and in each case is best translated with *"kind"*, *"kindness"*, *"kindly"*. It describes *goodness of heart*, and *a gracious character and attitude*.

Ungodly persons rarely, if ever, carry this quality. Even born-again Christians sometimes fail to manifest it. For example, those from differing denominations are often unable to deal *kindly* with each other. This is because humanly we cannot attain to kindness when dealing with others who disagree with us, or with those on another wavelength! But blessed be the Lord God, who through the work of His Holy Spirit is able to produce in us qualities which would otherwise be absent.

### Jesus and his yoke

The adjective *chrestos* is used to describe the yoke of Jesus. *"My yoke is kind,"* He says. His yoke speaks of a disciplined life of obedience to Him; of submission to His service and will. It speaks of companionship and cooperation in working together with Him. All this is *kind*, it springs from a relationship with the

Lord Jesus which is itself kind, gracious and pleasant. Your link with Him and your spiritual connection to Him will not result in stress. If you are overburdened, weighed down, in heaviness of heart, under a cloud or in distress, be sure to know that it is not the Lord who has put these things upon you. Other factors are responsible, since Christ is the One who can relieve you: *"Come to Me, all who labour and are weary, and I will give you rest. Take upon you My yoke and learn from Me because I am meek and lowly in heart, and your souls will find rest; for My yoke is kind and My burden is light."*

## Christ's life

Ephesians 4:30–32 instructs us about godly ways. On the negative side the content of this chapter implies that if we live in a depraved way we shall grieve the Holy Spirit of God, but on the positive side of things, we should be kind to one another, tender-hearted, forgiving one another, as God in Christ forgave us. This exhortation runs on into a conclusion in chapter 5, stating that we should be imitators of God and walk in love, as also Christ loved us, and gave Himself for us as a sweet-smelling offering and sacrifice to God. In other words, by the way we live we should permeate a fragrant odour of Christlikeness. However, such a fragrance does not automatically arise because we copy Jesus, or simply mimic what He did. Rather, it comes when we allow the Spirit to anoint us and produce His fruit within.

Peter asks if we have tasted the kindness of the Lord. Think for a moment about how kind Jesus was: dealing with Zacchaeus; with the woman caught in adultery; with Martha and Mary; with little children as they sat on His knee; with the sick and suffering, the hungry and the needy; with Jairus, whose daughter had just died; with the woman who touched the hem of His garment; with the prostitute who washed His feet; with the widow at the Temple treasury; with Mary on the resurrection morning; with two disciples on the Emmaus Road; with Thomas and Peter after Jesus had risen from the dead; with Saul on the Damascus Road. The Lord exuded *kindness* wherever He went, and the precious Holy Spirit of God seeks always to produce the same fruit in us.

## New wine and old wine

In Luke 5:39 we read, *"No one after drinking old wine desires new; for he says, 'The old is kind.'"* As far as I understand it, new wine may not be fully fermented; it is certainly not matured, and can taste bitter or have a sharp edge to it. But a fully matured old wine contains a mellowness, a sweetness, a fragrance and a smoothness which is kind to the palate. I suggest that the early Church experienced the old wine of the Holy Spirit. But as the centuries passed, a new wine was sought where Western and Eastern churches wanted dominance and desired to rule. New wine manufactured during the Middle Ages was offered, but from the Reformation onwards the Lord began to turn the churches back to the Biblical old wine. It is a pity if some today fail to see that *"the old is better"*.

## An illustration of kindness

I was making my way along some of the small country roads of Herefordshire, when I came to a complicated junction, and was unsure which way to go. I opted for straight on, but soon realised this was a mistake, and I needed to find a place to turn around. Then I saw a house in the distance, on its own by the roadside.

As I approached, I saw the driveway gates open of this medium-sized property. But I saw also on the wall by the driveway entrance a notice which read: "Private Property – No

Turning Here." Eventually I was able to turn in a farmyard much further on. I thought to myself, "Why would people put such an unhelpful and unfriendly notice at their entrance?" So I chatted to the Lord about it, and said, "If ever I own a house with a driveway entrance, I will put up a notice: "Private Property – You May Turn Here with Pleasure." Which of these two notices best express *kindness?* There is every chance that the people who owned the house in Herefordshire were unsaved; if that was so, they demonstrated their stark inability to show kindness, but without difficulty they ably expressed their selfishness!

Kindness is an inner quality of the heart, it is kindly disposition. Marvellously, when kindness is inside us it will come out in attitude, words and action.

## GOODNESS

### NT Greek: *agathousune* (αγαθουσυνη)

While kindness is an *inward* attitude of the heart, goodness is the *outward* expression of it. If *chrestotes* is kindly disposition, then *agathousune* is kindly activity. This word is used only four times in the Bible.

**Romans 15:14:** *"filled with goodness."* Paul is confident that the Christians in Rome are full of goodness. This confirms that in Christ, and by the power of the Holy Spirit producing His fruit within, we can be good – indeed, full of goodness! We have all met people like that. They stand out in stark contrast with the ungodly. Against the dark backdrop of rampant evil across our world today, there shines many of God's children who are full of goodness. Thank You, Lord!

**Galatians 5:22:** *"The fruit of the Spirit is . . . goodness."* Included in this list of Holy Spirit character fruit, we conclude that this type of goodness is something we are not naturally born with. It is not of human origin. It is not the product of human effort or the sheer dint of human will. It is the fruit of the Holy Spirit, and it is produced in us only by Him.

**Ephesians 5:9:** *"The fruit of the Spirit is in all goodness and righteousness and truth."* Although this text somewhat mirrors Galatians 5:22, marvellously it tells us other things. It infers that a good person must also be a righteous and truthful person. Think about it this way: have you ever known a good person who leads a wicked life, where righteousness, respectability, uprightness and virtue are absent? Similarly, have you ever known a good person who tells lies, and in whom truth does not dwell? We have touched upon an inappropriate mismatch, between goodness and its antithesis. Good people do not habitually live wickedly nor constantly tell lies.

1 John 3:9 is an interesting text, which simply translated says, *"Whoever is born of God does not sin because His seed remains in him; and He cannot sin because he has been born of God."* Does that mean that the born-again Christian is incapable of sinning? We know many born-again people who have done wrong things; they have sinned, if only in minor ways. The reason we do not take these words at face value is that they would be contradicted by another statement written by John: *"If we say we have no sin, we deceive ourselves and the truth is not in us."* The conclusion is that in 1 John 3:9 John is saying, *"Whoever is born of God does not habitually sin because His seed remains in him; and He cannot* **habitually** *sin because he has been born of God."* That makes good sense, and fits with the rest of the Scriptures.

**2 Thessalonians 1:11:** *"fulfil the good pleasure of His goodness"* is a literal translation, but this is a difficult verse to turn from NT Greek into English, as the following renditions show:

> Darby translation: *"[the] good pleasure of [his] goodness"*
>
> Wycliffe: *"fulfill all the will of his goodness"*
>
> Phillips: *"he will affect in you all his goodness desires to do"*

Good News: *"May he fulfill by his power all your desire for goodness"*

The Amplified Bible: *"[His] every gracious purpose of goodness"*

American Standard Version: *"and fulfil every desire of goodness"*

New King James: *"and fulfill all the good pleasure of His goodness"*

New International Version: *"he may bring to fruition your every desire for goodness"*

What filters down from these is the desire for God's goodness to be effective in our lives and fulfilled in us. The only way we can demonstrate His goodness in our lives is through the Spirit's fruit. It seems that goodness can go a step further than kindness, in that goodness can rebuke and discipline for the well-being of others. Goodness is strong to correct as well as to bless, yet it corrects graciously. The goodness of Jesus tackled head-on the hypocrisy of the Pharisees and Sadducees. Pulling no punches, the Lord gave graphic illustrations of their pride and their errors, and copiously warned them of the consequences of their deeds and of God's judgment. It was also Christ's intrinsic goodness that warned others to avoid the teaching and hypocrisy of the Jewish rulers.

Psalm 145:9 says, *"The LORD is good to all"* and Jesus confirmed that God causes the sun to rise on the evil and the good, and sends rain on the righteous and on the unrighteous. James 1:17 tells us that every good and perfect gift is from above, coming down from the Father. Even the godless enjoy God's goodness in the benefits of a created universe. Think of the food they eat, the joys of friendship, the means of reproductive procreation, the delight of scented flowers, the singing of the birds, the majesty of a landscape and the setting sun. These good gifts are enjoyed by all people, whatever their character.

## Godliness and goodness

These two cannot be disassociated. Godliness relies on our relationship with God and goodness concerns our relationship with others. The table below shows some of the connections:

| GODLINESS | GOODNESS |
|---|---|
| RELATIONSHIP WITH GOD – SALVATION | RELATIONSHIP WITH OTHERS – SERVICE |
| Genesis 3:9 "Where are you?" | Genesis 4:9 "Where is your brother?" |
| Luke 10:27 "Love the Lord your God" | Luke 10:27 "Love your neighbour" |

Paul's first letter was written to the Galatians about AD55, in which he presents four significant phrases:

**Galatians 5:16:** *"Walking in the Spirit"*. This refers to the way we live, how we conduct our lives. It involves both the inner state of our hearts and the outward actions of our bodies. Walking in the Spirit means keeping close to the Lord, manifesting His fruit and being willing to operate His gifts, and do His will.

**Galatians 5:18:** *"Led by the Spirit"*. This means the Holy Spirit guides, prompts and directs. He *leads*, we *follow*. Two classic examples in Scripture are firstly where the believers ministered to the Lord and fasted, and *"the Holy Spirit said . . ."* The Spirit gave directions for Barnabas and Saul to be sent out on mission. The next example is about a mission party who were *"forbidden by the Holy Spirit to preach the word in Asia. After they had come to Mysia, they tried to go into Bithynia, but the Spirit did not permit them"*. Paul, Silas and Timothy were not permitted to go in certain directions by the Holy Spirit. They could have disobeyed and struggled on in their own strength, but that way little would be accomplished for the Kingdom of God. If they obeyed, they would find that the Lord had already prepared the way for them into Macedonia in Europe!

**Galatians 5:22–23:** *"Fruit of the Spirit".* The nine-fold fruit of Christian character, produced in us by the Spirit. This is what we are now considering.

**Galatians 5:25:** *"Live in the Spirit".* This is more than action (walking), it is more than guidance (led), it is more than character (fruit), it is living, abiding, remaining, enclosed in the Holy Spirit's presence and Person. Paul says, *"If we live in the Spirit, let us also walk in the Spirit"* (Galatians 5:25 NKJV). Living in Him allows the fullness of His Being to be expressed through us – enabling us to *"do good to all".*

# FAITHFULNESS

## NT Greek: *pistis* (πιστις)

The NT Greek word *pistis* is rightly translated *"faith"* or *"faithfulness".* If faith is the tree, then faithfulness is the fruit. Faithfulness is the product of one who has faith, so the fruit of faithfulness describes qualities and attributes arising from faith itself. In Scripture, fullness of faith is always in God Himself and in His Word, especially His written Word (the Bible) but also His spoken word through the Holy Spirit, including words of wisdom or knowledge and prophecies. Faithfulness involves reliability, integrity, fidelity, loyalty, honesty and sincerity.

### The faithfulness of God

The faithfulness of God is seldom questioned, but it is often not understood. Primarily God is faithful to what He says, to all He has promised, to all He has stated and caused to be written.

Hence, we believe the Bible. Born-again believers accept the Bible as God's word – those things He wants us to know about Himself, about ourselves and about the cosmos and life. They do not accept that the Bible merely contains the word of God, or that God has left it to scholars to decipher and decide which parts are His word! Jesus Christ is called the *"Word of God"* (John 1:1,14; Hebrews 4:12–13), that is why we believe Him personally, all He is, all He said and did. If the Bible is God's written Word, then Jesus, the Son is God, is God's Living Word.

For these reasons we implicitly trust all the promises of God – what He has promised, He will perform. We believe in the face of any opposition, whether scientific, practical, personal or factual. To illustrate this, consider the Jewish nation of Israel. God gave the land of Canaan to Abraham, Isaac, Jacob (later named Israel, by God) and his twelve sons, who became heads of the tribes of Israel. God warned He would scatter Israel throughout the world if they forsook Him, but He also promised to bring them back again to their land. Israel indeed returned to their God-given land, and the modern state of Israel was set up in 1948. Between the scattering of Israel and her restoration has been almost 2,000 years!

During that period, sceptics demonstrated the impossibility of Israel returning to her land. Atheists used God's promise (to restore Israel) to prove His Word is false! But all have been silenced because God has done what He promised. Now, we may not like the practical outcome, but I would say this to everyone who opposes Israel: accept them as God's covenant people; accept that all the land of Israel is theirs by divine decree; treat them respectfully so that God can bless you; reject the false invention that Ishmael (not Isaac) was the inheritor of the promises made to Abraham. By doing this God will bless you.

Look at these amazing scriptures about the Lord's faithfulness:

Deuteronomy 7:9: *"The faithful God."*

Lamentations 3:23: *"Great is Your faithfulness."*

In Isaiah 11:5 He wears *"the sash of faithfulness".*

Romans 3:3: *"Will their unbelief destroy the faithfulness of God?"*

1 Corinthians 10:13: *"God is faithful"*

1 John 1:9: *"He is faithful and just to forgive us our sins and to cleanse us."* 1 Thessalonians 5:24: *"He who calls you is faithful, who also will do it."*

Hebrews 10:23: *"He who promised is faithful."*

The Name of Christ in Revelation 19:11 is *"Faithful and True".*

2 Corinthians 1:18: *"As God is faithful, our word to you was not Yes and No. For the Son of God, Jesus Christ, who was preached among you by us . . . was not Yes and No, but in Him was Yes. For all the promises of God in Him are Yes, and in Him Amen, to the glory of God through us."*

## *The faithfulness of believers*

George Canty said that faithfulness is often interpreted as being in a rut and sticking there! Little or nothing may be taking place in a church or in a believer's life for years, but he hangs in there, and that is often considered to be faithfulness! "I Shall Not Be Moved" is his favourite song – and he isn't moved, either by the church, the sermons or by the Holy Spirit! He sticks in the same place without complaint. There is no movement, and there is no life! Some might say, "Well, at least he's faithful," by which they relegate a fruit of the Spirit to the lowest common denominator concerning the things of God! This scenario is no more a reflection of the fruit of the Spirit than Ezekiel's dry bones. Jesus said He has come to give us abundant life. God sees the faithful of the land, that they may dwell with Him. We experience a powerful dynamic when we live with the Almighty, as His Spirit He touches our lives. The faithfulness produced by the Spirit is totally pragmatic – it carries a practical outcome.

### Faithfulness to truth

We know little about Gaius, but John the apostle wrote him a letter, and commended him for his faithfulness. Here was active faithfulness enabling Gaius to remain doctrinally true to God's word, unlike Diotrephes.

### Faithfulness to others

Once more Gaius is commended for his spiritual and practical help to others. *"Dear friend, you are faithful in what you do for the brothers, and for strangers"* (3 John 5–6). Here faithfulness is linked to love, showing how the nine-fold fruit of the Spirit works in harmony in a person's life.

### Faithfulness and blessing

Proverbs 28:20: *"A faithful man will abound with blessings."* An unfaithful man will not be so blessed.

### Faithfulness and suffering

Philippians 1:29 says *"For to you it has been granted on behalf of Christ, not only to believe in Him, but also to suffer for his sake."* Remaining faithful when persecuted means not losing your faith in God, which thousands have retained down the centuries. The opposite of faithfulness is told by Jesus in Luke 8:13, where those who received the word believe for a while, but then fall away during trials.

*Faithfulness and loyalty*

Matthew 25:21: *"Well done, good and faithful servant."* This parable teaches us to be loyal to God, also to friends, family and employers.

*Faithfulness and consistency*

Luke 9:62 says *"No one, having put his hand to the plough and looking back, is fit for the kingdom of God."* Faithfulness allows us to keep going, looking ahead, unlike Lot's wife who looked back at Sodom, or the mixed multitude with Israel in the desert who looked back to their days in Egypt and wanted to give up. Faithfulness to God, to others and to myself, is summed up in Galatians 6:7–10 about sowing and reaping: *"Let us not lose heart while doing good, for in due season we shall reap and not fail."*

## MEEKNESS

### NT Greek: *prautês* (πραυτης)

The NT Greek word *prautês* is translated by the word *"gentleness"* in most English versions, including the NKJV and NIV, but that is a pity. It might be popularly acceptable to use the more modern word *gentleness* in place of the archaic word *meekness*. But it makes for bad exegesis, as we shall see. At least six English translations (Authorised Version, Darby, Geneva Bible, Jubilee Bible 2000, Orthodox Jewish Bible and Young's Literal Translation) retain the word *meekness*. The Amplified Bible says, *"Gentleness (meekness, humility)"* and the Good News puts *humility*. So we'll need to sort this out!

*Meekness is different from gentleness*

The Bible uses both words, and gentleness is emphasised as much as meekness. The NT Greek word for gentleness is *epiekês*

– different altogether from meekness. Both words are used as adjectives by Paul in 2 Corinthians 10:1: *"We beseech you through the meekness (prautêtos) and gentleness (epiekês) of Christ . . ."* These are two separate words, and they have a separate and distinctive meaning. The table below clarifies the issue and shows the intrinsic difference between meekness and gentleness:

| MEEKNESS | GENTLENESS |
|---|---|
| NT GREEK – *prautês* | NT GREEK – *epiekês* |
| INWARD ATTITUDE | OUTWARD ACTION |
| EXAMPLES: Jesus was meek – 2 Corinthains 10:1 Moses was meek – Numbers 12:3 | EXAMPLES: Jesus was gentle – 2 Corinthians 10:1 Paul was gentle – 1 Thessalonians 2:7 |

The table indicates a most important difference between these two words. Meekness describes an *inner* quality of heart, an *inner* condition of mind and spirit. Gentleness describes *outward* action which can be seen and witnessed by others.

*What the NT Greek word prautês does not mean*

**Outward behaviour.** This can be mimicked and appear congenial, while inside the person can retain vicious motives; like the happy bandit who laughs while jocundly saying, "I think I have to kill you!"

**Our treatment of others.** It is possible to treat others cordially, but with hidden motives; like the man who fusses over the elderly lady in the hope of inheriting her estate! That is not meekness!

**A natural disposition of timidity.** Some men are more like mice, but their character is not meek. They may hold resentments and harbour revenge against others, somewhat like Dickens' Uriah Heep! Unlike him, God has not given us a spirit of fear (timidity, cowardice), but of power and of love and of a sound mind (2 Timothy 1:7).

**Weakness or faintheartedness.** Meekness often suggests *timidity* arising from lack of courage, but this is not what *prautēs* means. W.E. Vine says, "The meekness manifested by the Lord and commended to the believer is the fruit of power."[21]

*Examples of meekness*

### Moses

We read that Moses was very meek, more than all men. This was said after Moses had been attacked by Aaron and Miriam (his brother and sister). They attacked him for marrying a Cushite woman (a Gentile). How did Moses react to this? He could have done a number of things, such as:

a. Gain support from others, to back his cause and outwit his brother and sister.

b. Go crying on other people's shoulders, seeking sympathy and comfort.

c. Complain to God about his difficulties, pains and rejection by his family members.

d. Justify himself, by stating the situation which brought about his marriage to Zipporah.

e. Attack Aaron and Miriam, in an endeavour to subdue them.

In fact, Moses did none of these things. Being meek in heart and attitude, he left it to God to vindicate him, and when Miriam was struck with leprosy, straight away the meek Moses prayed for her healing. So you can see that meekness is an inner quality of character which harbours no malice, seeks no revenge and demands no redress.

## Paul

The apostle tells us to speak evil of no one; be gentle *(epiekês)*, showing all meekness *(prautês)* to all men. I would suggest that if the Spirit has produced meekness in your heart, generally it will be expressed in outward gentleness in your dealings with others. Paul wrote to the Galatians about how to treat believers who get it wrong and sin, saying if a man is overtaken in some trespass, you who are spiritual should restore him in a spirit of meekness *(prautês)*, considering yourself in case you also are tempted. Paul also advises Timothy to deal with people in meekness *(prautês)* correcting them, when they come with foolish arguments and stand in opposition. In 1 Thessalonians 2:7 Paul does not use the word *meekness* but rather *gentleness*, because he describes the outward conduct of himself and his companions towards the Thessalonian converts. He says, *"We were gentle among you, like a nurse caring for her little children."* He continues to say they were willing to impart not only the gospel, but their lives! Here is the opposite of the cult leader who uses his dominance and power to manipulate and control others.

## The Lord Jesus

Our Saviour is the supreme example of meekness. He said, *"I am meek and humble in heart"* and *"Blessed are the meek, for they shall inherit the earth."*

The inner meekness of Christ's heart is amply demonstrated throughout His life, including the time He was approaching the cross: by His washing the disciples' feet; in Gethsemane as He submitted to His Father's will; in His treatment of Judas, His betrayer; by taking time to heal Malchus during the skirmish at His arrest. Christ's meekness is beautifully summed up in 1 Peter 2:23 *"When they hurled their insults at him, he did not retaliate; when he suffered, he made no threats. Instead, he entrusted himself to him who judges justly."* (NIV).

### Meekness associated with other qualities

**Meekness and lifestyle** – Ephesians 4:1–2: *"Walk worthily with all humility, meekness, and with longsuffering."*

**Meekness and forgiveness** – Colossians 3:12–13: *"Put on tender mercies, kindness, humility, meekness, longsuffering; bearing with one another, and forgiving one another."*

**Meekness and godliness** – 1 Timothy 6:11: *"O man of God, flee these things and pursue righteousness, godliness, faith, love, endurance, meekness."*

**Meekness and God's word** – James 1:21: *"With meekness receive the engrafted word."*

**Meekness and wisdom** – James 3:13: *"Let him show by good conduct that his works are done in the meekness of wisdom."* That is, "wise meekness".

**Meekness and witnessing** – 1 Peter 3:15: *"Always be ready to give a defence to everyone who asks you a word concerning the hope that is in you, with meekness and fear."* We pastors are particularly tempted towards pride, and easily speak about *my* church, *my* position, *my* preaching and *my* ministry. Also pastors are prone to envy another person's gifts or acclaim. Romans 12:10 which says, *"In honour preferring one another"* is prevented from operating when meekness is absent. Remember that Scripture symbolizes the Holy Spirit as a dove (not a vulture); Jesus as a Lamb (not a wolf); God as a loving Father (not a despot); and believers as sheep or little lambs (not bulls)! All these are symbols of meekness and tenderness.

## SELF-CONTROL

**NT Greek:** *enkrateia* (ενκρατεια)

This word is found in only three verses in the New Testament. It is derived from *kratos,* meaning 'strength'. Its basic idea is the strength and power of mastery over self (self-discipline). Self-control is a fruit of the Holy Spirit, not something we produce ourselves! The secret of success for us is to concentrate on being continually filled with the Holy Spirit to allow His fruit to develop in us. When speaking to Felix, Paul reasoned about righteousness, self-control and the judgment to come. Peter lists a number of qualities which progress from one to the other, telling us to add to our faith goodness, to goodness knowledge, to knowledge self-control, to self-control perseverance, to perseverance godliness, to godliness brotherly kindness, and to brotherly kindness love.

### The world's lack of self-control

Most unbelievers today rarely show self-control; it is a quality which does not fit into their mode of life. They are gripped by passions and dominated by appetites which become stronger than reason. They are addicts.

### Addicted to illegal substances

So many in the world can only exist with the supporting buttress of drugs. Recently I asked a lady, "What is the drug situation in your area?" Nonchalantly she replied, "Oh! Drugs are everywhere, dear, you can't avoid them!" Casually she accepted illegal drugs as normal, and intimated that I (whom she patronisingly called "dear") was the one profoundly out of step with modern life. Discussion revolves around the legalisation of certain drugs, as the US state of Colorado has done with marijuana – the dried leaves and female flowers of the hemp plant, a narcotic hallucinogen used in cigarette form. Since it was legalised, problems with high school students have increased by two-thirds in that area. Is it churlish of me to ask why the principle, "If you can't stop it, legalise it" should not be used for other crimes? Consider road rage, or driving without insurance, or rape and child abuse, or murder. If these cannot be eradicated, should we legalise them?

## Addicted to alcohol

Binge-drinking is another problem the authorities are unable to control. Certain measures, such as raising the price of alcoholic drinks, and having alcohol-free areas in towns, have made little difference. Young people consider getting plastered is the basis of a great night out! Why not stem the supply of alcoholic beverages – or is such an idea totally repugnant to the economics of a business world?

## Addicted to hedonism

Young people particularly are bent on the gratification of the carnal nature, sensual indulgence and satisfaction. Night clubs, strip clubs, lap dancing and pole dancing, all designed to titillate and stimulate the human sex drive. Pornography is a multi-billion dollar industry which perverts those connected with it.

## Addicted to an adrenalin rush

Modern pastimes are designed to thrill – bungee-jumping, jet-skiing, paragliding, theme parks with corkscrew roller coasters, and a host of other machines. Extreme sports have been invented, and many have lost their lives needlessly when things went wrong. These activities confirm that ordinary living is just too boring for anyone unfamiliar with the power of God!

## Addicted to war and terrorism

On-line information in 2016 reported sixty countries involved with war, and 443 militia groups operating in the world. The history of humankind is the history of war. Conflicts are inspired by greed, envy, the acquisition of land or territory, false religion, racial hatred, revenge and petty disagreements, while some wars are perpetrated by ungodly warmongers and thugs.

The main motive behind most fighting is the control of a particular area of land, but some say it is religion which causes wars, as they point to the past troubles in Northern Ireland, or to Muslims who are taught that wherever they live they must get the land for Allah. Getting the land means owning it and ruling it for their god. In fact, territory, religion and wealth are merely some of the many excuses for fighting. The real cause behind it all is godlessness; unforgiven sin which inflames the bellicose nature of fallen human beings. It might be argued that this cannot apply to Muslims, since they fight for their god. But if their god is false and their religion is false, they merely add to their sins, making spurious all that they do, while becoming perfidious satanic agents.

## Addicted to religion

Communism in the nineteenth and twentieth centuries predicted and encouraged the abolition of religion. I agreed with that! However, communism is all but dead, while religion is stronger in the world today than ever. There is such a divergent variety of religions that indeed it would be helpful if they were all eliminated. They cannot all be right, despite the vain attempts to syncretise them. Every effort to harmonise, or show acceptance of all religions, is purely a mistaken human effort to avoid conflict. The word *religion* and *religious* is used only five times in the Bible. Paul refers to Judaism as a religion, but James tells us clearly what true religion is: *"Clean and undefiled religion before God the Father is this: to visit orphans and widows in their distress and to keep oneself from being polluted by the world"* (James 1:27).

Christianity is never described as a religion. Of course you can say it is, just as you can argue that soccer is a religion. Irrespective of definitions, religion is manmade, being comprised of human ideas aimed at betterment. Religion is also a satanic counterfeit for redemption. Jesus did not introduce a new religion, but a new relationship with God. *"As many as received Him to them He gave the right to become children of God"* (John 3:12). The New Testament speaks of God as *"Our Father who is in heaven"* and the use of the words, *Father, children, sons,* establishes the idea of a relationship with God, quite distinct from religion. Manmade religion is as far removed from God's relational redemptive project as chalk is from cheese!

Illegal drugs, alcohol, hedonism, an adrenalin rush, war and terrorism, and spurious religion are all crutches for a disabled world – they are false supports. They are stimulants, intended to make life worth living. They are efforts to prevent boredom. They are inventions to fill an empty, aching void in the human spirit when the Lord is absent. *"There is no peace for the wicked, says my God."* The truth of Isaiah 48:22 is demonstrated daily in the world today.

## The believer's self-control

There is nothing more stimulating and satisfying than meeting with the true and living God. Those who touched Jesus in faith were made perfectly whole, as Mark 6:56 tells us. Whole! Not empty, unsatisfied, depressed and disillusioned with life! Not militant or bent on revenge. Not broken, deranged or infirm. Biblical wholeness means being complete, healthy, strong, restored to the best possible condition. When Jesus Christ touches a human life, that person is transformed to wholeness in body, soul and spirit. Mentally he is clear-thinking and alert; spiritually he is God-conscious; socially he is acceptable, he is harmless as a dove. In reality the previously broken image of God in him is now in the process of being renewed. That person is rapidly becoming the glorious being that God originally intended all members of the human race to be. He is a small reflection of the Lord Jesus Christ – powerful but self-controlled. Self-control is part of the nine-fold fruit of the Holy Spirit, in which each part works together in perfect harmony within the life of the believer, so that the believer's actions and reactions are acceptable to God and to others. The work of the Spirit within us is the restoration of the image of God, which is reflected in the fruit of the Spirit. Consider godly men in the Bible and note their measure of self-control.

*Moses*

We have already considered the meekness of Moses above, but the incident we cited demonstrates not only his meekness but his self-control. Moses' brother and sister considered the fact that Moses had married a non-Israelite woman, and as such was ill-fitted to be the mouthpiece of God. Added to this, they were also jealous of Moses' position in God, and asked whether the Lord speaks only through Moses, or does He speak through them also? (Numbers 12:2) Succinctly we read, *"And the Lord heard it."* We have seen a number of ways in which Moses could have responded, but Moses remained full of self-control by doing nothing precipitous and by saying nothing inflammatory, but rather leaving the matter in God's hands. Then the Lord called them to the Tent of Meeting, where He explained to Miriam and Aaron that He spoke to Moses *"face to face"* and not at a distance as with other persons. The Lord was angry and asked, *"Why then were you not afraid to speak against My servant Moses?"*

## David

Read 1 Samuel 18:8–11 and 19:9–10, where we see that Saul's jealousy provoked him to try to kill David on two occasions by throwing a spear at the young man. In his book, *A Tale of Three Kings*,[22] Gene Edwards points out that David did not respond by throwing the spear back at Saul! There are two occasions when David could have killed Saul, recorded in 1 Samuel chapters 24 and 26, but he would not because he recognised his adversary as the *"anointed of God"*. In fact, David felt bad about cutting off part of Saul's robe! Here is extreme self-control, which flowed from David's relationship with God. Despite his obvious sins, David honoured and trusted God, and committed himself and his situation to the Lord, especially when people tried to harm him. The day comes when Shimei curses David, and Abishai, one of David's mighty warriors, was so indignant he asked permission to kill Shimei. Once again David exercises godly restraint, amazing self-control, and commits the incident into the Lord's hands.

## Jesus

Our Lord and Saviour is the supreme example of One Who exercises self-control. This is seen particularly during His trial before the Jewish Sanhedrin. Jesus often kept silent, and only when He was put under oath in the Name of His Father God, did He speak (Matthew 26:63–68). Then the Jewish leaders escorted him to Pontius Pilate, who had Jesus scourged in order to appease the mob. After being whipped, Jesus stood in front of the crowds and Pilate uttered what is now his immortalised dictum: *"Behold the Man!"* Then a little later he said, *"Behold your King!"* (John 19:5,14). Shortly after Jesus is nailed to a cross, but instead of cursing his tormentors, He prays, *"Father, forgive them, for they know not what they do."*

### Paul

Paul and his companion Silas are beaten and imprisoned, although they have done nothing wrong (Acts 16:16–34). Later an earthquake breaks open the prison, but they refuse to escape. They console the despairing prison guard, who thinks all his prisoners have escaped, telling him they are all present, before leading him to salvation. The next day they are released, but because they are Roman citizens who have been beaten and imprisoned without trial, they ask the now fearful magistrates to personally release them. After the magistrates plead with them to leave, they quietly do so. Self-control revealed.

Acts 22:1–29 is a remarkable incident in Paul's life. At Jerusalem he spoke to the angry crowd about his conversion to Christianity, and when he got to the part where God says He will send Paul to the Gentiles, the crowd became a howling mob demanding Paul's death. In order to control the situation, the Roman commander escorted Paul into the barracks intending to examine him under scourging. Through all this hatred, abuse and pain, Paul simply asks if it is lawful to scourge a man who is a Roman, and uncondemned. Self-control indeed!

Paul admonishes Timothy about the Old Testament law in 1 Timothy 1:9, stating that it was made for *"people who are disobedient and rebellious, who are ungodly and sinful, who consider nothing sacred and defile what is holy, who murder their father or mother.*"(NLT). But, there is no law against the fruit of the Spirit! Every fallen, sinful human being must choose which path to take. The wide gate and broad way is the way which is independent of the true and living God. Furthermore it is the life of godlessness, lawlessness, rebellion, sinfulness and depravity which leads to destruction. Conversely the Narrow Gate and Difficult Way is the Lord's way, the way of salvation with the fruit of the Spirit, leading to eternal life in God (see Matthew 7:13–14). One commentator says that the wide gate and broad way merely begin that way, and those who choose it find that the path narrows more and more until it ends in the black nothingness of a lost eternity! On the other hand, the narrow gate and difficult way is just the start. All those who progress along this path discover it becomes wider, smoother and easier until it opens out into the eternal blessedness of heaven! Which do you choose?

# CHAPTER SEVENTEEN

# DIVINE HEALING

W HEN I WAS ABOUT SIXTEEN YEARS OF AGE, AND regularly attending Brunswick Road Baptist Church, I received a number of dreams from the Lord. I know they were from God because of their potency and their powerful lasting effects; they have lingered with me over the years such that I remember them clearly to this day. Gloucester cross is the road system at the centre of the city, where Westgate, Eastgate, Southgate and Northgate streets meet together. It is now a pedestrianised area, but formerly this busy crossroads sported a policeman's plinth in the centre, on which an officer could stand to direct traffic from four directions. To protect pedestrians, galvanised iron rails had been erected on each pavement corner. People could lean on the barriers, and the person who sold the *Gloucester Citizen* newspaper could set up his box safely behind one of the rails. Also behind the rail situated on the left-hand corner of Westgate Street, there often sat a blind man with his cap on the ground ready to receive coins – mostly small change from passers-by.

In one dream I was walking up Westgate Street and approaching the blind man on Gloucester cross. I noticed his cap on the ground with small change in it. The words of Peter came flooding into my mind as he spoke to the lame man sitting at the Beautiful Gate leading to the Temple in Jerusalem. Peter said, *"Silver and gold I have none, but what I have I give you. In the Name of Jesus Christ of Nazareth rise up and walk."* In my dream I remembered how Peter took hold of the man's hand and lifted him to his feet, and that the man was immediately made whole, and began walking and leaping and praising God. I realised here in Gloucester was the same scenario. The essential need of the blind man was not small change, but his sight! Could I be the Lord's instrument, saying, "Sir, I don't have any money, but what I have I give you. In the Name of Jesus Christ, receive your sight?" It was at this point in my dream that my faith failed me, and I felt sick in heart and began to weep as I ran home. Indeed, at home in bed I woke from my dream weeping, and I began calling out in shame to the Lord about my unbelief and fear. In cowardice I kept away from Gloucester cross for some time, and when I did pass there much later, I am ashamed to say I was relieved to find the blind man was absent. What happened to him I do not know.

It would be impossible to attend Brunswick Road Baptist Church in those days without noticing an amazing Bible text painted above the central window arch behind the pulpit. It read, *"Jesus Christ the same yesterday, today and forever."* I wanted to know what that verse meant! Could it be taken at face value? I talked to Mr James, who was the Church Secretary, a kind and neatly dressed man. He told me it meant that the Lord Jesus Christ was indeed the same in the twentieth century as He had been in Bible days. I thought a lot about that. I saw from the

Scriptures that Jesus not only forgave sins but also healed bodies, and I knew that God was challenging me to believe Him for such things to happen today.

I went back to Mr James and asked, "If Jesus is still the same today, why doesn't He heal people today?" It was a sincere question which needed a sincere answer. Mr James replied, "Today the Lord heals through doctors and medical science." Of course He does – I saw it all now! Why hadn't I realised that it was through medical science that the Lord's ministry of healing continues today? I felt a bit foolish, and chided myself for thinking otherwise; after all, we constantly prayed for surgeons, doctors, nurses and medical staff to be granted wisdom, ability and skill to combat disease and perform surgical operations. My mind rested with that understanding.

Just a few weeks later dreadful news reached our youth group. Jane Williams' dad was dying with cancer! When Jane was a little girl her mum had died and now her dad was gravely ill. I learned also that medically nothing could save him. Here was a situation where medical science was powerless to save a life, but I reasoned, "If Jesus was here He would heal Jane's dad." I talked to the Lord about this, and after some time realised I had to put my faith into action – I must go and pray for him.

I had never met Jane's dad but I found out that he was in a hospital in Cardiff, so the next Saturday I boarded a train in Gloucester and settled into a compartment with my large Thompson Chain-Reference Bible, destined for the Welsh capital. A well-dressed man entered the compartment and sat opposite me. He appeared to be a businessman about thirty years of age. I read my Bible, looking at key verses, which I trusted would strengthen my faith in the Lord's ability to heal. After a while the man opposite commented about my reading the Bible, There was no disdain in his voice when he asked what I was going to do. I told him about my belief in the Lord Jesus;

about Jane's dad, and my intention to pray for healing. He was so gracious and encouraging and wished me well with my mission. I do not remember his name, or where he was from, but I will never forget him and I thank him for affirming me, and for not putting me down or deflating me in any way. Was he a businessman, or was he an angel sent to encourage me? Apart from the stranger on the train, and the Lord Himself, no one knew I was going to visit John to pray for him.

I arrived at the hospital and found the ward, and because mornings were outside normal visiting hours, the nurse told me to wait so that she could gain permission for me to see John. Fortunately they allowed me in, and when I first set my eyes on him I cringed –never had I seen a person so ill. He was hairless, completely jaundiced and alarmingly thin. With trepidation I walked to the side of his bed and gently told him who I was – Jane's friend from Brunswick Road Baptist Church. I told him I had decided to visit him, and that I would like to tell him about the Lord Jesus. Carefully I explained the way of salvation, and I was thrilled when he said he wanted to accept the Lord Jesus as His personal Saviour. What a delicate joy to lead him in a prayer of commitment to Christ, after which a beautiful quiet sense of assurance rested on my soul that Jesus had received John and saved him.

I then told John how Jesus had healed people in Bible days, and asked if he would permit me to show him some scriptures about healing. Then I asked permission to pray for his healing, and to place my hand gently upon him. John gave me permission and with some uncertainty I prayed and left him in God's hands. It was a week or so later that news reached us at church that John Williams had died. I went home with a heavy heart. My mind was full of misgivings and some confusion. I had tried to keep humble; I had tried to be sincere; I had tried to believe the Scriptures and to trust the Lord Himself for a miracle. Although

I had never seen anyone prayed for in this direct way, I had tried to remain calm and sensible in John's presence – but it had not worked, and I felt sick in heart and deeply discouraged.

In my room at home, I sought the Lord, hoping He would guide me. Quietly He spoke into my soul, explaining that I wanted John healed in order to boast in front of the people at Brun. I wanted to use John to prove that my theory about healing was correct. As He said this, I knew it was true! I had wanted to use John as a publicity stunt, as a confirmation that my beliefs were superior to those of my fellow believers. The prophet had written years before that, *"The heart is deceitful above all things, and desperately wicked. Who can know it?"* (Jeremiah 17:9). While I sat in the Lord's presence I realised I had let John down, and I had let Jane down, and worst of all I had let God down. My selfish motive had prevented the Lord healing John. I had loved my scriptural theories more than I had loved John or Jane. Not my compassion for John, but confirmation of my doctrine had been my motive!

The Lord said more. He was pleased that I had told John the gospel, and He assured me that John was with Him in heaven. This brought me comfort. He also told me that if I really wanted to see miracles I must remain humble and allow my love for others to enable miracles to happen.

Rev. Walter Quicke asked me if would cycle to Kendal Road Baptist Church to fetch a slide projector. I met the minister at the church and we went into a back room, where he handed me the projector. As we walked back to the church entrance he asked my name. "Tony Chamberlain," I said. Upon hearing it he stopped in his tracks and asked, "Are you the chap who is going about saying the Lord heals people today?" I told him, "Yes." He then proceeded to wipe the floor with me! I recall him saying that healing and miracles ceased after the apostles all died. He further explained that not only was I in error doctrinally, but that I was adding to people's difficulties and pains by giving them false hope – telling them that the Lord Jesus could heal them, when in fact He would not! He spoke about my bad influence on other believers and the fact that I was obviously arrogant, and needed to submit to the teachings of my superiors.

I felt utterly defeated. Having been severely rebuked, I left the church with a pain gnawing away in my soul. Was I so wrong, and was he so right? I had never seen the sick prayed for, and I had never seen a miracle happen. My short experience and his much longer experience of seeing no miracles seemed to testify that such things do not occur today. However, deep in my consciousness questions lingered, "Why has Jesus changed? Is the Bible untrue after all?"

Some things were beyond question, however. I knew that the Lord God had spoken to me, that He had forgiven me my sins, that He was my heavenly Father and that I was His son. I also knew He would show me the way forward, and with that I rested my case regarding divine healing. Shortly afterwards, my dear mother, Eileen, was taken ill and a number of visits to the doctor and to the hospital confirmed that she was suffering from stones in the kidneys. An operation to remove the stones was imminent. Then during the small hours one Friday night, she was in terrible pain, so much so that her cries of agony woke me up.

I got out of bed, fell onto my knees, and called on the Lord, pouring out my own distress for my mother. After a few minutes my bedroom door opened abruptly and Dad said he was going down the road to phone for an ambulance; he then apologised for interrupting my prayers. I heard the side door close, and got up and went into Mum's bedroom. There she was lying on the bed, writhing in agony, rolling from side to side with a contorted expression on her face. Her suffering made me angry – not with her, but angry at pain, with sin and with the distress the devil engineers.

Without thinking about strategy or protocol, standing over her I hastily put both hands on her body and ordered the devil to leave her, raising my voice loudly and rebuking Satan. I remember vividly that immediately Mum became calm and rested, and lay quietly on the bed. Then in softer tones as I took her hand and knelt by her bed, I asked the Lord to heal her, just as He had healed Peter's mother-in-law. Soon Dad returned and announced that an ambulance was on its way, and that night she was taken to the Gloucester Royal Infirmary in Southgate Street. Over the weekend she was X-rayed and on the Monday the specialist explained that more X-rays were required because the previous ones had failed to disclose the data they needed. When the next set of X-rays had been taken, they also showed no problems with mother's kidneys, so the specialist visited her in the ward and asked how she was and whether she was in pain.

Cheerfully she looked up at him and said she had suffered no pain at all since coming to the hospital and that she felt fine. She was discharged and came home that day. From that time to the end of her long life at almost ninety-six years of age, my mother never suffered again with her kidneys; she never had medication or any form of medical procedure to remove kidney stones. The Lord Jesus Christ Himself had performed a momentary operation and a life-long healing.

Like Mary over the birth of Jesus, I kept all these things, and pondered them in my heart. With a strengthened conviction, I had personally witnessed that Jesus is the Saviour of the soul and the healer of the body, and there are no valid arguments against that truth. Reluctant believers in divine healing might well accuse me of basing my beliefs on dreams! No, my beliefs and doctrine arose from the Scriptures, and it was these veritable truths that prompted my dreams. The Bible records many instances where the Lord spoke to people in dreams; that is not unusual. Inconsequential dreams quickly fade from the memory, and at best remain blurred and uncertain. My dreams remained vivid and drew me nearer to God. They were promptings from Him which confirmed His word, and sealed the truth of divine healing in my mind; a doctrine which was not practised or taught in most Protestant denominations at the time.

Under the subject of 'Gifts of healings' I listed previously eleven different means of divine healing included in the Bible. However, the list can be considerably extended as you can see, and doubtless further extended if all Biblical examples are included.

1. God's covenant of healing – Exodus 15:26; Mark 1:41

2. Obeying God's word – "wash in the Jordan seven times" 2 Kings 5:1–14. "Go to Siloam" John 9:7. "Go show yourselves to the priests" Luke 17:11–19

3. A prophetic word – Hezekiah, Isaiah 38:1–8; Naaman, 2 Kings 5:9–15

4. Speaking a word of wisdom/faith/instruction – 2 Kings 5:10; John 5:8; Acts 3:6–8

5. Healing bitter waters – Marah, Exodus 15:23–26; Elisha, 2 Kings 2:19–25

6. Making stew edible and feeding many people – 2 Kings 4:38–44

7. Touching the dead bones of a saint – Elisha, 2 Kings 13:20–21

8. Raising the dead to life – 2 Kings 4:32–37, Acts 9:36–43

9. Applying a poultice – Hezekiah, Isaiah 38:21

10. Healing wings of Christ – Malachi 4:2

11. Prayer to God – Luke 11:9–10; James 5:13–16; 1 John 3:22

12. Trusting in the Lord Jesus – Isaiah 53:4–5; Matthew 8:16–17; Mark 5:25–34

13. Breaking bread (communion) – 1 Corinthians 11:23–30

14. Laying on hands – Mark 16:18; Luke 13:13; Acts 9:17

15. Anointing with oil – Mark 6:13; James 5:14

16. Forgiveness/confession of sin – Mark 2:5–12; James 5:16

17. Gifts of healings – 1 Corinthians 12:9,28,30

18. Casting out demons – Mark 9:14–27; Luke 4:31–37; 10:17–20

19. The compassion of Christ – Matthew 9:35–36; Mark 6:34

20. The atonement of Christ – Isaiah 53:4–5; Matthew 8:16–17

21. Intimately reaching out to touch the Lord – Matthew 9:21, 14:36

22. Trusting God's word; *"He sent His word and healed them"* – Psalm 107:20

23. Instructions, power and authority from Christ – Luke 9:1–2, 10:9

24. Special miracles; Peter's shadow – Acts 5:15

25. Unusual miracles using handkerchiefs or cloths – Acts 19:11–12

26. Calling for the elders to pray – James 5:14–15

27. The prayer (vow) of faith – James 5:15

We live in a 'fallen' world – far removed from the glorious sinless beauty which the Creator desired, but which one day will be restored beyond its present condition and beyond its former glory. At present there are factors which deprive us of His glory: the strategy of Satan, the mischief of demons, the curse upon the planet, our own sinfulness and failure to walk with God. Nevertheless we can be saved through repentance and faith in Jesus Christ. We receive a new birth and become new creations in Christ, but even so, we are not yet perfected. The apostle John writes, *"If we say that we have no sin, we deceive ourselves, and the truth is not in us."* Henry Twells (1823–1900) wrote 'At even, ere the sun was set' with the fifth stanza ending:

> And they who feign would serve Thee best,
> Are conscious most of wrong within.

It would seem that the more we put effort into living a godly life, the more we become aware of our failure and frailty. Salvation in Christ is the only way forward here on earth, yet we must keep a true perspective on our state. We are forgiven, but not yet sinlessly perfect. We are Spirit-anointed but not yet faultless. Our bodies can be healed but not yet resurrected and immortalised. We are saved but not yet in heaven. We taste the powers of the age to come, but it is only a taste. God's word is seen only as a poor reflection in a mirror, and often we struggle to understand it.

Although we all have sinned and fall short of the glory of God, our bodies retain an amazing propensity for health and life. Whether we are unbelievers or saved, we all have amazing inbuilt natural self-healing properties. When assaulted by illness, the body activates its own defence mechanisms. Occasionally autopsies reveal that a person had suffered from a serious illness, but the body defences overcame it with the person merely feeling a little off colour. When the skin is punctured or cut, clotting agents in the bloodstream rush to repair the damage. Severed arteries have a shrink-back feature which helps prevent blood loss. We know the body can build up a certain amount of immunity against diseases. I caught dengue fever in Indonesia, but my doctor said that I would never catch that particular strain again, since my body would have built up a permanent defence mechanism against it.

This is all on the plus side, and testifies to the goodness of God who made us. Even so, our defence mechanisms are by no means as effective as the Lord intended, and on the minus side, new diseases constantly emerge, while old ones resurface after many years of almost complete elimination. Our personal defence mechanisms are supplemented by medical science, which also is His gift to the human race. The Lord has provided us with plants and herbal remedies, potions and medicines, while the added value of vaccinations and surgery enable people to live longer. But best of all is divine healing, by which the Lord overrules the disease and often speeds up the healing processes. The twenty-seven differing methods listed above of administering divine healing should reassure us that God is on the side of healing, and that He is not an ally of illness.

## THE WILL OF GOD

Many pastors dither over God's will regarding divine healing. When a person is sick they ask: Is this the result of sin? Is it the discipline of God? What is God's will in this case? Like the teaching of the Church in past centuries, they wonder if God has allowed that illness to teach a spiritual lesson, and that He wills it upon the hapless victim until the lesson is learned! Amidst all this uncertainty, however, there is one aspect that they are sure about, namely, "God doesn't heal everyone!" They are positive about this negative view, while remaining negative about the abundant positive promises, incidents and descriptions of divine healing presented throughout the Scriptures! Such uncertainties destroy faith, rendering leaders unable to believe God will do anything to help, and *"without faith it is impossible to please Him"* (Hebrews 11:6). Often believers end up with more faith in the doctor than in God! Are they those described as *"unstable, double-*

*minded persons who will receive nothing from the Lord"* according to James 1:6–8?

There are two simple remedies for this predicament. Firstly, accepting what the Bible teaches, and secondly, listening to what the Holy Spirit says. Even here church leaders muddy the waters by leaning on their head knowledge and personal experience rather than the plain statements of God's word. Also, without the baptism in the Holy Spirit, they encounter difficulty in hearing what the Spirit specifically says about a person or situation. The Lord does not present us with mysterious dilemmas, and has given us the baptism in the Spirit to guide us into all truth, to take the things of Christ and reveal them to us, to instruct us in the way we should go, and to provide the wisdom and knowledge of His will in every situation. Let's examine these two remedies.

## WHAT THE BIBLE TEACHES ABOUT DIVINE HEALING

In these last days God has spoken to us by His Son, the Lord Jesus Christ (Hebrews 1:2). Who Jesus is, what He did and what He said, embraces all that the Lord God desires us to know. Jesus is called the Word of God (John 1:1–4,14–17; Hebrews 4:12–13); these verses show Him to be the Living Word of God. In His wisdom God has taken the truths of the Living Word and recorded them in the Bible, which can be termed His Written Word. For this reason our doctrine and theology is based solely on what the Bible teaches.

Some might say, "But what the Bible says and shows I have never experienced. For example, I have never seen a miracle of healing!" Basing beliefs on experience (or lack of experience) leads to inaccurate assumptions, causing a person to believe that miracles did happen as recorded in the Bible, but they do not happen today! This faulty conclusion will produce a different belief system from what the Bible offers. We must acknowledge that our experience of God and His workings within our lives often falls far short of the dynamic He has promised in Scripture. But that is not because God has changed His mind, or altered His will; it is because of our own lack of holiness, desire, understanding, faith, prayer and commitment – and perhaps a lack of other virtues also. As a guide I would suggest that to grasp the truth about divine healing we need to firstly look at the Lord Jesus Christ. Secondly, we need to read the entire Bible to discover the whole trend of truth relating to this subject.

## What Jesus says and does

Jesus displayed a willingness to heal diseases and to cast out evil spirits. Early in His ministry He healed Peter's mother-in-law of a fever. In the evening we read that *"He healed many who were sick with various diseases, and cast out many demons".* Next day a leper came to Jesus, saying, *"If You are willing, You can make me clean"* (Mark 1:40–45). This is the only instance in Scripture where healing and God's will is questioned! The will of Jesus is of course the same as the will of God, since the Son did only what the Father would do, John 5:19,30. The leper had no doubts about the ability of Christ to heal; he openly said, *"You can make me clean."* What the leper was unsure about was whether Jesus would be *willing* to heal him! He had faith in Christ's power but was unsure of His purposes and character.

Many of us today are the same. Most believers have no doubts about the power and ability of Jesus to work miracles; they accept all the miracles recorded in the Bible. The main problem is that they are unsure about His character, His purposes today and the unchangeability of His Person. Does He have a different "will" for different people? Is His will inscrutable, like the will of

Allah? Is the true and living God unpredictable, making Him untrustworthy?

Often we have many reservations about ourselves which affect our view of Christ. For example, we might question whether we are good enough for Christ to heal us. We might also consider that Jesus knows us better than we know ourselves, so He might be unwilling to bless us because of our imperfections. In other words, we interpret His character and His willingness to hear and answer prayer by the estimation of our own holiness! Let's face it, many of us don't pray or believe because we think we are not good enough to be heard and answered in a positive way.

I'm glad it says Elijah was a man just like us in James 5:17–18, who prayed earnestly and his prayers were answered. A man *"just like us"* (ICB) means he had a similar moral character, a similar emotional nature, similar ups and downs in life, similar fears and failings, similar strengths and weaknesses, but his earnest prayers were heard and answered – that should encourage us to come boldly to the throne of grace. In its most simplistic form, divine healing is an answer to prayer. The 'problem' of not all being healed is the same as the 'problem' that not all our prayers are answered. Ironically for some strange reason we often hear the phrase, "God doesn't heal everyone" but we rarely hear a preacher teach that "God doesn't answer every prayer"! We must return to the leper who challenges Christ's will, and see the Lord's response which settles the matter. Three issues are apparent in Mark 1:41.

### Jesus is moved with compassion

Christ's compassion is the same today, because He is just the same today as in Bible days. Never measure the greatness of His compassion by the meanness of your own heart. The compassion of the Godhead is paramount throughout Scripture. *"Through*

*the Lord's mercies we are not consumed, because His compassions fail
not. They are new every morning; Great is Your faithfulness"*
(Lamentations 3:22–23). These words were uttered after
Jerusalem had been sacked by the Babylonians. The city was in
ruins, and most of its people escorted away into exile. But God's
compassion ensured that the city was not utterly destroyed, nor
its people totally obliterated.

Asaph contemplates Israel's rebellion against God, and states
in Psalm 78:38, *"He being full of compassion, forgave their iniquity,
and did not destroy them."* Psalm 86:15: *"You, O Lord, are a God
full of compassion, and gracious, longsuffering and abundant in
mercy and truth."* With a concordance, check out how many
times the Psalms say, *"The Lord is gracious and full of compassion."*
Jesus, the Son of God, displays identical characteristics. In
Matthew 9:36 Jesus exhibits compassion for multitudes of
ordinary folk. In Matthew 14:14 His compassion motivated
Him to heal the sick. In Mark 6:34 His compassion caused Him
to teach the multitude many truths.

### Jesus stretched out His hand and touched him

Jesus could have kept his distance and spoken a word of healing,
but He chose to touch the leper. Compassion leads to intimate
action, and touching a victim demonstrates that you accept
them; it demonstrates your fearlessness of diseases, and your
faith in the power of God to prevent you catching anything. In
church people with a fluey-cold sometimes keep their distance,
to kindly prevent others catching the virus. But I shake hands
and also hug people with a cold, in Jesus' Name, believing I will
not be adversely affected, and I do not recall catching a cold in
this way! Returning to Rev. Canon Henry Twells' (1823–1900)
beautiful hymn, 'At even, ere the sun was set', we find the last
stanza affirms the power and mercy of God to heal us all:

> Your touch has still its ancient power,
> No word from You can fruitless fall;
> Here in this solemn evening hour,
> And in Your mercy heal us all.

**Jesus replies, saying to the leper, "I am willing; be cleansed"**

There is no hesitation here. Christ does not fudge the issue by explaining the complexities of His will being done on earth, He simply forges ahead and states His willingness to heal this poor man. In verse 42 we read: *"As soon as He had spoken, immediately the leprosy left him, and he was cleansed."* In Mark's Gospel the word *immediately* (NT Greek: *eutheos* ευθεος) is used fourteen times in the first two chapters, and in many instances the word is linked to healing. Christ's response to the leper settles the matter regarding His willingness to heal. However, the human mind has learned many ways of circumventing the truth. Some postulate that Christ's response only settles the matter in this instance – His will might be different for somebody else!

Such mental manoeuvres will detrimentally affect our faith, so that we find it almost impossible to believe that God will answer our prayer for healing, and to believe He will answer immediately is completely beyond us! The human mind is one of the channels that Satan uses to influence us and lead us astray. We are so easily affected by the devil's insinuations that the Bible challenges us not to *"lean on our own understanding"*. The assertion that God's willingness to heal is different for individual people overlooks the fact that God is no respecter of persons.

**Does the Bible specifically say that God wills and desires to heal everyone?**

No! But it does say He *"wills all men to be saved"*, and since salvation includes healing for the complete person, soul and body, we have strong Biblical trends supporting the very positive stance taken by the Lord against illness.

**Are there texts which show that the Lord was unwilling to dispense healing to anyone?**

No! The nearest we get is where He challenged people's desire to be healed, such as the paralytic in John chapter 5, and the daughter of the Gentile woman from Syrophoenicia in Mark chapter 7 regarding her demonised daughter. There is no suggestion in these passages of Scripture that Jesus was unwilling to help. If fact He was willing, because He proceeded to heal them both!

**Are there passages of Scripture which show that Jesus did not heal everyone?**

Yes. John tells us about the pool of Bethesda, which had five porches where lay a great multitude of sick people. Here Jesus healed only one person – a man who had no faith, and who failed to recognise Him. At the pool it appears that no one else recognised the Lord of life! This incident does not prove that Jesus was unwilling to heal the others, but merely that He didn't. We cannot assume that the absence of healing rested on His unwillingness. There were other factors involved which must be considered, such as the fact that no one else asked Him for healing.

There are instances where Jesus neither saves nor heals people. The rich younger ruler was challenged by Jesus, but he walked away from His offer of salvation. That did not prove Christ was unwilling to save him; it proved only that the young man placed his riches above redemption, and desired earthly possessions more than eternal life. On one occasion the disciples failed to cast out a demon from a young lad. I wonder if they thought it might not be God's will to deliver him! Mark 9:14–27 sets the scene, and shows in verse 19 that Jesus expressed exasperation over the faithlessness of both the people and His disciples. Failure to deliver had nothing at all to do with the will of God, it hinged on the faithlessness and possibly the prayerlessness of Christ's followers.

Quite unlike the leper, the father of the demonised boy struggled to believe that Jesus had the power to set his son free, saying, *"If you can do anything have compassion and help us."* Jesus retorted, *"If you can! All things are possible to him who believes."* Was Jesus willing to deliver this lad from a tormenting demon? Of course He was willing, and He proved it by casting the demon out, despite everyone's uncertainties. Praise the Lord!

In Acts chapter 3 there was a lame man in Jerusalem whom Jesus hadn't healed. The Scriptures are silent as to when this man was first laid at the Beautiful Gate of the Temple. He could have arrived in Jerusalem only recently from a far country. In any case, the logistics are of little importance since two facts emerge: 1. He was lame from birth. 2. He was healed by Jesus through Peter and John. Therefore it was certainly God's will to heal him! I have already drawn attention to Mark 6:4–6 where Jesus could do no mighty work, except lay His hands on a few sick people and heal them. What a tragedy that the Lord's power was curtailed. Jesus was prohibited from exercising His full dynamic to produce mighty miracles. But this inability had nothing whatsoever to do with His will! It says He marvelled because of their unbelief. Many believers are too quick to place the onus on the Lord for the absence of miracles today; they prefer to think it is not God's will rather than to acknowledge their own inadequacy – their own faithlessness and human frailty. What did Jesus do to remedy this situation? It says He went about the villages in a circuit, teaching. Correct Bible teaching encourages faith because *"faith comes from hearing and hearing from the word of God"* (Romans 10:17).

**Are there verses which show that Jesus healed everyone present?**

Yes! Matthew 8:16 states, *"He cast out the spirits with a word, and healed all who were sick."* Mark 1:32–34 comments on this same instance, stating, *"Then He healed many who were sick with various diseases, and cast out many demons".* Do not jump to the conclusion that there is a discrepancy between Matthew and Mark. Matthew uses *"all"* to confirm that everyone who was sick was healed. But if we had only Matthew's text, some doleful person could suggest that healing everyone might refer only to one or two people! So Mark uses the word *"many"* to illustrate the great number of healings. Another instance is found in Matthew 12:15 which says, *"A great multitude followed Him, and He healed them all."* We cannot argue with that and retain our sanity! I like the poem based on Matthew's Gospel by Charlotte Murray:

> He healed them all – the blind the lame the palsied,
>
> The sick in body and the weak in mind;
>
> Whoever came, no matter how afflicted,
>
> Were sure a sovereign remedy to find.

Acts 5:16 describes the Lord dispensing healing through His followers in the early Church: *"A multitude gathered from the surrounding cities to Jerusalem, bringing sick people and those who were tormented by unclean spirits, and they were all healed."* And they were all healed! That is wonderful and we should allow such truth to banish unbelief as we pray for the sick today. Peter declared that Jesus healed them all, in Acts 10:38, *"God anointed Jesus of Nazareth with the Holy Spirit and with power, who went about going good and healing all who were oppressed by the devil, for God was with Him."*

Bible book after Bible book is loaded with the miracle power of God, saving, healing, delivering, restoring, reconciling, redeeming. We serve a mighty God who in the midst of a cursed and sinful earth releases His own powerful dynamic to save and heal. Gladly we find that the atmosphere of heaven excludes disease, illness, death and decay. There is no sickness in heaven where the perfect will of God is done. Revelation 21:4 says, *"God will wipe away every tear from their eyes; there shall be no more death, nor sorrow, nor crying. There shall be no more pain, for the former things have passed away."* Jesus bore not only our sins, but also our sicknesses, confirming that healing is His divine will for us, Isaiah 53:4–5; Matthew 8:16–17.

When I was in Bible college one popular subject for debate was, 'Is healing in the atonement?' The 'atonement' was assumed to be the cross. The matter was decisively answered when one lecturer pointed out that the atonement was in fact Christ Himself. He is the 'at-one-ment' between God and people. Since Christ is the divine healer of broken bodies and broken souls, then healing is indeed in the atonement!

## The will of God is often not done on earth

To accommodate evil and awful scenarios, Reformed theology makes a distinction between God's *sovereign will* and what is termed His *permissive will.* The Bible does not speak of such things, however, it speaks only of the will of God in all its fullness, which is *"good and acceptable and perfect"* (Romans 12:2). When Jesus was born, the wicked King Herod was filled with rage that another king would threaten his rule, so he had all the baby boys killed in Bethlehem. We might wonder how God could permit such a thing, or we might ask if this was merely

God's permissive will. Was this barbarity something God allowed but didn't really desire? Our minds could well go around in circles with such deliberations. Simply I see that the Bethlehem babies died, not because it was God's will, but because of the satanic grip on Herod's life, causing God's will to be thwarted on earth in this instance.

If the will of God was always done, there would be no need to pray as Jesus taught us, *"Thy will be done on earth as it is in heaven."* The Lord Jesus clearly indicated His will when He stated *"I would, but you would not!"* to the inhabitants of Jerusalem. *"I wanted to gather your children together, as a hen gathers her chicks under her wings, but you were not willing."* In John 5:40 Jesus stated, *"You are not willing to come to Me that you might have life."* It is evident from the Scriptures that demons and humans often resist the will of God. Paul points out that it was a common view that the will of God was irresistible: *"One of you will say to me: 'Then why does God blame us, for who resists His will?'"* (Romans 9:19). The plain fact is that people constantly resist God's will, just as Stephen declared, *"You stiff-necked and uncircumcised in heart and ears! You always resist the Holy Spirit; as your fathers did, so do you"* (Acts 7:51).

*Is sickness the result of sin?*

There is a connection between sin and illness. Sin has an effect on the whole person, spirit, soul and body. Jesus told the man He had healed at the pool of Bethesda, *"See, you have been made well. Sin no more, least a worse thing comes upon you."* Jesus forgave the woman who was caught in adultery, when He said, *"Neither do I condemn you: go and sin no more."*

The British National Health Service is overwhelmed by enormous numbers of sick people. In part this is because the institution endeavours to heal the physical symptoms but fails to deal with the spiritual root causes behind illness – namely Satan and sin. Also our nation continues to move further away from the Lord, resulting in more and more afflictions tormenting us. Until people turn back to God, the NHS will continue to be deluged. When will it be acknowledged that Jesus Christ forgives sin and heals sick bodies, failing minds and troubled souls? Ailments and anxieties are both relieved by the Lord of life.

We must be clear about this, however – sickness and disease may not be the direct result of personal sin in someone's life. The condition of a man born blind was questioned. Evidently the disciples had grasped that some sickness is the result of sin, but they had failed to understand that this is not so in every instance. They asked Jesus, *"Who sinned, this man or his parents, that he was born blind?"* Jesus answered, *"Neither this man nor his parents sinned."* Although sin is a possible cause of physical deformity, it was not the cause in this case. We are not given the reason for the blindness, but Jesus says it was an opportunity for *"the works of God to be revealed"* (see John chapter 9). The works of God are healings and restoration from deformity, as Jesus demonstrated by granting sight to the man born blind.

Romans 6:23 tells us *"the wages of sin is death"* and this result is not necessarily the discipline of God. We are told in Romans 5:12 that death came into the world through sin, and sin is the work of the devil. Early one morning at work I thought I was alone and I breathed the Name of Jesus. A voice came back at me, "He won't help you!" It was one of the cleaners, and I sensed she had suffered a great loss. "What happened?" I asked her. "God took my son who died when just a few years old." I felt great compassion for her and replied that I would be dead today if the Lord Jesus had not saved me. Then I said that it seemed to me that it wasn't God who took her son, but our old enemy, the devil. She had never thought of that!

Jesus said the devil *"was a murderer from the beginning, and the father of lies"*. One of the devil's lies is to portray the Lord as mean, vengeful and unloving, in direct contrast with the revelation of Him in Scripture. The devil incites us to blame the Lord for every tragedy; to hold Him responsible for world wars, for the convulsions of nature, for sickness in body and soul, and for death itself. I told the dear cleaner lady that it was a pity that she did not know the Lord Jesus when the devil took her son. If she had called on Him then, He would have saved her from years of bitterness and anger, just like he saved me from death. The enemy has done a good job of blinkering people to the reality of God's power and love; he also makes a good job of twisting the evidence so that God gets the blame for everything!

*Is sickness the discipline of God?*

God does discipline His children, as Hebrews 12:5–11 shows. He does so because He loves them, just like a caring father disciplines his own children. My older sister, Angela, and I would walk home from the Midland Road Primary School in Gloucester each school day. We passed the park, where there were swings and roundabouts for children to play. We could cross the busy road to get to the park, but the road was used not only by traffic but also by steam engines in those days. There was an underpass, however, which made things easier. But it was all risky, and we were solemnly instructed to go straight home and not to enter the park. Temptation was too strong one day, and to the park we went, causing us to arrive home late. Dad's belt come down on my tender bum, but what hurt me most was the indignity of being reprimanded. The result was we never strayed again. We needed to be a little older to realise that if Dad didn't love us, he wouldn't have cared what we did on the way home! The discipline was the result of his protective care and devotion.

It is the same with God. Occasions arise when the Lord's rebuke is required. For example, when we think and say the wrong thing, like Peter in Mark 8:33; or like James and John in Luke 9:54–56. Sometimes we do the wrong thing, like John in Mark 9:38–40; or we display a condemning attitude like the disciples in Mark 14:3–9, resulting in the Master's disapproval. In each of these instances the Lord did not discipline His followers by putting sickness upon them and the number of times this happened in Scripture is meagre.

Miriam's criticism of Moses resulted in her being leprous, but Moses prayed for her and she was healed (Numbers 12:9–15). The psalmist said, *"Before I was afflicted I went astray. But now I keep Your word"* (Psalm 119:67). We are not told what the psalmist's affliction was, or how it came, but the Lord enabled it to teach him to stay on God's path. Similarly, the Lord allowed Satan to afflict righteous Job, but within limits. God knew Job would still trust Him, and in his year of sorrow, sickness and loss, Job became a witness to the devil himself, that God can be trusted, that He is faithful and true. Indeed, he turns tears into joy and laughter. *"For His anger is for a moment, His favour is for life. Weeping may endure for a night, but joy comes in the morning"* (Psalm 30:5). The discipline of God doubtless involves pruning – cutting off, removing dead or unwanted growth, as Jesus explained in John 15:1–8, and as we mentioned above in chapter 15 – God the producer of fruit.

## THE GUIDANCE OF THE HOLY SPIRIT

After the followers of Christ were baptised in the Holy Spirit on the Day of Pentecost, their lives were directed by two factors: 1) the Holy Scriptures, and 2) the Holy Spirit. Today, those not baptised in the Holy Spirit in the Biblical way generally assume that the Holy Spirit is guiding them, but most of their actions and experience result from their own minds. I do not say the Holy Spirit does not guide them at all, but His sway in their lives is limited and His influence is tenuous. With an incomplete salvation much of what the Holy Spirit desires to do in them and through them is curtailed.

After Jesus received water baptism by John, the anointing of the Holy Spirit came upon Him like a dove. Then immediately the Spirit drove Him into the wilderness (Mark 1:12). "Drove" does not signify reluctance on Christ's part, but it emphasises the weight of conviction the Spirit placed on Him to go to the desert. Similar compulsions from the Holy Spirit rested on members of the early Church. Stephen, *"a man full of faith and the Holy Spirit"*, was chosen to be a deacon to help with the practical task of distributing food. But Stephen was *"full of faith and power, and did great wonders and signs among the people"*. His opposers *"were not able to resist the wisdom and the Spirit by which he spoke"*. Then there is Philip, who also was chosen to be a deacon, and *"multitudes with one accord heeded the things spoken by Philip, hearing and seeing the miracles which he did"*. After a great revival crusade in Samaria, Philip is instructed by an angel of the Lord to go to the desert road from Jerusalem to Gaza (Acts 8:26), where he sees an Ethiopian in a chariot. Then the Spirit told Philip to overtake the chariot – not merely catch up with it, but to overtake it, which suggests supernatural energy. After the Ethiopian is saved and water-baptised, the Spirit of the Lord caught Philip away and he was found thirty miles away at Azotus!

In Acts 13:1–12 we read that the Holy Spirit directed the proceedings, appointing Barnabas and Saul to specific ministry. In says, *"Being sent out by the Holy Spirit, they went . . ."* When writing to Gentile converts the apostles said that it seemed good to the Holy Spirit, and to them. Such Holy Spirit directives seem far from the experience of many believers today. In Acts

16:6–10 the Holy Spirit again directs proceedings by forbidding Paul, Silas and Timothy to preach in the Roman province of Asia. Then they tried to go to Bithynia, *"but the Spirit did not permit them."* Directions come through a vision given to Paul in the night, leading the evangelistic party to Macedonia and Europe. Paul was disturbed by opposition in the city of Corinth, but the Lord spoke to Paul in the night by a vision, telling him not to be afraid, but to speak and not keep silent; for God was with him, and no one would attack him.

The Lord also worked unusual miracles by the hands of Paul, so that even handkerchiefs or aprons were brought from his body to the sick, and the diseases left them and evil spirits went out of them. More information from the Holy Spirit reaches Paul, signifying what will happen to him if he goes to Jerusalem, namely that he will be arrested and bound. Then Paul is told to be of good cheer, for as he has testified for the Lord in Jerusalem, so he must also bear witness at Rome. See how God constantly assures, directs and informs His followers by the Holy Spirit, sometimes through a vision or a dream, sometimes through prophecy, and very often by drawing close and speaking. All this is normal Christianity!

We have the will of God spelled out clearly in the Bible, but there are specific situations where the Spirit's advice, instruction and direction are needed, including how to pray for the sick. We need the Spirit's mind on a person's true state and condition – are there specific spiritual forces behind the obvious illness or distress? Are words of knowledge required to deal with this particular condition? Would a word of wisdom clarify the way forward? If we are praying for a blind person, do we use spit and clay to anoint their eyes before instructing them where to wash? Do we anoint with oil? Do we lay on hands? Do we 'command' or 'pronounce' healing? Do we discern how much faith they have? Do we need to take measures to encourage their faith?

Does their lack of faith matter in this instance? Is this person's illness the binding of Satan? Is exorcism required? We need God the Holy Spirit to show us what to do. Yes, we need the Scriptures, but the Bible cannot contain instructions for every individual person, situation or scenario. We have listed twenty-seven Biblical methods for administering divine healing, but the Holy Spirit instructs us which one to use in each case. We cannot do without Him.

Jesus used many different methods to administer wholeness and healing, and similarly we need the guidance of the Holy Spirit in order to be effective. We may have prayed 100 times for sick people, but only relying on human experience is so often inadequate. Each person is a unique individual in God's eyes, and His knowledge and direction is required for each one. As it stands, the Bible may not help – in a given situation we may not have time to read through it, searching for a specific and immediate answer. Of course, the Holy Spirit can bring a certain scripture to mind in a moment of time, which will instruct us. He could remind us of James 5:16: *"Confess your trespasses to one another, and pray for one another, that you may be healed."* The Spirit alone knows the way forward, and we need His guidance in every situation.

Left to our own devices we might present a whole list of written reasons why a person is sick or not yet healed, asking them to read through and tick the boxes which apply! Sometimes new converts are presented with a long list of sins which they must repent of before they can be supposedly forgiven, or to prevent a future repetition of those sins. This method smacks of human intervention and it does not sit comfortably with me. I much prefer directives from the Holy Spirit, which are always effective.

I recall a prophet praying for a line of people. To each one a different and specific message was given and a unique prayer offered. I was the young assistant pastor of this church, and I noticed in the line was an unconverted young man. I wanted to warn the prophet that this person was not saved. I need not have worried. Operating in the power of the Holy Spirit, the prophet knew where this young person stood, and his words of challenge and his prayer for salvation was extraordinary. The Lord has not left us with mere human resources, which are pathetically inadequate for Kingdom ministry. Jesus said the Helper, the Holy Spirit, whom the Father would send in His Name, will teach us all things. So today we have the Holy Spirit to guide and instruct us and the Spirit never gets it wrong!

# CHAPTER EIGHTEEN

# CHRIST'S ASCENSION

THROUGHOUT THE CENTURIES, DIFFERENT THEMES OF Christ's life have been examined and debated and these have produced resultant theologies about many facets of the Being and life of our Lord – His pre-incarnate Being; His virgin birth, His baptism, His crucifixion and His resurrection. Accordingly, different denominational streams have arisen. The Roman Catholic Church is founded basically on the theology of the incarnation, while Protestantism is based broadly on the crucifixion. Evangelicalism rests on the cross and the resurrection. Modernist liberal ideas unreliably revolve around Christ's earthly life. But where is the theology of Christ's ascension? Doctrine about the ascension is meagre in quantity and shallow in quality. It is rarely mentioned or preached beyond consideration of Christ's High Priestly prayer ministry, or His preparing a home for us.

The Westminster Confession of Faith in chapter eight, article four, states:

> On the third day He arose from the dead, with the same
> body in which He suffered, with which also he ascended
> into heaven, and there sitteth at the right hand of His
> Father, making intercession, and shall return, to judge
> men and angels, at the end of the world.

The Second Helvetic Confession chapter eleven, article twelve, addresses the purpose and character of Christ's ascension:

> We believe that our Lord Jesus Christ, in the same flesh,
> did ascend above all visible heavens into the very highest
> heaven, that is to say, the seat of God and of the blessed
> spirits, unto the right hand of God the Father. Although
> it do signify an equal participation in glory and majesty,
> yet it is also taken to be a certain place; of which the
> Lord, speaking in the Gospel, says: "He will go and pre-
> pare a place for his" (John 14:2). Also the apostle Peter
> says: "The heavens must contain Christ until the time of
> restoring all things" (Acts 3:21).

Beyond such creedal statements information is scant. Rev. George Canty writes:

> The New Testament is vibrant with the fact the God has
> exalted Jesus. The Manger, the Cross, the Tomb were only
> steps to the Throne. He was born for us, He died for us,
> and He rose again for us, and this has all been translated
> into the common bread of Christian thought and daily
> life, yet, the fact that "He entered heaven for us", carried
> no practical or recent significance for Christians compa-
> rable to other statements about our Lord.[23]

Our hymn books contain little about Christ's ascent to glory because there can be no great hymns without great doctrine. Frances Ridley Havergal (1836–79) wrote 'Golden Harps are Sounding', in which the chorus states, "All His work is ended."

John 17:4 records Jesus as saying, *"I have glorified You on the earth. I have finished the work which you gave me to do."* Finished (Greek *teleioo*) means 'to complete, accomplish, conclude, reach a goal'. The context of Christ's finished work refers to His earthly accomplishments (although He was yet to go to the cross).

Until the Pentecostal revival which began in the early 1900s, the connection between Christ's ascension to the right hand of the Majesty on High and His granting of Holy Spirit baptism was not generally perceived. It has now become clear that the doctrine of the ascension and the doctrine of Pentecost are essentially the same. Jesus states in John 16:7: *"I tell you the truth. It is to your advantage that I go away; for if I do not go away, the Helper will not come to you; but if I depart, I will send Him to you."* There is the semblance of a toggle-switch here. If Jesus stays on earth, the Spirit stays in heaven, but if Christ goes, the Spirit comes! Explicitly Jesus says it is to our advantage that He goes away. Even so, we ask, could anything or anyone be better than the personal presence of the risen Lord Jesus Christ? Yes! Jesus said so. How is that? Is it so that we learn to *"walk by faith not by sight"* (2 Corinthians 5:7)? No, not merely that! It was because Christ's departure would initiate a Spirit baptism.

It is logical and clear that the Holy Spirit would be as equally dynamic as having the physical presence of Christ among us. It may be hard to accept that we are better off having the Spirit than having Jesus, but that is precisely what the Lord confirmed. Many will struggle with this, simply because their own personal experience of the Holy Spirit is woefully limited. The Holy Spirit is not limited by space and time, and anywhere in the world a believer can be baptised in the Holy Spirit by Jesus, by which they are filled and empowered. Here are a number of reasons why our Lord Jesus physically ascended into the heavens.

1. **Pre-eminence:** Christ is exalted and glorified – Mark 16:19; John 20:17; Eph.1:20; Hebrews 1:3, 8:1, 10:12, 12:2; 1 Peter 3:22

2. **Priestly prayers:** Christ's ministry of intercession – Romans 8:34; Hebrews 4:14, 7:25–26; 1 John 2:1

3. **Preparation:** Making a place in heaven for us – John 14:1–4, 17:24

4. **Power:** By activating Spirit baptism – John 16:7; Acts 2:33; Hebrews 2:4

5. **Persons:** To appoint His ascension gifts – Ephesians 4:11–14

6. **Provision:** Through the distribution of Spirit manifestations – 1 Corinthians 12:4–11,28–31, 14:4–5,12

7. **Proclamation:** Both declaring and demonstrating the gospel – Mark 16:15–20; Luke 24:45–49

In this list of seven reasons why Christ ascended, we see that it is generally only the first three which are declared by Bible teachers. The last four are most often omitted, resulting in converts being short-changed. The last four reasons are all connected with Spirit baptism, proving that the ascension and Pentecost are indelibly linked.

## CHRIST'S PRE-EMINENCE: Exalted and glorified

*From the lowest to the highest*

Luke 4:11: Jesus not only taught this principle, but also lived it. Philippians 2:6–11 are remarkable verses, in which we read that Christ *"made Himself of no reputation"* (NKJV) which is translated *"made himself nothing"* (NIV), and *"gave up his divine privileges"* (NLT), but closest to the Greek text is *"emptied Himself"(keno heautou* – Mounce Reverse-Interlinear). Theologically this is termed the *kenosis* (from the NT Greek word for emptiness: κένωσις, *kénōsis).* The New Testament does not use the actual noun *kénōsis* but the verb form *kenóō* occurs five times (Romans 4:14; 1 Corinthians 1:17, 9:15; 2 Corinthians 9:3; Philippians 2:7. These verses are often translated *empty* or *void*).

Of these five times it is Philippians 2:7, where it is said Jesus *"emptied himself"*, and this is the starting point for the Christian *kenosis* theory. A Jew was asked what this verse meant to him. He said the emptying is a pouring out, simply as milk is poured from a bottle into a jug; thus Jesus, the Son of God, poured Himself into a human body! I believe that He poured all of Himself into a human body, so that His majesty, power, authority, deity and every God-attribute came with Him.

I like the song, "You Laid Aside Your Majesty", but this opening phrase has never sat comfortably with me! So what did He leave behind? Simply He left behind the glory of heaven. He stepped from the palace of beauty down to the hovel of a fallen, sin-sick world; rather like the TV 'secret millionaire' who leaves his posh pad to live in poverty for a while, enabling him to get alongside the underprivileged. In Christ's case the contrast was immense and shockingly extreme. Clothing Himself with humanity was permanent and eternal!

Jesus spoke of the glory He had with the Father prior to His *kenosis*, before the world existed, John 17:5. Early on the resurrection morning, Mary Magdalene was the first to see the risen Lord, and it appears she wanted to hold on to Him because Jesus said, *"Do not touch Me, for I have not yet ascended to My Father; but go to My brethren and say to them, 'I am ascending to My Father and your Father, and to My God and your God'"* (John 20:17).

These words infer that Jesus made an unseen ascension prior to meeting up with His disciples later in Galilee. He presented Himself as the perfect, once-for-all sacrifice for sin to His Father in the heavenly tabernacle, just as the high priests of Israel had presented the blood of the atoning sacrifice within the veil of the earthly tabernacle. After the resurrection morning, a period of forty days elapsed before His visible ascension, and during this period, the Lord allowed people to handle His body and check the crucifixion marks.

Earlier in His ministry Jesus had challenged His disciples with the words in John 6:62: *"What if you see the Son of Man ascend where He was before?"* Later, Stephen cried out, saying, *"Behold, I see the heavens opened, and the Son of Man standing at the right hand of God!"* Peter says about Christ in his sermon in Acts 3:21, *"whom the heaven must receive until the times of restitution of all things, which God hath spoken by the mouth of all his holy prophets since the world began."*. Paul writes to Timothy, stating, *"Without controversy, great is the mystery of godliness: God was manifest in the flesh, justified in the Spirit, seen of angels, preached unto the Gentiles, believed on in the world, received up into glory."* Christ's ascension to the throne of glory validates all that He is, *"that in all things He may have the pre-eminence"* (Colossians 1:18). It also confirms the potency of all that He accomplished for us on earth. Remarkably we are instructed to identify with Christ in His ascension, Ephesians 2:6: *"God . . . made us alive with Christ . . . and has raised us with Christ, and seated us with Him in the heavenly realms."* Colossians 3:1: *"Since then you have been raised with Christ, set your hearts on things above where Christ is seated at the right hand of God."* George Canty says,

"However, the sharing of Christ's triumph and position is spoken of here only because of its practical reality in Christian consciousness by the giving of the Holy Spirit."[24] This is a crucial point. Without the tangible experience of Holy Spirit baptism, Christ's ascension is of little *practical* value to us. If the Lord who sits majestically in the heavens failed to provide Holy Spirit baptism, we would merely plod through the muck of this world, ill-equipped to face a multitude of demonic foes. Being baptised in the Holy Spirit was the essential requisite for all who belong to the Lord and who desire to serve Him. *"Wait . . . until"* said Jesus in Luke 24:49. It is this same Holy Spirit who takes the things about Christ, including His ascension, and reveals them to us. Without His anointing we would have little idea what it means to be *"raised with Christ"*.

## CHRIST'S PRIESTLY PRAYERS – ministry of intercession

Those who teach about the ascension tend to major on this point, using quotes from Romans 8:34, *"It is Christ who . . . is also risen, who is even at the right hand of God, who also makes intercession for us."* The wonder and importance of Christ literally praying for us as we pass through this troubled age cannot be denied. Christ's heavenly ministry is emphasised by the writer to the Hebrews, who calls Jesus our great High Priest. He writes in Hebrews 4:14 that *"we have a great High Priest, that is passed into the heavens, Jesus the Son of God, let us hold fast [our] profession"* and continues in 7:25 with, *"He always lives to make intercession for us."* John introduces another title for the Lord Jesus which reflects on His heavenly ministry of praying and pleading for us: *"If anyone sins, we have an Advocate with the Father, Jesus Christ the righteous"* (1 John 2:1).

## CHRIST'S PREPARATION – of a place in heaven for us

This facet of ascension truth is rarely overlooked, and it is indeed both an inspiration and comfort to know that Jesus is making a special place for us in heaven. *"In my Father's house are many mansions; if it were not so, I would have told you. I go to prepare a place for you."* The various King James versions translate *"dwellings"* as *"mansions"* while the NIV uses the English word *"rooms"*. Depending on your translation preference, you will anticipate either a palatial chateau or a bedsit! Irrespective of the size of our heavenly abode, the most wonderful news is that we shall be with Christ. Jesus prayed this for us: *"Father, I desire that they also whom You gave Me, be with Me where I am, that they may behold my glory which You have given Me"* (John 17:24).

We have seen so far that in heaven Christ is exalted and glorified; that He continues to pray for us; and that He prepares a home for us. Now, reasons four to seven for the ascension turn the spotlight of God's truth to the practical earthly effects of the ascension in our lives.

## CHRIST'S PROMISED POWER – by receiving the baptism in the Holy Spirit

The Lord explained that sending the Holy Spirit to His disciples was *"The promise of the Father"* and that this promise was *"The baptism in the Holy Spirit"*. Peter told the 3,000 converts on the Day of Pentecost that they too *"shall receive the gift of the Holy Spirit. For the promise is to you, and to your children, and to all who are afar off, as many as the Lord our God will call"*. How clearly Jesus explained the divine purpose of the promised baptism in the Spirit in Acts 1:8: *"you shall receive power when the Holy Spirit has come upon you, and you shall be witnesses to Me."* Power to be Jesus' witnesses. Not human power, but God's power, as Zechariah 4:6 emphasises: *"Not by might nor by power, but by My Spirit, says the Lord."*

Zerubbabel had a humanly impossible task to complete – building the Temple of the Lord, but what is impossible with men is possible with God. To attempt to do God's work without God's power is folly indeed. Christ warned His first apostles not to begin their service for Him until they were Spirit-baptised.

Finally, if the disciples (with the exception of the absent Thomas) had received the Holy Spirit when Jesus breathed on them before visibly ascending into the heavens, what they had not received was the promised baptism in the Holy Spirit, which was vitally necessary before commencing their gospel ministry in the world as witnesses of the risen Christ.

## CHRIST'S PEOPLE – distributing ascension ministry gifts

Ephesians 4:7–16 includes a quotation from Psalm 68:18: *"When He ascended on high, He . . . gave gifts to men."* This describes active ministry on earth, where Christ gives gifts to men, but the gifts themselves are men! That is to say they are *human* and could be men or women, (as were Priscilla and Junia). We read, *"He Himself gave some to be apostles, some prophets, some evangelists, and some pastors and teachers."* They are distinguishable from both the gifts from the Father (*charismata*, Romans 12:3–8), and those from the Holy Spirit (*phanerosis*, 1 Corinthians 12:7–11), for they are specifically seen to be gifts from Christ Himself (*domata*, Ephesians 4:8).

Generally, the historic churches have failed to link such ministries with the ascension of Christ, and for the most part fail to recognise such ministries in the Church today. Where are the apostles and the prophets? Most can name at least one evangelist, while pastors are accepted as church leaders, and teachers are those who lecture in Bible schools – all humanly mundane, and a far cry from the anointed and appointed ministries in the early Church.

## CHRIST'S PROVISION – through the distribution of Spirit manifestations

Notice the nine manifestations of the Holy Spirit are included in the *charismatic* list, for they are indeed *charismata*. But they are *special charismata* designated *phanerosis* – best translated *"manifestations"*. *"The manifestation of the Spirit is given to each one for the profit of all."* The word *gift* is not found in this verse, because what is given by the Spirit is a revelation of Himself! Most Bible translations use the word *manifestation*. A few paraphrased versions include the word *gifts*. Here are some alternative translations:

> Geneva Bible 1599 – footnote: *"The holy Ghost openeth and showeth himself freely in giving of these gifts."*
>
> Common English Bible: *"A demonstration of the Spirit is given to each person for the common good."*
>
> Expanded Bible: *"The manifestation/disclosure of the Spirit is given to each person, for the common good."*
>
> Holman Christian Standard Bible: *"A demonstration of the Spirit is given to each person to produce what is beneficial"*.
>
> Living Bible: *"The Holy Spirit displays God's power through each of us as a means of helping the entire church."*
>
> GOD'S WORD Translation: *"The evidence of the Spirit's presence is given to each person for the common good of everyone."*

From these texts we can see that what the Spirit actually gives is a nine-fold variety of manifestations of Himself. In other words, He reveals Himself by these separate means. He demonstrates His presence; He discloses His nearness; He displays His pervasiveness in the midst of the gathered Church; He provides evidence of His presence living in us. For this reason we must respect and honour each manifestation of the Spirit, since failing to do so is a reproach against the Person of the Holy Spirit Himself!

## GOSPEL PROCLAMATION – declaring and demonstrating the gospel

*Declaring the gospel*

Proclamation of God's word has occurred in every generation since the creation of humankind. Sometimes it is God personally who proclaims His truth, as He did in Eden. Sometimes He uses an angel messenger and sometimes He uses His human servants. He can even use an animal, like Balaam's donkey. God anoints and appoints prophets to convey His truth, and He speaks through anointed kings. But best of all, God has spoken to us by His Son, the Lord Jesus Christ, as Hebrews 1:1–2 declares. During His earthly ministry, Jesus appointed at least seventy (seventy-two, NIV) of His disciples to proclaim God's truth. Jesus also gave final instructions that believers must continue the work of declaring His truth to the end of the age, thus passing on His teaching from generation to generation.

*Demonstrating the gospel*

Declaration should be accompanied by demonstration! Jesus demonstrated truth through His miracle ministry. A classic example is told by Dr Luke, where Jesus is presented with a paralysed man. Firstly the Lord declares forgiveness of sins for him. This raises objections by the religious leaders who consider that God only has the right to forgive people. So Jesus asks them a question: *"Which is easier to say, 'Your sins are forgiven you,' or to say, 'Rise up and walk'?"* They do not answer this question, so Jesus demonstrates His authority and right to forgive people their sins by immediately healing the paralysed man. This demonstration enabled the religious leaders to know that Jesus is the Son of God with power to forgive and to save.

The Lord Jesus demonstrated the power of the gospel by the miraculous works He performed. When the imprisoned John the Baptist was beset by doubts, Jesus appealed to His works to assure John that He was the Messiah. His answer to John illustrated both declaration, *"the poor have the gospel preached to them"* and demonstration, *"the blind see, the lame walk, the lepers are cleansed, the deaf hear, the dead are raised."* Marvellously the Lord insisted that His followers would continue to do His works, and to an even greater extent. This is precisely what the first Christians did after Jesus had ascended to heaven. Their gospel declaration was confirmed to be true by their demonstration, as people were healed, raised from the dead, and as other miracles occurred.

It must be the same with us today. We owe it to this generation not only to declare the gospel, but to demonstrate it. Preaching has never been so unpopular in the West as it is today. You can sense people crying out, "Don't just preach it, prove it!" The Pharisees proudly thought that if Christ came only with words, they could possibly have won the argument. What perturbed them most was that they couldn't match His miracles! That galled them, and their only recourse was to get rid of Him – to kill Him; to nail His feet down in an effort to curtail His itineraries; to nail His hands down to prevent Him cleansing the lepers or raising the dead by His touch. But even that was not enough. He must be dead and buried in a sealed tomb to stop others touching Him and being healed. The Lord used these wicked plans of hostile men to provide eternal redemption for us all. Through His death, Jesus accomplished the sacrificial means by which all might be redeemed, forgiven, healed, delivered and set free.

The absence of miracles in Christian ministry is a denial of the gospel. Christ's ascension provides the gospel with the power to proclaim it, the dynamic to demonstrate it and the confidence to confirm it. To fail to see the connection between the ascension and Pentecost leaves believers bereft of the supernatural provision of Christ for His Church, necessary for Kingdom success until Jesus returns to earth.

# CHAPTER NINETEEN

# CESSATIONISM MUST CEASE

CESSATIONISM IS THE VIEW THAT MIRACULOUS SIGNS AND wonders ceased with the death of the first apostles and/or with the completion of the New Testament canon. Such teaching has its foundation in the sands of human invention rather than the Word of God. This idea is tares among wheat!

*Cessationism is based on lack of experience*

In order to be credible, doctrine must be based only on what the Bible says. The silences of Scripture are inadequate for establishing doctrine. One cessationist says that because the baptism in the Spirit is not mentioned in the Book of Acts after chapter 19, then the experience must have ceased – but it may not have! In fact, long after the events in Acts chapter 19, various passages of the New Testament talk about the power of the Spirit, miracles, gifts of the Spirit, and being filled with the Spirit. Such phenomena had not ceased, as the cessationist asserts. We must face the fact that often our experience of God falls far short of what it should be. This is not God's fault! We lack experience of His dynamic power in our lives, because we lack Him – His presence. Our dedication to God is shallow and distant. The lack of miracles in our own lives and ministry does not mean signs and wonders have ceased, but rather that we falter in our walk with God.

## Cessationism is anti-scriptural

Many passages of Scripture show that the Holy Spirit age continues until Jesus returns, and specifically mentions that prophecy continues as long as those who call on the Name of the Lord can be saved, and until the sun is turned into darkness at the Lord's return. Jesus said, *"These signs shall follow those who believe"* (Mark 16:17). Those *"who believe"* include me! Jesus said that future converts must be taught to observe everything He had commanded His disciples. Since Jesus commanded them to heal the sick, they were to teach others to do the same, *"even to the end of the age"*.

In Acts 1:8 Jesus said that Holy Spirit power would accompany His disciples *"to the end of the earth"*. The apostles never reached the end of the earth – they reached Rome, the Middle East, Europe and possibly India. It was those who followed on after them that took the gospel to the Americas, the Orient and Australasia. Jesus' words *"to the end of the earth"* indicate global *extent,* and *time* until Jesus returns! Peter said the promise of Holy Spirit baptism is *"to as many as the Lord our God shall call"* (Acts 2:39) and that also includes me! Peter saw clearly that, *"God is no respecter of persons"* (Acts 10:24), meaning He deals with each one on the same basis, irrespective of race, gender or social standing.

Cessationists discredit many Scripture passages by inventing reasons why they do not apply today. The experience of millions of today's Spirit-baptised Christians throughout the world cause them to invent numerous human explanations, and these are added to bad exegesis, and it must cease! One false doctrine spawns a second or third false idea in order to substantiate the original anti-scriptural theory. Some cessationists associate the Spirit's manifestations (such as prophecy, faith and word of knowledge) with natural terms. They say prophecy is "preaching", a word of knowledge is "human instinct", and faith is simply "what you believe". How incredulous that such people turn what the Bible describes precisely as "manifestations of the Spirit" into "manifestations of the human psyche"!

*Cessationism invents its own theories*

Human ingenuity suggests that the early Church needed a kick-start in order to successfully launch the gospel. The fact that about 120 believers were expected to take the gospel everywhere seems unreasonable, when viewing this immense task from a purely human perspective. However, we find that God Himself provided the needed propulsive power through His Holy Spirit, as Jesus explained, *"You will receive power after the Holy Spirit comes upon you, and you will be witnesses to Me"* (Acts 1:8).

Are cessationists suggesting that because there are now millions of Christians throughout the world, the power of the Holy Spirit is no longer needed – we can do the job in our own strength? Such reasoning is not only unsupported Biblically, it contradicts Christ's words, *"Without Me you can do nothing"* (John 15:5). Jesus also made it clear that He is the One who builds His Church. Whilst we have a part to play as His servants, salvation remains a supernatural phenomenon. The early Church began in the power of the Spirit, so must we continue now in the power of the flesh? There is not the scantiest idea in Scripture that today we do not need what God granted to the first

Christians. In fact, both Scripture and society demand that what the first Christians experienced we certainly require.

The Bible is silent about the apostolic era being supernaturally distinct. But the Bible is not silent about the fact that miracles will continue throughout this age until Jesus returns.[24] In Hebrews we read how God bore witness with signs and wonders, with various miracles and gifts of the Holy Spirit, according to His will. The Bible nowhere suggests that God has changed His will concerning miraculous works. Indeed, if His will has changed, then He has changed and His character has changed, but this refutes the doctrine of the Lord's immutability, and the plain Biblical statements about His unchanging character. God is not capricious, and we are meant to discern and to know His will. Biblically there is not even a hint that what the first Christians experienced was to cease after the first century, and that the following 2,000 years plus (until Christ returns) would be entirely different in character.

Those who say signs and wonders were for the early Church only, relegate most of the New Testament record to historic prose, of no more use today than informing us of what once was! If the apostolic era was supernaturally distinct, it was not because such was God's will, but because believers moved away from the model and experience of the early Church.

## Cessationism leans on two factors

There are two main planks in the cessationist platform, the first of which is the death of the apostles. The New Testament says that prophecies, tongues and knowledge will pass away when that which is perfect arrives. However, it is shamefully unacceptable to assert that the death of the first apostles was the 'perfect arriving'! This is nonsense, so cessationists offer a second assertion, namely the completion of the New Testament canon,

314

which was finally agreed by the Council of Carthage in AD397.[25] They claim that this was the 'perfect arriving'. We have thousands of ancient copies of the twenty-seven New Testament books, but we have no original manuscripts. The copies differ in some details, due it is thought to copyist errors. Is this the 'perfect arriving'? Is this seeing *"face to face"*? With the New Testament canon completed, do we no longer see through *"a glass darkly"* or observe *"a poor reflection as in a mirror"* (1 Corinthians 13:12)? It is better to accept that the return of Christ to earth is the arrival of the perfect, and the moment we shall see face to face, as the Scriptures state.

*Cessationism is a convenient excuse for lack of faith*

Such lack of faith is brought about by the absence of Holy Spirit baptism and by the fear of failure. It is a flaw in the systematic theology of Reformed doctrine. It is responsible for lack of the miraculous in the experience of many believers. The Vicar of Bagdad saw only a few healed in Britain, but almost everyone healed in Bagdad! We read that Jesus *"could do no mighty miracles except lay His hands on a few sick folk and heal them"*. The sad reason was the people's lack of faith, trust and acceptance of Christ, and this caused the Lord to marvel. Unbelief tied His hands; it affected His ability to do God's will on earth as it is done in heaven! To remedy this, Jesus went around in a circuit teaching, because *"faith comes from hearing, and hearing from the word of God"*. Correct teaching of God's word is a powerful remedy for faithlessness.

We consider that one modern miracle is sufficient to blow the cessationist argument to shreds, and the millions of miracles occurring today through the Spirit's ministry in worldwide believers are overpoweringly sufficient to refute this false teaching. Purely on Biblical grounds, cessationism must cease.

But if Biblical grounds are not enough for some, then the testimony of multitudes which have experienced their own tangible miracle must avail, to the glory of our God and Saviour, Jesus Christ. To counteract the abundance of modern miracles, cessationists have argued that God does indeed perform miracles today, but not through his servants as in the early Church! This justifies their personal lack of a miraculous ministry, but it remains Biblically untenable.

### Cessationism wrongly influences others

If cessationism were merely a matter of personal preference which was kept to oneself, it would do little damage. But false teachers have surely arisen who belligerently pontificate their unbiblical doctrines, teaching in theological colleges, preaching in churches, and publishing their spurious tenets in books or on the internet.

How tragic that people who claim to be saved and who accept that the Bible is the out-breathed Word of God, retain the same spiritual blindness as the Pharisees of Christ's day. They may own Jesus as their personal Saviour, but know little about the Holy Spirit who desires to lead them into all truth. Their stubborn refusal to accept at face value that Jesus continues to work miracles through His Spirit-filled Church today is a tragedy, not only for them, but for a world which needs to meet the true, unchanging Biblical Christ.

Peter Masters introduces a new human theory.[26] He says it was only the first apostles of Christ who worked signs and wonders! This not only overlooks others who were not apostles but who performed miracles, it also contradicts Jesus' words recorded in John 14:12, *"Truly, I say to you, he who believes in Me, the works that I do he will do also; and greater works than these he will do, because I go to My Father."* Beginning His utterance with

*"Truly"* indicates that what Jesus says is unequivocally and unalterably correct and without hidden meanings. Therefore Christ's words cannot refer only to the apostles of Christ. *"He who believes in Me"* is anyone who believes in Jesus Christ, a fact confirmed by many in the Bible who were not apostles but who worked miracles.

### 1. Stephen – Acts 6:5-10

Stephen was not an apostle, in fact he was one of the first deacons, chosen by the Church to serve communion and distribute food to the people. But, he was a man full of faith and the Holy Spirit and we read that he did great wonders and signs among the people. Further, his antagonists were unable to resist the wisdom and the Spirit by which he spoke.

### 2. Philip – Acts 6:5, 8:5-8

Philip was also chosen as one of the deacons, and this man preached and multitudes with one accord heeded the things spoken by Philip, hearing and seeing the miracles he did. What a marvel, another man who was not an apostle, but one who believed in Jesus so that the works that Jesus he did also! Later Philip led an Ethiopian to Christ, baptised him in water, and then miraculously the Spirit of the Lord caught Philip away and he was found at Azotus.

### 3. Ananias – Acts 9:10-19

Ananias was not an apostle. He is simply described as a disciple. This man had a vision in which God spoke to him, instructing him to visit the repentant Saul, lay hands on him, heal his blindness, and fill him with the Holy Spirit. It appears Ananias also water-baptised Saul.

## 4. Prophets from Jerusalem: one named Agabus – Acts 11:27–28

Agabus and his fellow believers were prophets, not apostles, but brought the supernatural word of prophecy to the Church in Antioch.

## 5. Prophets and teachers: Barnabas, Simeon, Lucius, Manaen, Saul – Acts 13:1–4

Each of these were not apostles, but prophets and teachers who were foretelling and forthtelling God's word to the Church. However, Barnabas and Saul are instructed to begin the work God had arranged for them to do as they are sent out by the Holy Spirit. This was the beginning of their first missionary journey, and being sent out by the Lord, we understand they had been promoted to apostleship from their previous prophetic and teaching ministry.

## 6. Philip's daughters who are prophets – Acts 21:8–9

This is the same Philip who took up the duties of a deacon, and who also was an evangelist who performed many miracles of healing and deliverance. He is never called an apostle, and he has four unmarried daughters who prophesy. As we know, prophesying is not preaching. It is a spontaneous, supernatural utterance from the Spirit of God, declaring the word of God.

These many persons performing miraculous works and utterances defeat Peter Masters' theory. But how foolish it is to invent a theory which is anti-Biblical!

### Cessationism presents a truncated gospel

Personally I want New Testament Christianity, a New Testament Jesus and a New Testament gospel. Anything less, whether considered better or worse, is not Christianity. True Christianity is Christ in all His fullness and glory, as recorded in the Bible. Please don't offer me a different Jesus, who acts differently, who changes His will and character. The Scriptures assure us that God doesn't change – He cannot change because He is perfection, and any change would be less than perfect!

Owing to some people preaching only a part of the gospel, the phrase "full gospel" was introduced, indicating that no part of the Biblical gospel was left out of a Church's belief system. When less than the entire gospel is declared, then it is truncated. It is an abridged version; a cropped rendition; a curtailed and variant narrative. Those who teach against miracles happening today are absurdly unscriptural, but when they ignore the whole subject of the miraculous they present an abridged gospel.

Paul testified about mighty signs and wonders, by the power of the Spirit of God, stating that from Jerusalem and round about to Illyricum he fully preached the gospel of Christ. This verse does not say that Paul preached the full gospel of Christ, but that he fully preached the gospel of Christ. If *fully preached* means anything it includes the fact that not only did Paul preach everywhere – his geographical extent, but that he preached everything – his Biblical inclusiveness. Paul testifies to the Ephesians that he did not shun to declare *"the whole counsel of God"*. In modern parlance he is saying, "I have preached the full gospel." The phrase *"whole counsel of God"* indicates the extent of truth delivered; it was the whole gamut of salvation; it was every aspect of Christ and the gospel; it included the complete and whole body of teaching as contained now in the Bible, of which he says he kept nothing back.

The expression *full gospel* would be unnecessary, were it not for the declarers of a cropped gospel version. This is because the Good News of Jesus Christ is in fact Christ Himself, in all His fullness! The gospel is not just the cross, or the resurrection, or

319

forgiveness of sins, or Christ's return to earth. It is all of these and much, much more. The gospel is all of Christ Himself. It is not merely some of the words He spoke, or some of the deeds He performed, or some of the ways in which He lived while on earth. It is all that He said and says; all that He did and does and all that He was and is. The gospel is everything recorded in the Old and New Testament Scriptures about Him – it is the whole Book!

Luke tells us, beginning at Moses and all the Prophets, Jesus expounded to them in all the Scriptures the things concerning Himself. Paul explained to the Christians in Corinth that on his first visit to them he determined not to know anything among them except Jesus Christ and Him crucified. Many will breathe a sigh of relief here, observing that Paul did not mention the Holy Spirit! This is the crux of the whole issue. If Paul determined to know nothing except Jesus Christ, that is enough, because Christ is God the Son, always obedient to the will of the Father. Christ is the Saviour from sin and hell, who died on the cross; He is the divine Healer of broken hearts, bodies and lives; He is the Baptiser in the Holy Spirit; and He is the coming King! To fully know Christ is to know also the Father and the Holy Spirit. If you do not fully preach Christ, but pick and choose certain aspects of His life and ministry, you will present a clipped and distorted gospel. You could easily omit His return to earth, or His promise to baptise in the Holy Spirit.

A person may be truly justified before God, with sins forgiven, but without water baptism or Spirit baptism his experience is incomplete.

## SIGNS AND WONDERS ATTEST THE LEGITIMACY OF THE TRUE AND LIVING GOD

The Old Testament designates the Lord as the *"God of wonders"*[27] in contrast to heathen gods which produced no wonders!

Occasionally subnatural, demonic instances occur, but other than that, false religions manifest very few, if any, signs and wonders and this notable lack of the miraculous confirms the falseness of their god(s). Signs and wonders by the true and living God confirm the truth of Christianity. Any other religion is proved spurious by its lack of the miraculous in everyday life. I once asked a Muslim how we could know that the Koran was not a false book. He said if it is true, it will agree with previous revelations from God! In that case the Koran is spurious, since in most places it disagrees with the Old Testament and New Testament Scriptures revealed by God centuries before.

Jesus foretold the rise of false prophets *"who come in sheep's clothing, but inwardly they are ravenous wolves. You shall know them by their fruits"*. Do Muslims display the fruits of miracles, of divine healing and dynamic works of service? There is a stark absence of these demonstrable and wholesome signs. Some replace such positive deeds by nefarious acts of terrorism and death, mostly towards their fellow Muslims! Such acts confirm the falseness of their god and their faith! Some of my wife's family are Muslims, and they asked, "Why is it when you pray you get answers, but when we pray nothing happens?" A false deity cannot answer, as the prophets of Baal discovered in Elijah's time. The failure to hear and answer prayer and to perform mighty miracles confirms that people are associating with a fictitious god. Time to call on *Jehovah Jehoshua Christos*!

As I consider this state of affairs, I am reminded of Paul's reference to centuries of idol worship, saying, *"These times of ignorance God overlooked, but now commands all men everywhere to repent"* (Acts 17:30). This well applies to cessationist teaching, which was invented during times of ignorance. But there is a more sinister matter at work here! Most cessationists accept that Bible miracles were genuine, but that modern-day miracles (of healing or anything else) are spurious. This position is abundantly familiar – they are standing in the shoes of the Pharisees of Christ's day, who said, *"We know that God spoke to Moses: as for this fellow, we know not where He is from"* (John 9:30). How amazing that the Pharisees had complete faith that Moses was a man of God and that all his works were genuine, despite the fact that they were absent in Moses' time! They accepted Moses whom they never heard or saw, but rejected Jesus whom they did hear and see! Cessationists display a parallel situation: they believe the miracles of Christ and the early Church were legitimate, but they reject miracles occurring in the ministry of Christ's servants today. How amazing that they accept what they did not see, but reject what they can see! Surely an enemy has done this!

We must not make the abnormal the norm, yet many church leaders do this as they stifle any expectancy in the miraculous today. So much so that Christ has been unable to do any mighty work, except lay His hands upon a few sick folk, and heal them. Mark 6:5–6 are some of the saddest verses in the New Testament, because they show that our unbelief prohibits the work of Christ. Unbelief closes the door on His ability to deliver us from sin and sickness. Unbelief is a sin, and probably the greatest sin of all, since it can eventually escort the human soul to the blackness of hell. The time is far past when we should acknowledge that the absence of the miraculous in our Christian experience today is the result of our own sinful unbelief, just as it was in Christ's day. Inventing unscriptural and anti-scriptural theories will not do. Cessationists perilously shift the blame for not experiencing the miraculous from ourselves, and place it squarely on the Lord's shoulders! It is a demonic idea to postulate that Christ has altered His programme, changed His procedures, adjusted His will and modified His character! Wake up, disbelieving believers!

It was taught by one modern mission group that "God does not respond to need, but only to faith". The foundation for this adage is not a Bible statement, but an interpretation of texts. Such axioms are well-meaning and generally contain an element of truth – but they are rarely the whole truth. When they said, "God does not respond to need, but only to faith", it was explained that if God responded to needs there would be none left in the world! Surely suspect reasoning. The Bible gives instances where God responded to need when no faith was present. For example in John 5:1–9 Jesus miraculously healed a paralysed man who had been in that state for thirty-eight years. Jesus asked him if he wanted to be made well. The man did not recognise who was talking to him, and had no faith that this person could heal him. He simply stated the hopelessness of his situation. The Lord of life did not enter into dialogue, but spoke creative, healing words, *"Rise, take up your bed and walk. And immediately the man was made well."* No faith, but needs met. Praise the Lord!

Another instance was when the disciples were in a ferocious storm and cried out in fear for their lives, *"Teacher, don't you care that we are perishing?"* In response Jesus rebuked the wind and peace reigned, but He asked them, *"Why are you so fearful? How is it that you have no faith?"* (Mark 4:40). No faith, but their needs were met. In the Old Testament, the Syrian army had besieged Jerusalem and people were starving. Outside the city were four lepers whose logic was impeccable. They reasoned that if they entered the city, they would die of starvation. If they stayed outside the city, they would die of starvation. If they submitted to the Syrian army, they might, or might not, be killed – but there was a slim chance of being fed and of staying alive. On reaching the Syrian camp they found it was deserted, and they were able to eat and drink to the full. No faith, just a slim chance, but their needs were met.

Many examples could be quoted from the Bible which refute the words, "God does not respond to need." Consider how He meets the needs of multitudes for food and drink –multitudes not only of Christian believers, but unbelievers, adherents to pagan religions and evil persons, indeed, He sends the rain on the just and the unjust. However, the adage continues to say, "God responds to faith." As it stands, that is true. The Lord does respond to faith, since Jesus said, *"Have faith in God. For assuredly I say to you, whoever says to this mountain, 'Be removed and cast into the sea,' and does not doubt in his heart, but believes that those things he says will be done, he will have whatever he says. Therefore I say to you, whatever things you ask when you pray, believe that you receive them, and you will have them"* (Mark 11:22–24).

## CAN GOD?

A "mixed multitude" of people left Egypt with the Israelites. They lacked love for, and faith in, the Lord. As they craved for meat they badly influenced the people of God. Their faithlessness displeased the Lord, and Asaph described the episode this way, *"Yes, they spoke against God: They said, 'Can God prepare a table in the wilderness? Can He give bread also? Can He provide meat for His people?'"* (Psalm 78:19–22). We read that the Lord heard this and was furious because they did not believe in Him. If they had faith and trust in God, their many questions would have been turned into statements; not, "Can God?" but "God can!" The Bible is explicit that nothing is too difficult for the Lord, who asks Jeremiah the rhetorical question, *"I am the LORD, the God of all flesh. Is there anything too hard for Me?"* (Jeremiah 32:27).

A similar question was put to Ezekiel (Ezekiel 37:1–14), when he was shown a valley of very dry bones. The Lord asked the prophet if those dead bones can live. Ezekiel knew the anointing of God and something of His power, and was not going to declare his doubts, so he wisely replies, *"O LORD GOD,*

*You know.*" The Lord proceeded to demonstrate His power which arrived through the operation of His Word and His Spirit. The Lord instructed Ezekiel to prophesy to the bones, and say to them, *"O dry bones, hear the word of the LORD . . . Come from the four winds, O breath, and breathe on these slain, that they may live."* This, of course, was a promise that God would deliver Israel from her exiled death and place her once again in her own land.

This scenario shows that God's word and Spirit together can accomplish anything.

Even the angel Gabriel teaches, *"For nothing is impossible with God."* Jesus said the inability of the disciples to deliver a demonised boy was the result of their unbelief. He went on to say that if they had faith as a grain of mustard seed, mighty miracles would occur and nothing would be impossible for them. On another occasion the disciples were astonished by Jesus' words about the difficulty for the rich entering God's Kingdom. They wondered and asked who then could be saved. Jesus looked at them and said, *"With men this is impossible, but with God all things are possible."* Luke also explains that Jesus said, *"The things which are impossible with men are possible with God."*

I sometimes wonder if those who oppose the miraculous are reading the same Bible as I; or whether they acknowledge the same God as I; or whether they have the same Lord Jesus as I, or the same Holy Spirit! Are their minds poisoned and their senses dulled by false teaching? Have they leaned on their own understanding and failed to hear what the Spirit says? Their theology may be systematised, but it is often humanised and in some cases demonised. I advocate only Biblical theology. If a doctrine is not Biblically supported by clear statements and trends, ditch it! It is perilous to formulate doctrine on ideas not entertained by the Bible, because the result is not Christianity!

You might consider it to be better than what the early Church experienced, but it will not be Christianity. It will not be "the Way" but a different, erroneous way.

The sin of unbelief has permeated, and in many cases deluged, Bible schools and seminaries. Unsuspecting students complete their course having been brainwashed not to expect God to work miracles today. The scribes and Pharisees travelled over land and sea to win a proselyte, and Jesus said when he is won, they make him twice as much a son of hell as themselves! How many seminaries turn students into rank unbelievers, even more disbelieving than their tutors? How many students have lost their faith while studying at a Christian institution? How many seminaries are actually spiritual cemeteries where living converts are buried under a huge weight of human academia and the deadness of the letter, while being denied the life-giving Spirit?

Recently I have spoken about these matters with an evangelical preacher, who said that he and his denomination adhere to "the conservative theological view that everyone saved is automatically baptised in the Holy Spirit", without any Spirit manifestations or outward evidences, of course! The crux of the matter is that "conservative theological views" should be re-examined in the light of Scripture and adjusted to conform to what the Bible actually says.

Prayer for revival dominated the historic Protestant churches during the nineteenth century, and God answered those prayers with a Pentecostal outpouring. But the main-line churches would have none of it. When I was a teenager, they said tongues were of the devil. After well over a century of worldwide Spirit-filled ministry accompanied by mighty signs and wonders, many still repudiate it – many certainly don't want it, nor like it! Let it be acknowledged that no other revival has come since the Pentecostal outpouring of the Spirit. There is no other, because the Pentecostal baptism in the Holy Spirit is the only revival promised in the Bible –it is *"the Promise of the Father"*, and to negate it, neglect it or ignore it, leaves us bereft of heaven's resources.

# APPENDIX – NEW TESTAMENT VERSES ABOUT THE HOLY SPIRIT

LISTED BELOW ARE 104 VERSES IN THE NT REFERRING TO the Person of the Holy Spirit, and sixty-three verses referring to the baptism in the Holy Spirit. Eleven verses apply to both the Person and the baptism in the Holy Spirit. For example, Luke 11:13: *"How much more will God give the Holy Spirit to those who ask Him."* This verse certainly applies to a Pentecostal Spirit baptism experience, but it might also apply to the personal ongoing presence and filling of the Holy Spirit in a believer's life. In Acts 4:29–31 the believers pray for boldness to speak and for signs and wonders to be done in Jesus' Name, with the result that they were all filled with the Holy Spirit. They all had been granted Spirit baptism at Pentecost but they continued to experience subsequent fillings. Saul is filled with the Spirit in Acts 9:17, just as the disciples were on the Day of Pentecost. To argue that Saul could be filled but not baptised in the Holy Spirit places him back in Old Covenant times. In the New Covenant, people are initially Spirit-baptised, which includes being filled with the Spirit, and which activates a constant filling.

The purpose of this chart is to show the importance of distinguishing between the work of the Spirit's Person from His work of Spirit baptism. Romans 8:9–10 says, *"If anyone does not have the Spirit of Christ, he is not His"*, which some have misinterpreted, hoping to prove that we are baptised in the Holy Spirit at the moment of our conversion! If we acknowledge that the Spirit of Christ is the Holy Spirit, the verse is saying that anyone without the Holy Spirit is not a Christian. Romans chapter 8 essentially refers to our son-ship in Christ through the Holy Spirit, not our equipping for service through baptism in the Spirit. That is why it does not say, "If anyone is not baptised in the Holy Spirit they do not belong to Christ!" Such a statement baulks against the whole trend of teaching in the New Testament regarding Spirit baptism. Failure to differentiate between the Spirit's Person and His specific work as the medium into whom Christ baptises us has led to muddled thinking and erroneous conclusions about how and when the Spirit operates in our lives.

| REFERENCE | SUBJECT | PERSON OF THE SPIRIT | BAPTISM IN THE SPIRIT |
|---|---|:---:|:---:|
| Matthew 1:20 | Mary conceived by the Holy Spirit | ✓ | |
| 3:11 | John Baptist: Jesus will baptise with the Holy Spirit | | ✓ |
| 3:16 | Spirit descending like a dove upon Jesus | | ✓ |
| 12:18 | Isaiah 42:1–4 My Beloved . . . I will put My Spirit upon Him | | ✓ |
| 28:19 | The triune Name of God in water baptism | ✓ | |
| Mark 1:8 | Jesus will baptise you with the Holy Spirit | | ✓ |
| 1:10 | Spirit descending like a dove upon Jesus | | ✓ |
| 1:12 | Spirit drove Jesus into the wilderness | ✓ | |
| Luke 1:35 | Holy Spirit will come upon Mary | ✓ | |
| 1:41 | Elizabeth filled with the Holy Spirit | ✓ | |
| 1:67 | Zacharias filled with the Holy Spirit and prophesies | ✓ | |
| 2:25–27 | Holy Spirit upon Simeon enters Temple by the Spirit | ✓ | |
| 3:16 | Jesus will baptise you with the Holy Spirit | | ✓ |
| 3:22 | Spirit descending like a dove upon Jesus | | ✓ |
| 4:1 | Jesus filled with the Spirit, led into the wilderness | ✓ | |
| 4:14 | Jesus returns in the power of the Spirit | ✓ | |
| 11:13 | How much more will God give the Holy Spirit | ✓ | ✓ |

| REFERENCE | SUBJECT | PERSON OF THE SPIRIT | BAPTISM IN THE SPIRIT |
|---|---|---|---|
| 24:49 | Promise of the Father – endued with power from on high | | ✓ |
| John 1:32 | Spirit descending like a dove and remaining upon Jesus | | ✓ |
| 1:33 | Jesus will baptise you with the Holy Spirit | | ✓ |
| 3:5,6,8 | Born of the Spirit | ✓ | |
| 3:34 | God does not give the Spirit by measure to Jesus | | ✓ |
| 4:24 | God is Spirit . . . worship in spirit and truth | ✓ | |
| 7:37-39 | The Holy Spirit was not yet (given) | | ✓ |
| 14:12 | Greater works because Jesus' goes to the Father | | ✓ |
| 14:16–17 | Another Comforter, the Spirit of truth who dwells with you | ✓ | ✓ |
| 14:26 | Holy Spirit will teach us all things and remind us | ✓ | |
| 15:26 | Holy Spirit will testify about Jesus | ✓ | |
| 16:7 | If Jesus departs, the Holy Spirit will take over | | ✓ |
| 16:8–11 | Holy Spirit brings conviction of sin, righteousness, judgment | ✓ | |
| 20:22 | Jesus breathed on them, saying receive Holy Spirit | ✓ | |
| Acts 1:2 | Jesus gave commandments through the Holy Spirit | ✓ | |
| 1:4 | Wait for the Promise of the Father | | ✓ |
| 1:5 | You will be baptised with the Holy Spirit | | ✓ |
| 1:8 | You will receive power when the Holy Spirit comes upon you | | ✓ |
| 1:16 | The Holy Spirit spoke through David | ✓ | |

| 2:3–4 | All filled with the Holy Spirit, began to speak in tongues | | ✓ |
|---|---|---|---|
| 2:17–18 | Joel 2:28–32 I will pour out My Spirit on all flesh | | ✓ |
| 2:33 | The Promise of the Holy Spirit | | ✓ |
| 2:38–39 | Gift of Holy Spirit for all | | ✓ |
| 4:31 | All filled with Holy Spirit | ✓ | |
| 5:3–4 | Lie to God the Holy Spirit | ✓ | |
| 5:32 | Holy Spirit a witness and given to those who obey Him | | ✓ |
| 6:3 | Men full of the Holy Spirit | | ✓ |
| 6:5 | Stephen, a man full of faith and the Holy Spirit | | ✓ |
| 6:10 | Not able to resist the wisdom and the Spirit | ✓ | |
| 7:51 | You always resist the Holy Spirit | ✓ | |
| 7:55–56 | Stephen full of the Holy Spirit | ✓ | |
| 8:15-17 | Prayed for them to receive the Holy Spirit | | ✓ |
| 8:29 | Spirit said to Philip | ✓ | |
| 8:39 | Spirit of the Lord caught away Philip | ✓ | |
| 9:17–18 | Saul filled with the Spirit | | ✓ |
| 9:31 | Comfort of the Holy Spirit | ✓ | |
| 10:19 | Spirit spoke to Peter | ✓ | |
| 10:38 | God anointed Jesus of Nazareth with the Holy Spirit | | ✓ |
| 10:44–48 | Gift of the Holy Spirit poured out on the Gentiles | | ✓ |
| 11:15–17 | Holy Spirit fell on them … baptised with the Holy Spirit | | ✓ |
| 11:24 | Barnabas full of the Holy Spirit | ✓ | |
| 11:28 | Agabus showed by the Spirit | ✓ | |
| 13:2–4 | Saul and Barnabas separated and sent out by the Holy Spirit | ✓ | |

| REFERENCE | SUBJECT | PERSON OF THE SPIRIT | BAPTISM IN THE SPIRIT |
|---|---|---|---|
| 13:9 | Saul who is called Paul is filled with the Holy Spirit | ✓ | |
| 13:52 | Disciples filled with joy and the Holy Spirit | ✓ | |
| 15:8 | God gave Holy Spirit to Cornelius as He did at Pentecost | | ✓ |
| 15:28 | It seemed good to the Holy Spirit and to us | ✓ | |
| 16:6–7 | Holy Spirit forbade entry to Asia and Bithynia | ✓ | |
| 18:5 | Paul compelled by the Spirit | ✓ | |
| 19:2 | Did you receive the Holy Spirit when you believed? | | ✓ |
| 19:6 | Paul laid hands upon them, the Holy Spirit came upon them | | ✓ |
| 20:23 | The Holy Spirit testifies about Paul's trials | ✓ | |
| 20:28 | Holy Spirit made then shepherding overseers | ✓ | |
| 21:4 | They told Paul by the Spirit not to go to Jerusalem | ✓ | |
| 21:9–10 | Philip's four daughters prophesy, and Agabus | ✓ | |
| Romans 1:4 | Son of God with power according to the Spirit of holiness | | ✓ |
| 2:29 | Circumcision of the heart, in the Spirit | ✓ | |
| 7:6 | Serve in the newness of the Spirit | | ✓ |
| 8:1-2 | Walk according to the Spirit | ✓ | |
| 8:5 | Set their minds on the things of the Spirit | ✓ | |
| 8:9–10 | If anyone does not have the Spirit of Christ he is none of His | ✓ | |

| | | | |
|---|---|---|---|
| 8:11 | Spirit will quicken your mortal bodies | ✓ | |
| 8:14 | Those led by the Spirit are the sons of God | ✓ | |
| 8:15 | Spirit of adoption by whom we cry Abba, Father | ✓ | |
| 8:23 | The firstfruits of the Spirit | | ✓ |
| 8:26–27 | Spirit Himself makes intercession for us | ✓ | |
| 9:1 | Conscience bearing witness in the Holy Spirit | ✓ | |
| 12:6–8 | Differing gifts and manifestations of the Spirit | ✓ | ✓ |
| 14:17–18 | God's Kingdom is righteousness, peace, joy in the Holy Spirit | ✓ | |
| 15:19 | Signs and wonders by the power of the Spirit of God | ✓ | |
| 15:30 | Through the love of the Spirit | ✓ | ✓ |
| 1 Corinthians 2:4 | In demonstration of the Spirit and of power | ✓ | |
| 2:10 | Revealed to us through the Spirit, who searches all things | ✓ | |
| 2:11 | No one knows the things of God except the Spirit of God | ✓ | |
| 2:12 | We have received the Spirit who is from God | | ✓ |
| 2:13 | The Holy Spirit teaches comparing spiritual things | ✓ | |
| 2:14 | Natural man does not receive the thing of the Spirit of God | ✓ | ✓ |
| 3:16 | You are the temple of God in whom the Spirit dwells | ✓ | ✓ |
| 6:19 | Your body is the temple of the Holy Spirit | ✓ | ✓ |
| 12:7–11 | The nine manifestations of the Spirit | ✓ | ✓ |

| REFERENCE | SUBJECT | PERSON OF THE SPIRIT | BAPTISM IN THE SPIRIT |
|---|---|---|---|
| 12:13 | The Spirit baptises us into the body of Christ | | ✓ |
| 2 Corinthians 1:21–22 | God has anointed us, sealed us and given us the Spirit | | ✓ |
| 3:3 | Written by the Spirit of the living God | ✓ | |
| 3:6 | Of the Spirit who gives life | ✓ | |
| 3:8 | Ministry of the Spirit is more glorious | ✓ | |
| 3:17–18 | The Lord is the Spirit who transforms us from glory to glory | ✓ | |
| 5:5 | Given us the Spirit as a guarantee | | ✓ |
| 13:14 | The communion of the Holy Spirit be with you all | ✓ | |
| Galatians 3:2–3 | Did you receive the Spirit by law, or by faith? | | ✓ |
| 3:5 | He who supplies the Spirit and works miracles | | ✓ |
| 3:14 | That we might receive the promise of the Spirit | | ✓ |
| 4:6 | Sent forth the Spirit of His Son into our hearts | ✓ | |
| 5:16 | Walk in the Spirit | ✓ | |
| 5:17–18 | Spirit and flesh are contrary, so be led by the Spirit | ✓ | |
| 5:22–23 | Nine-fold fruit of the Spirit | ✓ | |
| 5:25 | Live in the Spirit and walk in the Spirit | ✓ | |
| 6:8 | Sow to the Spirit and reap everlasting life | ✓ | |
| Ephesians 1:13 | Having believed – sealed with the Holy Spirit of promise | | ✓ |

| 2:18 | Access to the Father by one Spirit | ✓ | ✓ |
|---|---|---|---|
| 2:21–22 | A dwelling place of God in the Spirit | ✓ | |
| 4:3 | Keep the unity of the Spirit | ✓ | |
| 4:30 | Do not grieve the Holy Spirit by whom you were sealed | | ✓ |
| 5:18–19 | Be filled with the Spirit, singing spiritual songs | ✓ | |
| 6:17 | The sword of the Spirit which is the word of God | ✓ | |
| Philippians 3:3 | Who worship God in the Spirit . . . no confidence in the flesh | ✓ | |
| 1 Thessalonians 4:8 | God who has also given us His Holy Spirit | | ✓ |
| 5:19–20 | Do not quench the Spirit or despise prophesies | ✓ | |
| 2 Thessalonians 2:13 | Sanctification by the Spirit and belief in the truth | ✓ | |
| Timothy 4:1 | The Spirit expressly speaks about latter times | ✓ | |
| Timothy 1:14 | That good thing keep by the Holy Spirit who dwells in us | ✓ | |
| Titus 2:5 | The washing of regeneration and renewing of the Holy Spirit | ✓ | ✓ |
| Hebrews 2:4 | Various miracles and gifts of the Holy Spirit | ✓ | ✓ |
| 6:5 | Partakers of the Holy Spirit | ✓ | ✓ |
| 10:15 | The Holy Spirit witnesses to us | ✓ | |
| 10:26 | Insulted the Spirit of grace | ✓ | |
| James 4:5 | The Spirit who dwells in us yearns jealously | ✓ | |
| 1 Peter 1:2 | In sanctification of the Spirit | ✓ | ✓ |
| 1:11 | The Spirit of Christ who was in them | ✓ | |

| REFERENCE | SUBJECT | PERSON OF THE SPIRIT | BAPTISM IN THE SPIRIT |
|---|---|---|---|
| 1:12 | Preached . . . by the Holy Spirit sent forth from heaven | ✓ | ✓ |
| 1:22 | Obeying the truth through the Spirit in sincere love | ✓ | |
| 3:18 | Made alive by the Spirit | ✓ | |
| 2 Peter 1:20–21 | Holy men of God spoke as they were moved by the Holy Spirit | ✓ | |
| 1 John 2:20 | You have an anointing from the Holy One | | ✓ |
| 2:27 | The anointing you have received abides in you | | ✓ |
| 3:24 | We know He abides in us by the Spirit whom He has given us | | ✓ |
| Jude 20 | Praying in the Holy Spirit | ✓ | ✓ |
| Revelation 2:7 | Ephesus, hear what the Spirit says to the Churches | ✓ | |
| 2:11 | Smyrna, hear what the Spirit says to the Churches | ✓ | |
| 2:17 | Pergamos, hear what the Spirit says to the Churches | ✓ | |
| 2:29 | Thyatira, hear what the Spirit says to the Churches | ✓ | |
| 3:8 | Sardis, hear what the Spirit says to the Churches | ✓ | |
| 3:13 | Philadelphia, hear what the Spirit says to the Churches | ✓ | |
| 3:22 | Laodicea, hear what the Spirit says to the Churches | ✓ | |
| 22:17 | The Spirit and the bride say, "Come!" | ✓ | |
| | **Eleven verses refer to both Spirit Person and Spirit Baptism** | 104 | 63 |

# BIBLIOGRAPHY

THE FOLLOWING LIST IN ALPHABETIC ORDER COMPRISES A few publications which are recommended by the author to all who are serious about the dynamics of the Holy Spirit today.

"ENCOUNTER THE HOLY SPIRIT" by Jeannie Morgan.
Clays Ltd, St Ives plc. ISBN 978 0 85721 168 2

"FREE INDEED!" by Tom Marshall.
Sovereign World, Chichester. ISBN 1 85240 002 1

"I BELIEVE IN THE HOLY SPIRIT" by Michael Green.
Hodder & Stoughton, London. ISBN 0 340 72179 0

"IN MY FATHER'S HOUSE" by George Canty.
Marshall, Morgan & Scott, London. ISBN 0 551 05166 3

"MIGHTY MANIFESTATION" by Reinhard Bonnke.
Kingsway Publications, Eastbourne. ISBN 0 85476 481 X

"JESUS BAPTISES IN ONE HOLY SPIRIT" by David Pawson.
Anchor Recordings, Ashford. ISBN 978-1909886452

"PARADIGM SHIFT" by Professor Roy Peacock.
Authentic Media Ltd. ISBN 978 1 78078 098 6 & ebook: 978 1 0787 099 3

"SPIRITUAL GIFTS" by Donald Gee.
Gospel Publishing House, Missouri. ISBN 0 65802 2 592

"SURPRISED BY THE POWER OF THE SPIRIT" by Jack Deere.
Kingsway Publications, Eastbourne. ISBN 1 84291 270 4

"THE HALLMARKS OF PENTECOST" by George Canty.
Marshall Pickering. ISBN 0 551 01843 7

"THE NORMAL CHRISTIAN BIRTH" by David Pawson.
Hodder & Stoughton, London. SBN 0 340 489723

"THE PRACTICE OF PENTECOST" by George Canty.
Marshall Pickering. ISBN 0 551 01430 X

"THE PRODIGAL SPIRIT" by Graham Tomlin.
Alpha International, London, SW7 1JA. ISBN 978 1 905887 00 2

"WHAT'S GOING ON?" by George Canty.
Grenehurst Press, Cheltenham, Glos. 1977 ISBN 0 905857 02 X

"WORD AND SPIRIT TOGETHER" by David Pawson.
Anchor Recordings, Ashford, TN24 9HS. ISBN 978 1909886469

# NOTES

1.  Billy Graham, The Holy Spirit Copyright © 1978. Used by permission of Thomas Nelson

2.  Jeannie Morgan, *Encounter the Holy Spirit* (Oxford: Monarch Books, 2011).

3.  Joel 2:28; Luke 24:49; Acts 1:4, 2:4,33,38, 4:8,31, Acts 5:32, 8:15–17, 9:6,17, 10:38,44,47, 11:17, 15:8, 19:6; Galatians 3:14; 2 Corinthians 1:21–22, 5:5; Ephesians 1:13, 4:30; 1 Thessalonians 4:8; Titus 3:6; 1 John 2:20,27.

4.  David Pawson, *Word and Spirit Together* (Ashford: Anchor Recordings, 2014).

5.  David Pawson, *The Normal Christian Birth* (London: Hodder & Stoughton, 1991).

6.  *Is Spirit baptism a one-time event?* Grace to You website, Tuesday 25 June 2013.

7.  Tom Marshall, *Free Indeed!* (Lancaster: Sovereign World Ltd., 2000).

8.    Matthew 5:17–19; Luke 24:44; 2 Timothy 3:16–17; Hebrews 4:11–13; 2 Peter 1:16–21

9.    Romans 5:14–19; 1 Corinthians 15:22,45–49; 1 Timothy 2:13–14; Jude 14

10.   Jack Deere, *Surprised by the Power of the Spirit* (Eastbourne: Kingsway Communications Ltd., 1994).

11.   *"Revival Library"*. From the web, quoting Charles Finney, Autobiography, Chapter 2 Conversion to Christ.    Accessed 2015.

12.   *Vine's Expository Dictionary of New Testament Words* (Peabody, MA: Hendrickson, 2005), pp.1085–1087.

13.   R.F. Weymouth, *The New Testament in Modern Speech* (London: James Clarke & Co., 1903).

14.   Donald Gee, *Concerning Spiritual Gifts* (Springfield, MO: Gospel Publishing House, 2012).

15.   *Eastons 1897 Bible Dictionary* Online at dictionary.com.

16.   *Vine's Expository Dictionary of New Testament Words* (Peabody, MA: Hendrickson, 2005).

17.   Harold Horton, *The Gifts of the Spirit* (Springfield, MO: Gospel Publishing House, 1975).

18.   Tom Marshall, *Free Indeed!* (Chichester: Sovereign World Ltd., 1986).

19.   George Canty, *What's Going On?* (Grenehurst Press, Cheltenham. Glos. 1977).

20.   Tom Marshall, *Free Indeed!* (Chichester: Sovereign World Ltd., 1986), p.196.

21.   *Vine's Expository Dictionary of New Testament Words* (Peabody, MA: Hendrickson, 2005), p.738

22.   Gene Edwards, *A Tale of Three Kings* (Carol Stream, IL: Tyndale House, 1992).

23.   George Canty, *In My Father's House* (London: Marshall, Morgan & Scott Ltd, 1969).

24.   Joel 2:28–32; Mark 16:15–20; John 14:12–14; 1 Corinthians 13:8–14:1.

25.   In AD363 the Council of Laodicea stated that only the Old Testament and the twenty-seven books of the New Testament were to be read in the churches. Athanasius cited the twenty-seven books of the New Testament as being the only true books in AD367. The Council of Hippo (AD393) recognised the twenty-seven books. The Council of Carthage (AD 397) affirmed that only canonical books were to be read in the churches.

26.   Peter Masters, *The Healing Epidemic* (London: Wakeman Trust, 1988).

27.   Exodus 7:3; Deuteronomy 6:22, 7:19; 1 Chronicles 16:12; Psalm 136:4; Jeremiah 32:20; Joel 2:30.